BOLLINGEN SERIES XX

THE COLLECTED WORKS

OF

C. G. JUNG

VOLUME 19

EDITORS

† SIR HERBERT READ

MICHAEL FORDHAM, F.R.C.PSYCH., HON. F.B.PS.S.

† GERHARD ADLER, PH.D.

WILLIAM MCGUIRE, *executive editor*

GENERAL
BIBLIOGRAPHY
of C. G. Jung's Writings

Revised Edition

COMPILED BY LISA RESS AND WILLIAM McGUIRE

BOLLINGEN SERIES XX

PRINCETON UNIVERSITY PRESS

PUBLISHED BY PRINCETON UNIVERSITY PRESS
41 WILLIAM STREET, PRINCETON, NEW JERSEY 08540
99 BANBURY ROAD, OXFORD OX2 6JX

PRESS.PRINCETON.EDU

FIRST PUBLISHED IN 1979
REVISED AND UPDATED, 1992
NEW PAPERBACK PRINTING, 2024

CLOTH ISBN 9780691098937
PAPERBACK ISBN 9780691259437

LIBRARY OF CONGRESS CATALOG CARD NUMBER: 75-156

EDITORIAL NOTE TO THE REVISED EDITION

This edition, succeeding the first, which was published in 1979, has been prepared to meet the needs primarily of students of C. G. Jung's writings working in English. Accordingly, it records (through 1991) only publications in English and in German, besides the very few writings in other languages for which Jung was, in some sense, directly responsible. Those include a few short works that he wrote in French.

The first edition recorded through 1975 not only publications in German and English but those translated into seventeen other languages: Danish, Dutch, Finnish, French, Greek, Hebrew, Hungarian, Italian, Japanese, Norwegian, Portuguese, Russian, Serbo-Croatian, Slovenian, Spanish, Swedish, and Turkish. The bibliography volume of the *Gesammelte Werke*, published by Walter-Verlag, Olten, Switzerland, in 1983, extended the chronology to that year and recorded translations in nineteen languages besides English (a few works in Persian and Polish having been added). Regrettably, it has not been possible for the editors of either of the collected editions to trace the numerous translations that have appeared subsequently—a task for the next generation. Thus the limitation of the present version of the bibliography to the German and English publications.

At this point, the canon of Jung's work is virtually complete in print. The twenty volumes of the *Collected Works* are published, including those devoted to the bibliography and the index. Some of the text volumes are in second editions (and reprints have been frequent, though not recorded here). Two supplementary volumes, unanticipated in the original plan, have now appeared. The project of editing and publishing Jung's "seminar notes," which had been canceled, has been revived; three of the seminars have been published and others are in preparation. Several anthologies and numerous paperback extracts are now available in the United States, the United Kingdom, and the other English-speaking countries. Most if not all of the paperbacks are accounted for in the bibliography.

v

The eighteen text volumes of the *Gesammelte Werke*, as well as the bibliography volume and two volumes of the seminars, have now been published by Walter-Verlag, successors to Rascher Verlag; the index volume is in preparation. A large number of anthologies and paperback extracts have issued from Swiss and German houses.

In the preparation of the present edition, the editor has had indispensable cooperation from Helga Egner, of Walter-Verlag. Others who gave significant assistance were David Stonestreet, of Routledge (successors to Routledge & Kegan Paul); Ingeborg Meyer-Palmedo, of S. Fischer Verlag; Doris Albrecht, of the Kristine Mann Library, New York; Joan Alpert, of the Virginia Allan Detloff Library, C. G. Jung Institute of San Francisco; and Verena Maag, of the C. G. Jung Institute, Küsnacht/Zurich. At Princeton University Press, Deborah Tegarden and Timothy Mennel have been notably constructive colleagues.

*

From the editorial note in the first edition, the following information is relevant. It has been the editors' intention to record the initial publication of each original work by Jung, each translation (in the first edition, into any language; now, into English or German), and substantial revisions and/or expansions, with reciprocal cross-references. Unrevised reprints have not been recorded unless brought out by a different publisher or altered in format. The *Collected Works* and the *Gesammelte Werke* are listed separately, in volume sequence, on facing pages.

Michael Fordham, who originally compiled the bibliography in the late 1940s as a working tool for the planning of the English collected edition, based his draft on a list published by Jolande Jacobi in her *The Psychology of C. G. Jung* (cf. E. 1942c); he was indebted also to Professor Jung's secretary at that time, Marie-Jeanne Schmid. Fordham's version underwent revision and augmentation by the editorial staff in a printed version privately distributed to workers in the field. The preparation of a definitive general bibliography was undertaken by A.S.B. Glover. After his death, in 1966, the work was carried on, under the present editor's supervision, first by Jasna P. Heurtley (who was notably effective in locating foreign translations) and then by the former librarian of the Kristine Mann Library, Lisa Ress, who was responsible for what achieved publication. Assistance that is reflected in the present edition came from Aniela Jaffé, Mr. and Mrs. Franz Jung (whose house, at Küsnacht, was the repository of Professor Jung's library), and the editors and publishers of the *Gesammelte Werke*.

WILLIAM McGUIRE

CONTENTS

ABBREVIATIONS

CW = *Collected Works*; GW = *Gesammelte Werke*; B.S. = Bollingen Series. An asterisk preceding an entry indicates that the publication could not be examined. Standard bibliographical abbreviations are used.

PERIODICALS

Aus d. Jhrsb. = Aus dem Jahresbericht
Basl. Nach. = Basler Nachrichten
Bull. APC = Analytical Psychology Club of New York. Bulletin
CorrespBl. schweizer Ärzte = Correspondenzblatt für schweizer Ärzte
Eran. Jb. = Eranos-Jahrbuch
Europ. Rev. = Europäische Revue
J. abnorm. Psychol. = Journal of Abnormal Psychology
J. Psychol. Neurol. = Journal für Psychologie und Neurologie
Jb. psychoanal. psychopath. Forsch. = Jahrbuch für psychoanalytische und psychopathologische Forschungen
Neue Schw. R. = Neue schweizer Rundschau
Neue Zür. Z. = Neue Zürcher Zeitung
New Repub. = New Republic
Psychoanal. Rev. = Psychoanalytic Review
Schweiz. Z. Strafrecht. = Schweizerische Zeitschrift für Strafrecht
Revta Occid. = Revista de Occidente
Z. angew. Psychol. = Zeitschrift für angewandte Psychologie und psychologische Sammelforschung
Zbl. Nervenhk. = Zentralblatt für Nervenheilkunde und Psychiatrie
Zbl. Psychoanal. = Zentralblatt für Psychoanalyse
Zbl. Psychotherap. = Zentralblatt für Psychotherapie und ihre Grenzgebiete

I

THE PUBLISHED WRITINGS OF C. G. JUNG

Original Works and Translations

GERMAN

1902a *Zur Psychologie und Pathologie sogenannter occulter Phänomene. Eine psychiatrische Studie.* Leipzig: Oswald Mutze. pp. 121. Repub. as GW 1,1. Inaugural dissertation for the doctoral degree, presented to the Universität Zürich, Medizinische Fakultät. TR.—English: 1916a,2/CW 1,1.

1902b "Ein Fall von hysterischem Stupor bei einer Untersuchungsgefangenen." *J. Psychol. Neurol.*, I:3, 110–22. Repub. as GW 1,5. TR.—English: CW 1,5.

1903a "Über manische Verstimmung." *Allgemeine Zeitschrift für Psychiatrie und psychisch-gerichtliche Medizin*, LXI:1, 15–39. Repub. as GW 1,4. TR.—English: CW 1,4.

1903b "Über Simulation von Geistesstörung." *J. Psychol. Neurol.*, II:5, 181–201. Repub. as GW 1,6. TR.—English: CW 1,6.

1904a With F. Riklin: "Experimentelle Untersuchungen über Assoziationen Gesunder." (Diagnostische Assoziationsstudien, I. Beitrag.) *J. Psychol. Neurol.*, as follows: Pt. I—III:1/2, 55–83; Pt. II—III:4, 145–64; Pt. III—III:5, 193–215; Pt. IV—III:6, 283–308; Pt. V—IV:1/2, 24–67. Combined and pub. as G.1906a.

1904b "Über hysterisches Verlesen: eine Erwiderung an Herrn Hahn (pr. Arzt in Zürich)." *Archiv für die gesamte Psychologie*, III:4 (May), 347–50. Repub. as GW 1,2. TR.—English: CW 1,2.

1904c "Ärztliches Gutachten über einen Fall von Simulation geistiger Störung." *Schweiz. Z. Strafrecht*, XVII, 55–75. Repub. as GW 1,7. TR.—English: CW 1,7.

1905a "Kryptomnesie." *Die Zukunft*, Jhg. 13, L (25 Feb.), 325–34. Repub., slightly rev., as GW 1,3. TR.—English: CW 1,3.

1905b Review of Willy Hellpach: *Grundlinien einer Psychologie der Hysterie.* *Zbl. Nervenhk.*, XXVIII (n.s. XVI) (15 Apr.), 318–21. GW 18,19. TR.—English: CW 18,19.

1905c "Experimentelle Beobachtungen über das Erinnerungsvermögen." *Zbl. Nervenhk.*, XXVIII (n.s. XVI):196 (1 Sept.), 653–66. Repub. as GW 2,4. TR.—English: CW 2,4.

1905d "Zur psychologischen Tatbestandsdiagnostik." *Zbl. Nervenhk.*, XXVIII (n.s. XVI):200 (1 Nov.), 813–15. Repub. as GW 1,9. TR.— English: CW 1,9.

1905e "Über spiritistische Erscheinungen." *Basl. Nach.*, Nos. 311–16 (12–17 Nov.). Extract pub. in *Volksrecht* (22 Nov.). Given as lecture at the Bernoullianum, Basel, 5 Feb. 1905. GW 18,4. TR.—English: CW 18,4.

1905f "Die psychologische Diagnose des Tatbestandes." *Schweiz. Z. Strafrecht*, XVIII, 369–408. Repub. as G. 1906k with last (minor) sentence omitted.

1905g "Analyse der Assoziationen eines Epileptikers." (Diagnostische Assoziationsstudien, III. Beitrag.) *J. Psychol. Neurol.*, V:2, 73–90. Repub. as G. 1906a,2.

1905h "Über das Verhalten der Reaktionszeit beim Assoziationsexperimente." (Diagnostische Assoziationsstudien, IV. Beitrag.) *J. Psychol. Neurol.*, VI:1/2, 1–36. Also issued as pamphlet, Leipzig: Barth. pp. 38. Jung's "Habilitationsschrift," Universität Zürich, Medizinische Fakultät. Repub. as G. 1906a,3.

1906a *Diagnostische Assoziationsstudien: Beiträge zur experimentellen Psychopathologie.* Ed. by C. G. Jung. Vol. I. Leipzig: Barth. pp. 281. Subsequently issued bound as one with G. 1909a. Contains the following works wholly or partly by Jung:
   1. With F. Riklin: "Experimentelle Untersuchungen über Assoziationen Gesunder." (7–145) G. 1904a repub. Repub. as GW 2,1. TR.—English: 1918a,1/CW 2,1.
   2. "Analyse der Assoziationen eines Epileptikers." (175–92) G. 1905g repub. Repub. as GW 2,2. TR.—English: 1918a,2/CW 2,2.

3. "Über das Verhalten der Reaktionszeit beim Assoziationsexperimente." (193–228) G. 1905h repub. Repub. as GW 2,3.
TR.—English: 1918a,3/CW 2,3.

4. "Psychoanalyse und Assoziationsexperiment." (258–81) G.
1906i repub. Repub. as GW 2,5. TR.—English: 1918a,4/CW
2,5.

Contents also summarized in French by Jung. Cf. Fr. 1908a.

1906b "Die psychopathologische Bedeutung des Assoziationsexperi-
mentes." *Archiv für Kriminalanthropologie und Kriminalistik,* XXII:2–
3 (15 Feb.), 145–62. Given as inaugural lecture upon Jung's ap-
pointment as Lecturer in Psychiatry, Universität Zürich, 21 Oct.
1905. Repub. as GW 2,8. TR.—English: CW 2,8.

1906c "Statistisches von der Rekrutenaushebung." *CorrespBl. Schweizer
Ärzte,* XXXVI:4 (15 Feb.), 129–30. Repub. as GW 2,15. TR.—English: CW 2,15.

1906d "Obergutachten über zwei sich widersprechende psychiatrische
Gutachten." *Monatsschrift für Kriminalpsychologie und Strafrechts-
reform,* II:11/12 (Feb.–Mar.), 691–98. Repub. as GW 1,8 with minor
title change. TR.—English: CW 1,8.

1906e Review of L. Bruns: *Die Hysterie im Kindesalter. CorrespBl. schweizer
Ärzte,* XXXVI:19 (1 Oct.), 634–35. GW 18,20. TR.—English: CW
18,20.

1906f Review of E. Bleuler: *Affektivität, Suggestibilität, Paranoia. CorrespBl.
schweizer Ärzte,* XXXVI:21 (1 Nov.), 694–95. TR.—English: CW
18,20.

1906g "Die Hysterielehre Freuds. Eine Erwiderung auf die Aschaffenburgsche Kritik." *Münchener medizinische Wochenschrift,* LIII:47 (20
Nov.), 2301–02. Repub. as GW 4,1. TR.—English: CW 4,1.

1906h Review of Carl Wernicke: *Grundriss der Psychiatrie in klinischen Vorlesungen. CorrespBl. schweizer Ärzte,* XXXVI:23 (1 Dec.), 790–91.
GW 18,20. TR.—English: CW 18,20.

1906i "Psychoanalyse und Assoziationsexperiment." (Diagnostische Assoziationsstudien, VI. Beitrag.) *J. Psychol. Neurol.,* VII:1/2, 1–24.

Also pub. in *Schweiz. Z. Strafrecht*, XVIII, 396–403. Repub. as G. 1906a,4. TR.—English: 1918a,4.

1906j "Assoziation, Traum und hysterisches Symptom." *J. Psychol. Neurol.*, VIII:1/2, 25–60. Repub. as G. 1909a,1.

1906k "Die psychologische Diagnose des Tatbestandes." *Juristisch-psychiatrische Grenzfragen*, IV:2, 3–47. Also pub. as pamphlet (bound with article by another author). Halle: Carl Marhold. At head of title: "Aus der psychiatrischen Universitätsklinik in Zürich." G. 1905f repub. with omission of last (minor) sentence. Repub. as monograph: G. 1941d; and as GW 2,6. TR.—English: CW 2,6.

1907a *Über die Psychologie der Dementia praecox: Ein Versuch.* Halle a. S.: Carl Marhold. pp. 179. 1972: (Frühe Schriften II; "Studienausgabe.") Olten: Walter. pp. 180.

Vorwort. (Dated July 1906.)

    I. Kritische Darstellung theoretischer Ansichten über die Psychologie der Dementia praecox.

    II. Der gefühlsbetonte Komplex und seine allgemeinen Wirkungen auf die Psyche.

    III. Der Einfluss des gefühlsbetonten Komplexes auf die Wertigkeit der Assoziation.

    IV. Dementia praecox und Hysterie. Eine Parallele.

    V. Analyse eines Falles von paranoïder Demenz, als Paradigma. Schlusswort.

Repub. as GW 3,1. TR.—English: 1909a/CW 3,1.

1907b Review of Albert Moll: *Der Hypnotismus, mit Einschluss der Hauptpunkte der Psychotherapie und des Occultismus. CorrespBl. schweizer Ärzte*, XXXVII:11 (1 June), 354–55. GW 18,20. TR.—English: CW 18,20.

1907c Review of Albert Knapp: *Die polyneuritischen Psychosen. CorrespBl. schweizer Ärzte*, XXXVII:11 (1 June), 355. GW 18,20. TR.—English: CW 18,20.

1907d Review of M. Reichhardt: *Leitfaden zur psychiatrischen Klinik. CorrespBl. schweizer Ärzte*, XXXVII:23 (1 Dec.), 742–43. GW 18,20. TR.—English: CW 18,20.

1907e "Über die Reproduktionsstörungen beim Assoziationsexperiment." (Diagnostische Assoziationsstudien, IX. Beitrag.) *J. Psychol. Neurol.*, IX:4, 188–97. Repub. as G. 1909a,2.

1907f Contribution to discussion of paper by Frank and Bezzola: "Über die Analyse psychosomatischer Symptome," p. 185, in "II. Vereinsbericht. 37. Versammlung südwestdeutscher Irrenärzte in Tübingen am 3. und 4. November 1906." *Zbl. Nervenhk.*, n.s. XVIII:5, 176–91.

1908a *Der Inhalt der Psychose.* (Schriften zur angewandten Seelenkunde, 3.) Leipzig and Vienna: Franz Deuticke. pp. 26. Repub. with supplement as G. 1914a. Academic lecture, given at the Rathaus, Zurich, 16 Jan. 1908.

1908b With E. Bleuler: "Komplexe und Krankheitsursachen bei Dementia praecox." *Zbl. Nervenhk.*, XXXI (n.s. XIX), (Mar.), 220–27.

1908c 7 abstracts. *Folia neuro-biol.*, 1:3 (Mar.), 493–94, 497–99. Listed but not trans. at the end of CW 18,26 (not in GW). Articles abstracted by Jung:

1. 388) Jung, C. G. "Associations d'idées familiales."
2. 389) Métral, M. "Expériences scolaires sur la mémoire de l'orthographe."
3. 394) Lombard, Emile. "Essai d'une classification des phénomènes de glossolalie."
4. 395) Claparède, Ed. "Quelques mots sur la définition de l'hystérie."
5. 396) Flournoy, Th. "Automatisme téléologique antisuicide. . . ."
6. 397) Leroy, E.-Bernard. "Escroquerie et hypnose. . . ."
7. 398) Lemaître, Aug. "Un nouveau cycle somnambulique de Mlle. Smith. Les peintures religieuses."

All of the above articles reviewed appeared originally in the *Archives de psychologie 1907*, VII:25&26. Cf. CW 18,26,ii (not in GW).

1908d "Über die Bedeutung der Lehre Freuds für Neurologie und Psychiatrie" (Autorreferat). *CorrespBl. schweizer Ärzte*, XXXVIII:7 (1 Apr.), 218. Summary of lecture given to the Gesellschaft der Ärzte des Kantons Zürich, autumn meeting, 26 Nov. 1907. GW 18,21.
    TR.—English: CW 18,21.

1908e Review of Franz C. R. Eschle: *Grundzüge der Psychiatrie. CorrespBl. schweizer Ärzte*, XXXVIII:8 (15 Apr.), 264–65. GW 18,20. TR.—English: CW 18,20.

1908f Review of P. Dubois: *Die Einbildung als Krankheitsursache. CorrespBl. schweizer Ärzte*, XXXVIII:12 (15 June), 399. GW 18,20. TR.—English: CW 18,20.

1908g Review of Georg Lomer: *Liebe und Psychose. CorrespBl. schweizer Ärzte*, XXXVIII:12 (15 June), 399–400. GW 18,20. TR.—English: CW 18,20.

1908h Review of E. Meyer: *Die Ursachen der Geisteskrankheiten. CorrespBl. schweizer Ärzte*, XXXVIII, 706. GW 18,20. TR.—English: CW 18,20.

1908i 9 abstracts. *Folia neuro-biol.*, II:1 (Oct.), 124–25, 132–35. Listed but not trans. at the end of CW 18,26 (not in GW). Articles abstracted by Jung:

1. 122) Piéron, H. "La théorie des émotions et les données actuelles de la physiologie."
2. 123) Revault d'Allones, [G.] "L'explication physiologique de l'émotion."
3. 124) Hartenberg, P. "Principe d'une physiognomie scientifique."
4. 130) Dumas, G. "Qu'est-ce que la psychologie pathologique?"
5. 131) Dromard, [G.] "De la dissociation de la mimique chez les aliénés."
6. 132) Marie, A. "Sur quelques troubles fonctionnels de l'audition chez certains débiles mentaux."
7. 133) Janet, P. "Le renversement de l'orientation ou l'allochirie des représentations."
8. 134) Pascal, [Constanza]. "Les maladies mentales de Robert Schumann."
9. 135) Vigouroux, [A.] et Juquelier, [P.] "Contribution clinique à l'étude des délires du rêve."

All the articles reviewed appeared originally in the *Journal de psychologie normale et pathologique*, IV (Sept.–Oct. 1907), V (Mar.–Apr. 1908). Cf. CW 18,26,ii (not in GW).

1908j Review of Wilhelm Stekel: *Nervöse Angstzustände und ihre Behandlung. Medizinische Klinik*, IV:45 (8 Nov.), 1735–36. GW 18,22. TR.—English: CW 18,22.

1908k Review of Sigmund Freud: *Zur Psychopathologie des Alltagslebens.* *CorrespBl. schweizer Ärzte,* XXXVIII:23 (1 Dec.), 775–76. GW 18,20. TR.—English: CW 18,20.

1908l 5 abstracts. *Folia neuro-biol.,* II:3 (Dec.), 366–68. Listed but not trans. at the end of CW 18,26 (not in GW). Articles abstracted by Jung:
  1. 348) Varendonck, J. "Les idéals des enfants."
  2. 349) Claparède, Ed. "Classification et plan des méthodes psychologiques."
  3. 350) Katzaroff, Dimitre. "Expériences sur le rôle de la récitation comme facteur de la mémorisation."
  4. 351) Maeder, Alphonse. "Nouvelles contributions à la psychopathologie de la vie quotidienne."
  5. 352) Rouma, Georges. "Un cas de Mythomanie. . . ."
All of the above articles reviewed appeared originally in the *Archives de psychologie 1908,* VII:27&28. Cf. CW 18,26,ii (not in GW).

1908m "Die Freudsche Hysterietheorie." *Monatsschrift für Psychiatrie und Neurologie,* XXIII:4, 310–22. Repub. as GW 4,2. Lecture given to the First International Congress of Psychiatry and Neurology, Amsterdam, Sept. 1907. TR.—English: CW 4,2.

1908n "Zur Tatbestandsdiagnostik." *Z. angew. Psychol.,* I:1/2, 163.

1908o Contribution entitled "Deutsche Schweiz" to "Der gegenwärtige Stand der angewandten Psychologie in den einzelnen Kulturländern." *Z. angew. Psychol.,* I, 469–70. GW 18,9. TR.—English: CW 18,9.

1909a *Diagnostische Assoziationsstudien: Beiträge zur experimentellen Psychopathologie.* Ed. by C. G. Jung. Vol. II. Leipzig: Barth. Subsequently issued bound as one with G. 1906a. Contains the following works by Jung:
  1. "Assoziation, Traum und hysterisches Symptom." (31–66) G. 1906j repub. Repub. as GW 2,7. TR.—English: 1918a,5/CW 2,7.
  2. "Über die Reproduktionsstörungen beim Assoziationsexperiment." (67–76) G. 1907e repub. Repub. as GW 2,9. TR.—English: 1918a,6/CW 2,9.

1909b "Vorbemerkung der Redaktion." *Jb. psychoanal. psychopath. Forsch.*, I:1. 1 p. Dated Jan. 1909. GW 18,23. TR.—English: CW 18,23.

1909c "Die Bedeutung des Vaters für das Schicksal des Einzelnen." *Jb. psychoanal. psychopath. Forsch.*, I:1, 155–73. Also pub. as pamphlet, Leipzig and Vienna: Franz Deuticke. pp. 19. "Zweite, unveränderte, mit einer Vorrede versehene Auflage." Pub., rev. and exp., as G. 1949a. TR.—English: 1916a,4/ (Pts. only) CW 4,14.

1909d Review of Karl Kleist: *Untersuchungen zur Kenntnis der psychomotorischen Bewegungsstörungen bei Geisteskranken. CorrespBl. schweizer Ärzte*, XXXIX:1 (1 Jan.), 176. GW 18,20. TR.—English: CW 18,20.

1909e Review of L. Loewenfeld: *Homosexualität und Strafgesetz. CorrespBl. schweizer Ärzte*, XXXIX:1 (1 Jan.), 176. GW 18,20. TR.—English: CW 18,20.

1909f Review of Oswald Bumke: *Landläufige Irrtümer in der Beurteilung von Geisteskranken. CorrespBl. schweizer Ärzte*, XXXIX:6 (15 Mar.), 205. GW 18,20. TR.—English: CW 18,20.

1909g Review of Christian von Ehrenfels: *Grundbegriffe der Ethik. CorrespBl. schweizer Ärzte*, XXXIX:6 (15 Mar.), 205. GW 18,20. TR.—English: CW 18,20.

1909h Review of Isidor Sadger: *Konrad Ferdinand Meyer. Eine pathographisch-psychologische Studie. Basl. Nach.* (Nov.), 1 p. GW 18,11. TR.—English: CW 18,11.

1909i Review of Louis Waldstein: *Das unbewusste Ich und sein Verhältnis zur Gesundheit und Erziehung. Basl. Nach.* (9 Dec.), 1 p. GW 18,12. TR.—English: CW 18,12.

1910a Review of Christian v. Ehrenfels: *Sexualethik. CorrespBl. schweizer Ärzte*, XL:6 (20 Feb.), 173. GW 18,20. TR.—English: CW 18,20.

1910b Review of Alexander Pilcz: *Lehrbuch der speziellen Psychiatrie für Studierende und Aerzte. CorrespBl. schweizer Ärzte*, XL:6 (20 Feb.), 174. GW 18,20. TR.—English: CW 18,20.

1910c Review of Max Dost: *Kurzer Abriss der Psychologie, Psychiatrie und gerichtlichen Psychiatrie . . . CorrespBl. schweizer Ärzte*, XL:6 (20 Feb.), 174. GW 18,20. TR.—English: CW 18,20.

1910d Review of W. v. Bechterew: *Psyche und Leben. CorrespBl. schweizer Ärzte*, XL:7 (1 Mar.), 206. GW 18,20. TR.—English: CW 18,20.

1910e Review of M. Urstein: *Die Dementia praecox und ihre Stellung zum manisch-depressiven Irresein. CorrespBl. schweizer Ärzte*, XL:7 (1 Mar.), 206. GW 18,20. TR.—English: CW 18,20.

1910f Review of Albert Reibmayer: *Die Entwicklungsgeschichte des Talentes und Genies.* I. Band. *CorrespBl. schweizer Ärzte*, XL:8 (10 Mar.), 237. GW 18,20. TR.—English: CW 18,20.

1910g Review of P. Näcke: *Ueber Familienmord durch Geisteskranke. CorrespBl. schweizer Ärzte*, XL:8 (10 Mar.), 237–38. GW 18,20. TR.— English: CW 18,20.

1910h Review of Th. Becker: *Einführung in die Psychiatrie. CorrespBl. schweizer Ärzte*, XL:29, 942. GW 18,20. TR.—English: CW 18,20.

1910i Review of A. Cramer: *Gerichtliche Psychiatrie. CorrespBl. schweizer Ärzte*, XL:29, 942. GW 18,20. TR.—English: CW 18,20.

1910j Review of August Forel: *Ethische und rechtliche Konflikte im Sexual-leben in- und ausserhalb der Ehe. CorrespBl. schweizer Ärzte*, XL:29, 942–43. GW 18,20. TR.—English: CW 18,20.

1910k "Über Konflikte der kindlichen Seele." *Jb. psychoanal. psychopath. Forsch.*, II:1, 33–58. Also pub. as monograph: Leipzig and Vienna: Franz Deuticke. pp. 26. Repub., with addn. of new foreword, as G. 1916b. Cf. E. 1910a,3 for English version. Lecture delivered to the Depts. of Psychology and Pedagogy, Clark University, Worcester, Mass., Sept. 1909.

1910l "Randbemerkungen zu dem Buch von [Fritz] Wittels: *Die sexuelle Not.*" *Jb. psychoanal. psychopath. Forsch.*, II:1, 312–15. GW 18,24. TR.—English: 1973d,2. CW 18,24.

1910m "Referate über psychologische Arbeiten schweizerischer Autoren (bis Ende 1909)." *Jb. psychoanal. psychopath. Forsch.*, II:1, 356–88. GW 18,26. TR.—English: CW 18,26.

1910n "Bericht über Amerika." In "Bericht über die II. private psychoanalytische Vereinigung in Nürnberg am 30. und 31. März." *Jb. psychoanal. psychopath. Forsch.*, II:2, 737. Abstract, recorded by Otto Rank, of Jung's paper. Briefer abstract, also by Rank, pub. in *Zbl. Psychoanal.*, I:3 (Dec.), 130. GW 18,64. TR.—English: CW 18,64.

1910o "Zur Kritik über Psychoanalyse." *Jb. psychoanal. psychopath. Forsch.*, II:2, 743–46. Repub. as GW 4,7. TR.—English: CW 4,7.

1910p "Buchanzeige." Review of Erich Wulffen: *Der Sexualverbrecher. Jb. psychoanal. psychopath. Forsch.*, II:2, 747. GW 18,25. TR.—English: CW 18,25.

1910q "Ein Beitrag zur Psychologie des Gerüchtes." *Zbl. Psychoanal.*, I:1/2, 81–90. Repub. as GW 4,4. TR.—English: 1916a,5/CW 4,4.

1910r "Die an der psychiatrischen Klinik in Zürich gebräuchlichen psychologischen Untersuchungsmethoden." *Z. angew. Psychol.*, III, 390. Contribution to a survey of clinical methods. Repub. as GW 2,17. TR.—English: CW 2,17.

1910s "Über Dementia praecox." *Zbl. Psychoanal.*, I:3 (Dec.), 128. Summary of lecture given at the I. private Psychoanalytische Vereinigung, Salzburg, 27 Apr. 1908. GW 18,10. TR.—English: CW 18,10.

1911a "Wandlungen und Symbole der Libido. Beiträge zur Entwicklungsgeschichte des Denkens." [Pt. I.] *Jb. psychoanal. psychopath. Forsch.*, III:1, 120–227. Contents:
1. Einleitung.
2. Über die zwei Arten des Denkens.
3. Vorbereitende Materialien zur Analyse der Miller'schen Phantasien.
4. Der Schöpferhymnus.
5. Das Lied von der Motte.
Repub., with G. 1912c, as G. 1912a. The 1st of 2 pts.

1911b "Morton Prince, M.D.: *The Mechanism and Interpretation of Dreams. Eine kritische Besprechung.*" *Jb. psychoanal. psychopath. Forsch.*, III:1, 309–28. Repub. as GW 4,6. TR.—English: CW 4,6.

1911c "Kritik über E. Bleuler: 'Zur Theorie des schizophrenen Negativismus.'" *Jb. psychoanal. psychopath. Forsch.*, III:1, 469–74. Repub. as GW 3,3. TR.—English: 1916a,7/CW 3,4.

1911d "Buchanzeige." Review of Eduard Hitschmann: *Freud's Neurosenlehre. Jb. psychoanal. psychopath. Forsch.*, III:1, 480. GW 18,27. TR.—English: CW 18,27.

1911e "Ein Beitrag zur Kenntnis des Zahlentraumes." *Zbl. Psychoanal.*, I:12, 567–72. Repub. as GW 4,5. TR.—English: 1916a,6/CW 4,5.

1911f "Beiträge zur Symbolik." *Zbl. Psychoanal.*, II:2 (Nov.), 103–04. Summary by Otto Rank of lecture given at the 3d Congress of the Internationale Psychoanalytische Vereinigung, Weimar, 22 Sept. 1911. (Ms. of lecture never discovered.) GW 18,34. TR.—English: CW 18,34.

1911g "Bericht über das Vereinsjahr 1910–11." *Korrespondenzblatt der Internationalen Psychoanalytischen Vereinigung*, pp. 16–17, in *Zbl. Psychoanal.*, II:3 (Dec.), 233–34. Annual report by the president, delivered to the 3d Congress of the Internationale Psychoanalytische Vereinigung, Weimar, 21–22 Sept. 1911. GW 18,28. TR.—English: CW 18,28.

1911h Contribution on ambivalence to the discussion following a paper by E. Bleuler. *Psychiatrisch-neurologische Wochenschrift*, XII:43 (21 Jan.), 406. (Also pub. in *Zbl. Psychoanal.*, I:5 (Feb.–Mar.), 267–68, and in *CorrespBl. schweizer Ärzte*, XLI:6 (20 Feb.).) Brief remarks to papers by Von Speyr and Riklin follow. Recorded at a Winter Meeting of the Verein Schweizer Irrenärzte, Bern, 27 Nov. 1910. GW 18,33. TR.—English: CW 18,33.

1912a *Wandlungen und Symbole der Libido. Beiträge zur Entwicklungsgeschichte des Denkens.* Leipzig and Vienna: Franz Deuticke. pp. 422. With 8 text illus. G. 1911a and 1912c repub., combined as one. Repub., with addn. of new foreword, as G. 1925a. TR.—English: 1916b.

1912b *"Über Psychoanalyse beim Kinde." Ier congrès international de Pédagogie, Brussels, August, 1911. [Published Papers.] Vol. II, pp. 332–43. Brussels: Librairie Misch et Thron. Subsequently incorporated into G. 1913a.

1912c "Wandlungen und Symbole der Libido. Beiträge zur Entwicklungsgeschichte des Denkens." [Pt. II.] *Jb. psychoanal. psychopath. Forsch.*, IV:1, 162–464. Contents:
  1. Einleitung.
  2. Über den Begriff und die genetische Theorie der Libido.
  3. Die Verlagerung der Libido als mögliche Quelle der primitiven menschlichen Erfindungen.
  4. Die unbewusste Entstehung des Heros.
  5. Symbole der Mutter und der Wiedergeburt.
  6. Der Kampf um die Befreiung von der Mutter.
  7. Das Opfer.
  Repub., with G. 1911a, as G. 1912a. The 2d of 2 pts.

1912d "Neue Bahnen der Psychologie." *Raschers Jahrbuch für schweizer Art und Kunst* (Zurich), III, 236–72. Repub. as GW 7,3. Pub., rev. and exp., with title change, as G. 1917a. TR.—English: 1916a,15/CW 7,3 (2d edn.).

1912e "Psychoanalyse." *Neue Zür. Z.*, CXXXIII:38 (10 Jan.). Jung's response to article by J[ohann] M[ichelsen], "Psychoanalyse," which appeared earlier in the same paper, 2 Jan. 1912. Cf. G. 1912f and 1912g. GW 18,29. TR.—English: CW 18,29.

1912f "Zur Psychoanalyse." *Neue Zür. Z.*, CXXXIII:72 (17 Jan.). Jung's reply to a response to his G. 1912e. Cf. G. 1912e and 1912g. GW 18,29. TR.—English: CW 18,29.

1912g "Zur Psychoanalyse." *Wissen und Leben*† IX:10 (15 Feb.), 711–14. Jung's reply to the editor's request for a concluding word on the controversy carried in the *Neue Zür. Z.* (cf. G. 1912e and 1912f) in the form of a letter to the editor, dated 28 Jan. 1912. Repub. as GW 4,8. TR.—English: CW 4,8.

† *Neue Schweizer Rundschau* published as *Wissen und Leben*, 1907–1918.

1912h "Über die psychoanalytische Behandlung nervöser Leiden." (Autorreferat.) *CorrespBl. schweizer Ärzte*, XLII:28 (1 Oct.), 1079–84.

Abstract of a report given at a meeting of the Medizinisch-pharmazeutischer Bezirksverein, Bern, 4 June 1912. GW 18,30. TR.— English: CW 18,30.

1913a "Versuch einer Darstellung der psychoanalytischen Theorie. Neun Vorlesungen, gehalten in New-York im September 1912." *Jb. psychoanal. psychopath. Forsch.*, V:1, 307–441. The text of 9 lectures written in German but given in an English trans. as an Extension Course at Fordham University, Sept. 1912. Cf. E. 1913b. Repub. as monograph: Leipzig and Vienna: Franz Deuticke, pp. 135. Pub. with addns. as G. 1955b. Incorporates G. 1912b. TR.— English: 1913b/1914a/1915b/CW 4,9.

1913b "Erklärung der Redaktion." *Jb. psychoanal. psychopath. Forsch.*, V:2, 757. Repub. in G. 1974a following 357J. TR.—English: 1974b.

1913c "Zur Psychologie des Negers." *Korrespondenzblatt der Internationalen Psychoanalytischen Vereinigung*, p. 8, in *Internationale Zeitschrift für ärztliche Psychoanalyse*, I:1, 115. Abstract of lecture given to the Zurich Branch Society of the Internationale Psychoanalytische Vereinigung, Zurich, 22 Nov. 1912. GW 18,65. TR.—English: CW 18,65.

1913d "Eine Bemerkung zur Tauskschen Kritik der Nelkenschen Arbeit." *Internationale Zeitschrift für ärztliche Psychoanalyse*, I:3, 285–88. GW 18,31. TR.—English: 1973d,3/CW 18,31.

1914a *Der Inhalt der Psychose.* (Schriften zur angewandten Seelenkunde, 3.) Leipzig and Vienna: Franz Deuticke. pp. 44. G. 1908a exp. by the addn. of the rev. German version of E. 1915c as Suppl. Repub. as GW 3,2. TR.—English: 1916a,14/CW 3,2&3.

1914b *Psychotherapeutische Zeitfragen. Ein Briefwechsel mit Dr. C. G. Jung.* Ed. by Dr. R. Loÿ. Leipzig and Vienna: Franz Deuticke. pp. 51. Repub. as GW 4,12. TR.—English: 1916a,10/CW 4,12.

1914c Editorial note to *Psychologische Abhandlungen*, 1, ed. by C. G. Jung. Leipzig and Vienna: Franz Deuticke. 1 p. GW 18,134. TR.—English: CW 18,134.

1916a *VII Sermones ad Mortuos. Die sieben Belehrungen der Toten.* Geschrieben von Basilides in Alexandria, der Stadt, wo der Osten den Westen berührt. Übersetzt aus dem griechischen Urtext in die deutsche Sprache. Printed for private circulation by the author. pp. XXVIII. Repub. as G. 1962a,15,x. TR.—English: 1925a/ 1966a,19. Presentation copy examined, inscribed: "To R.F.C. Hull. A souvenir from C. G. Jung. June, 1959."

1916b *Über Konflikte der kindlichen Seele.* Leipzig and Vienna: Franz Deuticke. pp. 35. G. 1910k repub. with the addn. of the "Vorwort zur zweiten Auflage," dated Dec. 1915. Pub. with further addns. as G. 1939a.

1917a *Die Psychologie der unbewussten Prozesse. Ein Überblick über die moderne Theorie und Methode der analytischen Psychologie.* (Schweizer Schriften für allgemeines Wissen, 1.) Zurich: Rascher. pp. 135. G. 1912d, rev. and exp., with title change and the addn. of a preface dated Dec. 1916. Repub., slightly rev. and with new preface, as G. 1918a. TR.—English: 1917a,15.

1918a *Die Psychologie der unbewussten Prozesse. Ein Überblick über die moderne Theorie und Methode der analytischen Psychologie.* Zurich: Rascher. pp. 149. G. 1917a, slightly rev., pub. with the addn. of a preface to the second edition, dated Oct. 1918. Pub., further rev. and exp., with title change, as G. 1926a.

1918b "Über das Unbewusste." *Schweizerland,* IV:9, 464–72; IV:11–12, 548–58. In 2 pts. Repub. as GW 10,1. TR.—English: CW 10,1.

1921a *Psychologische Typen.* Zurich: Rascher. pp. 704. Repr. with varying pp. Index added 1930. Contents:
    Einleitung. (7–13)
    I. Das Typenproblem in der antiken und mittelalterlichen Geistesgeschichte. (17–94)
    II. Über Schillers Ideen zum Typenproblem. (97–189)
    III. Das Apollinische und das Dionysische. (193–207)
    IV. Das Typenproblem in der Menschenkenntnis. (211–36)
    V. Das Typenproblem in der Dichtkunst. (239–380)
    VI. Das Typenproblem in der Psychiatrie. (383–404)
    VII. Das Problem der typischen Einstellungen in der Ästhetik. (407–21)
    VIII. Das Typenproblem in der modernen Philosophie. (425–55)

IX. Das Typenproblem in der Biographik. (459–70)
X. Allgemeine Beschreibung der Typen. (473–583)
XI. Definitionen. (587–691)
Schlusswort. (693–704)
Repub. as GW 6,1&3. TR.—English: 1923a/CW 6,1,2,&4.

1922a "Über die Beziehungen der analytischen Psychologie zum dichterischen Kunstwerk." *Wissen und Leben*, XV:19 (1 Sept.), 914–25; XV:20 (15 Sept.), 964–75. (Parts I and II respectively.) Repub. as G. 1931a,3. Given as lecture to the Gesellschaft für deutsche Sprache und Literatur, Zurich, May 1922, and to the Psychologischer Club Zurich, same year. TR.—English: 1923b/CW 15,6.

1925a *Wandlungen und Symbole der Libido. Beiträge zur Entwicklungsgeschichte des Denkens.* Leipzig and Vienna: Franz Deuticke. pp. 428. G. 1912a repub., with addn. of the "Vorrede zur zweiten Auflage," dated Nov. 1924, which appears on the recto and verso of the unnumbered page between the title page and the table of contents. Repub., with new foreword, as G. 1938b.

1925b "Die Ehe als psychologische Beziehung." *Das Ehebuch.* pp. 294–307. Ed. by Hermann Keyserling. Celle: Kampmann. Repub. as G. 1931a,11. TR.—English: 1926a/1928a,6.

1925c "Psychologische Typen." *Zeitschrift für Menschenkunde; Blätter für Charakterologie* . . . , I:1 (May), 45–65. Repub. as GW 6,5. Lecture given at the Congrès international de Pédagogie, Territet/Montreux, 1923. TR.—English: 1925b/CW 6,6.

1926a *Das Unbewusste im normalen und kranken Seelenleben . . . Ein Überblick über die moderne Theorie und Methode der analytischen Psychologie.* "III. vermehrte und verbesserte Auflage." Zurich: Rascher. pp. 166. Contents:
    Vorworte. (5–10)
    I. Die Anfänge der Psychoanalyse. (11–28)
    II. Die Sexualtheorie. (29–45)
    III. Der andere Gesichtspunkt. Der Wille zur Macht. (46–59)
    IV. Die zwei psychologischen Typen. (60–92)
    V. Das persönliche und das überpersönliche oder kollektive Unbewusste. (93–115)
    VI. Die synthetische oder konstruktive Methode. (116–29)

VII. Die Dominanten des kollektiven Unbewussten. (130–58)
VIII. Zur Auffassung des Unbewussten. Allgemeines zur Therapie. (159–64)
Schlusswort. (165–66)
G. 1918a rev. and exp. with title change. Again rev. and exp., with title change, as G. 1943a. TR.—English: 1928b,1/CW 7,1.

1926b *Analytische Psychologie und Erziehung. 3 Vorlesungen gehalten in London im Mai 1924.* Heidelberg: N. Kampmann. pp. 95. Repr. 1936: Zurich: Rascher. pp. 95. First written and given as lectures in English (cf. E. 1928a,13, Lectures II–IV, London, May 1924). First pub., however, in this German version. Pub., rev. and exp., as G. 1946b,1.

1926c "Geist und Leben." *Form und Sinn*, II:2 (Nov.), 33–44. Repub. as G. 1931a,13. Lecture given to the Literarische Gesellschaft Augsburg, 29 Oct. 1926, contributed to the series "Natur und Geist." TR.—English: 1928a,2.

1927a "Die Erdbedingtheit der Psyche." *Mensch und Erde.* pp. 83–137. Ed. by Hermann Keyserling. (Der Leuchter; Weltanschauung und Lebensgestaltung, 8.) Darmstadt: Otto Reichl. Subsequently divided and largely rewritten as G. 1931a,8 and G. 1928d. Originally given as lecture to the Conference of the Gesellschaft für freie Philosophie, Darmstadt, 1927.

1927b "Die Frau in Europa." *Europ. Rev.*, III:7 (Oct.), 481–99. Repub. as G. 1929a. TR.—English: 1928a,5.

1928a *Die Beziehungen zwischen dem Ich und dem Unbewussten.* Darmstadt: Reichl. pp. 208. Repr. 1933: Zurich: Rascher. Half title: *Das Ich und das Unbewusste.* Contents:
    I. Die Wirkungen des Unbewussten auf das Bewusstein.
      1. Das persönliche und das kollektive Unbewusste. (11–30)
      2. Die Folgeerscheinungen der Assimilation des Unbewussten. (31–60)
      3. Die Persona als ein Ausschnitt aus der Kollektivpsyche. (61–73)
      4. Die Versuche zur Befreiung der Individualität aus der Kollektivpsyche. (74–88)

II. Die Individuation.
1. Die Funktion des Unbewussten. (91–116)
2. Anima und Animus. (117–58)
3. Die Technik der Unterscheidung zwischen dem Ich und den Figuren des Unbewussten. (159–83)
4. Die Mana-Persönlichkeit. (184–208)

Orig. given as lecture, in German, and pub. in trans. as Fr. 1916a. Subsequently much rev. and exp. from the German ms., and pub. as above. Pub. with the addn. of a new foreword as G. 1935a. TR.—English: 1928b,2.

1928b *Über die Energetik der Seele.* (Psychologische Abhandlungen, 2.) Zurich: Rascher. pp. 224. Contents:
1. Vorwort. Repub. as G. 1948b,1.
2. "Über die Energetik der Seele." (9–111) Repub. as G. 1948b,2. TR.—English: 1928a,1.
3. "Allgemeine Gesichtspunkte zur Psychologie des Traumes." (112–84) First pub. in an English trans. (cf. E. 1916a,13). Orig. German text considerably rev. and exp., and pub. here. Subsequently pub., rev. and exp., as G. 1948b,4.
4. "Instinkt und Unbewusstes." (185–99) First pub. in an English trans. (cf. E. 1919b). Pub., rev. and with the addn. of brief concluding note, as G. 1948b,6. Contribution to symposium, "Instinct and the Unconscious," presented at a joint meeting of the Aristotelian Society, The Mind Association, and the British Psychological Association, London, July 1919. TR.—English: 1919b.
5. "Die psychologischen Grundlagen des Geisterglaubens." (200–24) Pub., rev., as G. 1948b,7. Paper read in an English trans. before the Society for Psychical Research, London, 4 July 1919. TR.—English: 1920b.

Whole book pub., exp., with addns. and title change, as G. 1948b.

1928c "Heilbare Geisteskranke? Organisches oder funktionelles Leiden?" *Berliner Tageblatt*, 189 (21 Apr.), 1. Beiblatt. The orig. ms. bears the title "Geisteskrankheit und Seele" and was presumably given as a lecture before a meeting of the III. Allgemeiner Ärztlicher Kongress für Psychotherapie, Baden-Baden, 20–22 Apr. 1928. Repub. under the orig. title as GW 3,6. TR.—English: CW 3,7.

1928d "Die Struktur der Seele." *Europ. Rev.*, IV:1 (Apr.), 27–37; and IV:2 (May), 125–35. (In two parts.) Derived from G. 1927a. Pub., rev. and exp., as G. 1931a,7.

1928e "Die Bedeutung der schweizerischen Linie im Spektrum Europas." *Neue Schw. R.*, XXXIV:6 (June), 1–11, 469–79. A retort to Keyserling's *Das Spektrum Europas*. Repub. as GW 10,19. TR.—English: 1959k/ CW 10,19.

1928f "Das Seelenproblem des modernen Menschen." *Europ. Rev.*, IV:9 (Dec.), 700–15. Brief, much simplified version pub. as G. 1929e. Pub., rev. and exp., as G. 1931a,14. Read before the Tagung des Verbandes für intellektuelle Zusammenarbeit, Prague, Oct. 1928. TR.—English: 1931c.

1928g "Psychoanalyse und Seelsorge." *Ethik (Sexual- und Gesellschafts-Ethik)* (Halle), V:1, 7–12. Repub. as GW 11,8. TR.—English: CW 11,8.

1929a *Die Frau in Europa*. Zurich: Verlag der Neuen Schweizer Revue. pp. 46. Reset, 1932: "Zweite Auflage." Zurich: Rascher. pp. 39. Reset, 1965: "Rascher Paperback," pp. 25. G. 1927b repub. as monograph. Repub. as G. 1971a,2. TR.—English: CW 10,6.

1929b With Richard Wilhelm: *Das Geheimnis der goldenen Blüte. Ein chinesisches Lebensbuch*. Munich: Dorn. pp. 161. A 1929 Berlin edn. with 150 pp. has been reported but not seen. Contains the following work by Jung:
    I. "Einführung." (7[88])
       1. Einleitung. (9–27)
       2. Die Grundbegriffe. (28–40)
       3. Die Erscheinungen des Weges. (41–57)
       4. Die Loslösung des Bewusstseins vom Objekt. (58–64)
       5. Die Vollendung. (65–73)
       6. Schlusswort. (74–75)
       7. Beispiele europäischer Mandalas. ([77–88]) Includes 10 black and white plates.
G. 1929h pub., rev. and exp. Pub., rev. and with addns., as G. 1938a. TR.—English: 1931a,1&2.

1929c *"Ziele der Psychotherapie." *Bericht über den IV. allgemeinen ärztlichen Kongress für Psychotherapie* in Bad Nauheim [April]. pp. 1–14. Given as lecture to the Congress, 12 Apr. 1929. Repub. as G. 1931a,5.

1929d "Die Probleme der modernen Psychotherapie." *Schweizerisches medizinisches Jahrbuch.* pp. 74–86. Repub. as G. 1931a,2. Lecture given to the Ärztlicher Verein and to the Psychotherapeutische Gesellschaft, Munich, 21 March 1929. TR.—English: 1931d.

1929e "Das Seelenproblem des modernen Menschen." *Allgemeine Neueste Nachrichten* (23 Jan.). A much abbreviated, simplified version of G. 1928f.

1929f "Der Gegensatz Freud und Jung." *Kölnische Zeitung,* Saturday, 4 May and Tuesday, 7 May. (In two parts.) Repub. as G. 1931a,4.

1929g "Paracelsus. Ein Vortrag gehalten beim Geburtshaus an der Teufelsbrücke bei Einsiedeln am 22. Juni 1929." *Lesezirkel,* XVI:10 (Sept.), 117–25. Repub. as G. 1934b,5. Lecture given at Paracelsus' birthplace to the Literarische Club Zurich, 22 June 1929.

1929h With Richard Wilhelm: "Tschang Scheng Schu. Die Kunst das menschliche Leben zu verlängern." *Europ. Rev.,* V:8 (Nov.), 530–56. Contains the following work by Jung:
   1. "Einleitung." (530–42)
Pub., rev. and exp., as G. 1929b.

1929i "Die Bedeutung von Konstitution und Vererbung für die Psychologie." *Die Medizinische Welt,* III:47 (Nov.), 1677–79. Repub. as GW 8,4. TR.—English: CW 8,4.

1930a "Psychologie und Dichtung." *Philosophie der Literaturwissenschaft.* pp. 315–30. Ed. by Emil Ermatinger. Berlin: Junker und Dünnhaupt. Pub., rev. and exp., as G. 1950a,2. TR.—English: 1930c/1933a,8.

1930b "Einführung." W. M. Kranefeldt: *Die Psychoanalyse.* pp. 5–16. (Sammlung Göschen, 1034.) Berlin and Leipzig: Walter de Gruyter. Reset, 1950: new title: *Therapeutische Psychologie.* Jung's intro-

duction, pp. 5–17. Repub. as GW 4,15. TR.—English: 1932a / CW
4,15.

1930c "Nachruf für Richard Wilhelm." *Neue Zür. Z.*, CLI:422 (6 Mar.), 1.
Repub. as G. 1931b. Delivered as contribution to a memorial ser-
vice for Wilhelm, Munich, 10 May 1930. Cf. G. 1931b and
1938a,2. TR.—English: 1931a,3.

1930d "Die seelischen Probleme der menschlichen Altersstufen." *Neue
Zür. Z.* (14 and 16 Mar.). (In 2 pts.) Pub., largely rewritten, as G.
1931a,10, with title change.

1930e "Der Aufgang einer neuen Welt." A review of Hermann Keyserling: *Amerika; der Aufgang einer neuen Welt. Neue Zür Z.*, no. 2378,
iv (7 Dec.), Bücherbeilage, p. 6. Repub. as GW 10,20. TR.—English: CW 10,20.

1931a *Seelenprobleme der Gegenwart.* (Psychologische Abhandlungen, 3.)
Zurich: Rascher. pp. 435. 1932: new edn. 1950: rev. edn. pp. 392.
Reset, 1969: "Rascher Paperback." pp. 323. Repr., 1973: ("Studienausgabe.") Olten: Walter. pp. 323. Contents:
  1. Vorwort(e). (v–vii) Dated Dec. 1930 and July 1932. TR.—English: CW 18,67 with addn.
  2. "Die Probleme der modernen Psychotherapie." (1–39) G.
  1929d repub. Repub. as GW 16,6. TR.—English: CW 16,6.
  3. "Über die Beziehungen der analytischen Psychologie zum
  dichterischen Kunstwerk." (40–73) G. 1922a repub. Repub.
  as GW 15,6. TR.—English: CW 15,6.
  4. "Der Gegensatz Freud und Jung." (74–86) G. 1929f repub.
  Repub. as GW 4,16. TR.—English: 1933a,6 / CW 4,16.
  5. "Ziele der Psychotherapie." (87–114) G. 1929c repub. Repub. as GW 16,5. TR.—English: 1933a,3 / CW 16,5.
  6. "Psychologische Typologie." (115–43) A lecture to a meeting of the Schweizer Irrenärzte, Zurich, 1928. Repub. as
  GW 6,6. TR.—English: 1933a,4 / CW 6,7.
  7. "Die Struktur der Seele." (144–75) G. 1928d rev. and exp.
  Repub. as GW 8,7. TR.—English: CW 8,7.
  8. "Seele und Erde." (176–210) Derived from G. 1927a; title
  changed. Repub. as GW 10,2. TR.—English: 1928a,3 / CW
  10,2.

9. "Der archaïsche Mensch." (211–47) G. 1931f, somewhat rev. Repub. as GW 10,3. TR.—English: 1933a,7 / CW 10,3.
10. "Die Lebenswende." (248–74) G. 1930d, much rev., with title change. Repub. as GW 8,16. TR.—English: 1933a,5.
11. "Die Ehe als psychologische Beziehung." (275–95) G. 1925b repub. Repub. as GW 17,8. TR.—English: CW 17,8.
12. "Analytische Psychologie und Weltanschauung." (296–335) A rev. and exp. version of the orig. unpub. ms, 1st pub. in trans. as E. 1928a,4. Repub. as GW 8,14. Lecture given in Karlsruhe, 1927, and to the Philosophische Gesellschaft, Zurich, 4 March 1930. TR.—English: CW 8,14.
13. "Geist und Leben." (369–400) G. 1926c repub. Repub. as GW 8,12. TR.—English: CW 8,12.
14. "Das Seelenproblem des modernen Menschen." (401–35) G. 1928f, rev. and exp. Repub. as GW 10,4. TR.—English: 1933a,10 / CW 10,4.

1931b * "Richard Wilhelm." *Chinesisch-Deutscher Almanach für das Jahr 1931.* pp. 7–14. Frankfurt a. M.: China-Institut. G. 1930c repub. Repub. as G. 1938a,2 with title change.

1931c * "Die praktische Verwendbarkeit der Traumanalyse." *Bericht über den VI. allgemeinen ärztlichen Kongress für Psychotherapie.* Dresden. Delivered as a lecture to the 6th Congress of the Allgemeine ärztliche Gesellschaft für Psychotherapie, Dresden, 31 Apr. 1931. Cf. G. 1934b,4. TR.—English: 1933a,1.

1931d "Vorwort." H. Schmid-Guisan: *Tag und Nacht.* pp. vi–x. Zurich and Munich: Rhein. GW 18,108. TR.—English: CW 18,108.

1931e "Einführung." Francis [error for Frances] G. Wickes: *Analyse der Kindesseele. Untersuchung und Behandlung nach den Grundlagen der Jungschen Theorie.* pp. 13–20. Stuttgart: Julius Hoffmann. The first 3 1/2 paragraphs only of the above were previously pub. in trans. as E. 1927a. Repub. as GW 17,2. TR.—English: (Pt. only) 1927a / 1966c / CW 17,2.

1931f "Der archaische Mensch." *Europ. Rev.*, VII:3 (Mar.), 182–203. Pub., rev. somewhat, as G. 1931a,9. Lecture delivered to the Hottinger Lesezirkel, Zurich, 22 Oct. 1930, and pub. abridged as the above.

1931g "Die Entschleierung der Seele." *Europ. Rev.*, VII:7 (July), 504–22. Pub. with minor alterations and title change as G. 1934b,2. Lecture given to the Kulturbund, Vienna, 1931. TR.—English: 1933a,9.

1932a *Die Beziehungen der Psychotherapie zur Seelsorge.* Zurich: Rascher. pp. 30. Reset, 1948; pp. 39. Repub. as GW 11,7 with title change. Text of lecture to the Elsässische Pastoralkonferenz, Strassburg, May 1932, and to the Psychologischer Club Zurich, 1932. TR.—English: 1933a,11 / CW 11,7.

1932b "Vorwort zum Märchen vom Fischotter." O. A. Schmitz: *Märchen aus dem Unbewussten.* pp. 7–12. Munich: Hanser, GW 18,110. TR.— English: CW 18,110.

1932c * Answers to questions on Goethe. *Kölnische Zeitung*, (22 Mar.) Letter to the editor, Max Rychner (28 Feb. 1932). Letter pub. in G. 1972a, and trans. in E. 1973b.

1932d "Dr. Hans Schmid-Guisan: In memoriam." *Basl. Nach.*, (25 Apr.). Obituary article. TR.—English: CW 18,109.

1932e "Ulysses." *Europ. Rev.*, VIII:2/9 (Sept.), 547–68. Pub. with the addn. of "forenote" as G. 1934b,7.

1932f "Sigmund Freud als kulturhistorische Erscheinung." *Charakter*, I:2 (Sept.), 65–70. Repub. as G. 1934b,6. Excerpts pub. as "Entlarvung der viktorianischen Epoche. Freud kulturhistorisch gesehen." *Vossische Zeitung* (4 Aug.). Simultaneously issued in trans. in the U.S. edn. of this journal as E. 1932b. TR.—English: 1932b.

1932g "Picasso." *Neue Zür. Z.*, CLIII:2 (Sun., 13 Nov.), 1. Repub. as G. 1934b,8.

1932h "Wirklichkeit und Überwirklichkeit." *Querschnitt*, XII:12 (Dec.), 844–45. Repub. as GW 8,15. TR.—English: CW 8,15.

1932i "Die Hypothese des kollektiven Unbewussten." (Autorreferat.) *Vierteljahresschrift der Naturforschenden Gesellschaft in Zürich*, LXXVII:2, "Sitzungsberichte," IV–V. Abstract of lecture read before a meeting of the Naturforschende Gesellschaft held at the

Eidgenössische Technische Hochschule, Zurich, 1 Feb. 1932. Lecture ms not discovered. GW 18,51. TR.—English: CW 18,51.

1933a "Blick in die Verbrecherseele. Das Doppelleben des Kriminellen. Ungewöhnliche Fälle von Übertragung verbrecherischer Absichten auf Andere. . . . Aus einem Gespräch." *Neues Wiener Journal* (15 Jan.). 1 p. For English versions, see E. 1932c.

1933b "Über Psychologie." *Neue Schw. R.*, n.s. I:1 (May), 21–28 and 1:2 (June), 98–106. (In 2 pts.) Rev. and expanded into G. 1934b,3 with change of title. An expanded version of a lecture originally delivered in Dresden, 1931, then at a conference, Town Hall, Zurich, 18 Dec. 1932, and in Cologne and Essen, Feb. 1933.

1933c "Bruder Klaus." *Neue Schw. R.*, n.s. I:4 (Aug.) 223–29. Repub. as GW 11,6. TR.—English: 1946c / CW 11,6.

1933d Review of Gustav Richard Heyer: *Der Organismus der Seele. Europ. Rev.*, IX:10 (Oct.), 639. GW 18,124. TR.—English: CW 18,124.

1933e "Geleitwort." *Zbl. Psychotherap.*, VI:3 (Dec.), 139–40. Repub. as GW 10,25. TR.—English: CW 10,25.

1933f Contribution on hallucination to the "Discussion-Aussprache" following papers on "Das Problem der Sinnestäuschungen" in "Bericht über die Wissenschaftlichen Sitzungen der 84. Versammlung der Schweizerischen Gesellschaft für Psychiatrie in Prangins près Nyon, 7–8 Octobre 1933." *Schweizer Archiv für Neurologie und Psychiatrie. . .*, XXXII:2, 382. GW 18,38. TR.—English: CW 18,38.

1934a *Allgemeines zur Komplextheorie.* (Kultur- und staatswissenschaftliche Schriften der Eidgenössischen Technischen Hochschule, 12.) Aarau: Sauerländer. pp. 20. Pub., slightly rev. and with minor title change, as G. 1948b,3. Text of lecture originally entitled "Über Komplextheorie," given as "Antrittsvorlesung," at the Eidgenössische Technische Hochschule, 5 May 1934, and at the 7. [Allgemeiner ärztlicher] Kongress für Psychotherapie, Bad Nauheim, 10–13 May 1934. Summary of lecture pub. in *Zbl. Psychotherap.*, VII: 3, 139–42.

1934b *Wirklichkeit der Seele. Anwendungen und Fortschritte der neueren Psychologie.* With contributions by Hugo Rosenthal, Emma Jung and W. M. Kranefeldt. (Psychologische Abhandlungen, 4.) Zurich: Rascher. pp. 409. Reset, 1969: Olten: Walter. pp. 265. Contains the following works by Jung:

1. Vorwort. (vii–viii) Dated Sept. 1933. GW 18,113. TR.—English: CW 18,113.
2. "Das Grundproblem der gegenwärtigen Psychologie." (1–31) G. 1931g, slightly rev. and with title change. Repub. as GW 8,13. TR.—English: CW 8,13.
3. "Die Bedeutung der Psychologie für die Gegenwart." (32–67) G. 1933b, rev. and exp. with title change. Repub. as GW 10,7. TR.—English: CW 10,7.
4. "Die praktische Verwendbarkeit der Traumanalyse." (68–103) Cf. G. 1931c. Repub. as GW 16,12. TR.—English: 1933a,1 / CW 16,12.
5. "Paracelsus." (104–18) G. 1929g repub. Repub. as G. 1952c. TR.—English: CW 15,1.
6. "Sigmund Freud als kulturhistorische Erscheinung." (119–31) G. 1932f repub. Repub. as GW 15,3. TR.—English: CW 15,3.
7. "Ulysses." (132–69) G. 1932e pub. with the addn. of a forenote. Repub. as GW 15,8. TR.—English: 1949c / CW 15,8.
8. "Picasso." (170–79) G. 1932g repub. Repub. as GW 15,9. TR.—English: 1940a / 1953i / CW 15,9.
9. "Vom Werden der Persönlichkeit." (180–211) Lecture delivered to the Kulturbund, Vienna, Nov. 1932, titled "Die Stimme des Innern." Repub. as GW 17,7. TR.—English: 1939a,6 / CW 17,7.
10. "Seele und Tod." (212–30) G. 1934h repub. Pub., abridged and with title change, as G. 1935i. Repub. as whole as GW 8,17. TR.—English: 1945a / 1959c / CW 8,17.

1934c "Zur Empirie des Individuationsprozesses." *Eran. Jb. 1933.* pp. 201–14. Includes 5 black and white plates. (The *Eranos Jahrbuch* articles were originally given as lectures at the Eranos Tagung, Ascona, in August of the year indicated.) Pub., completely rewritten and exp., as G. 1950a,4. TR.—English: 1939a,2.

1934d "Geleitwort." Gerhard Adler: *Entdeckung der Seele. Von Sigmund Freud und Alfred Adler zu C. G. Jung.* pp. vii–viii. Zurich: Rascher. Dated Dec. 1933. GW 18,52. TR.—English: CW 18,52.

1934e "Geleitwort." Carl Ludwig Schleich: *Die Wunder der Seele*. pp. 3–11. Berlin: S. Fischer. Reset, 1953: Frankfurt: G. B. Fischer. pp. 5–11. GW 18,39. TR.—English: CW 18,39.

1934f Rejoinder to Dr. Bally's article "Deutschstämmige Psychotherapie," headlined "Zeitgenössisches." *Neue Zür. Z.*, CLV:437,1 (13 Mar.) and CLV:443,1 (14 Mar.). (In 2 pts.) Cf. G. 1934g. Repub., with G. 1934g, as GW 10,26. TR.—English: CW 10,26 (with trans. of G. 1934g).

1934g "Ein Nachtrag." *Neue Zür. Z.*, CLV:457 (15 Mar.). Second and third paragraphs *only* by Jung. Cf. G. 1934f. Repub., with G. 1934f, as GW 10,26. TR.—English: CW 10,26 (p. 544, last 3 parags., ftnote 5) with trans. of G. 1934f.

1934h "Seele und Tod." *Europ. Rev.*, X:4 (Apr.), 229–38. Extract pub. in *Berliner Tageblatt*, (17 Apr.). Entire article repub. as G. 1934b,10.

1934i "Ein neues Buch von Keyserling." Review of Hermann Keyserling: *La Révolution mondiale*. *Basl. Nach.*, Sonntagsblatt, XXVIII: 19 (13 May), 78–79. Repub. as GW 10,21. TR.—English: CW 10,21.

1934j Circular letter: "Sehr geehrte Kollegen! . . . Zürich-Küsnacht 1.12.34." *Zbl. Psychotherap.*, VII:6 (Dec.), 1p. (separatum). Repub. as GW 10,27. TR.—English: 1946d,1 / CW 10,27.

1934k "Zur gegenwärtigen Lage der Psychotherapie." *Zbl. Psychotherap.*, VII:1, 1–16. Repub. as GW 10,8. TR.—English: CW 10,8.

1934l With M. H. Göring: "Geheimrat Sommer zum 70. Geburtstag." *Zbl. Psychotherap.*, VII, 313–14.

1935a *Die Beziehungen zwischen dem Ich und dem Unbewussten.* Zurich: Rascher. pp. 208. 1966: 7th rev. edn. ("Rascher Paperback.") pp. 151. 1971: ("Studienausgabe.") Olten: Walter. pp. 160. G. 1928a pub. with addn. of the "Vorrede zur zweiten Auflage," dated Oct. 1934, on 4 unnumbered pp. between the title page and the table of contents. (An insignificant, prefatory parag. was added to the 1938 repr.) Repub. as GW 7,2, with slight title change. TR.—English: CW 7,2.

1935b "Über die Archetypen des kollektiven Unbewussten." *Eran. Jb. 1934.* pp. 179–229. (See G. 1934c.) Pub., rev., as G. 1954b,2. TR.— English: 1939a,3.

1935c "Einleitung." M. Esther Harding: *Der Weg der Frau.* pp. 9–13. Zurich: Rhein. The original German version, of which an English trans. was previously pub. as E. 1933b. TR.—English: 1933b / CW 18,130.

1935d "Geleitwort." Olga von Koenig-Fachsenfeld: *Wandlungen des Traumproblems von der Romantik bis zur Gegenwart.* pp. iii–vi. Stuttgart: F. Enke. TR.—English: CW 18,115.

1935e "Vorwort." Rose Mehlich: *J. H. Fichtes Seelenlehre und ihre Beziehung zur Gegenwart.* pp. 7–11. Zurich: Rascher. TR.—English: (Pts. only) 1950e / CW 18,114.

1935f "Einführung." *Das tibetanische Totenbuch.* pp. 15–35. Ed. by W. Y. Evans-Wentz. Zurich: Rascher. 1973: Repr., Olten: Walter. Jung's "Einführung" consists of:
    1. "Geleitwort." (15–16)
    2. "Psychologischer Kommentar zum Bardo Thödol." (17–35)
Repub. as GW 11,11. TR.—English: 1957f.

1935g "Was ist Psychotherapie?" *Schweizerische Ärztezeitung für Standesfragen,* XVI:26 (28 June), 335–39. Repub. as GW 16,3. Contribution to a symposium of the Allgemeine ärztliche Gesellschaft für Psychotherapie, "Psychotherapie in der Schweiz," May 1935. Cf. G. 1935h. TR.—English: CW 16,3.

1935h "Votum C. G. Jung." *Schweizerische Ärztezeitung für Standesfragen,* XVI:26 (28 June), 345–46. Repub. as GW 10,31, with sl. title change. Contribution to discussion at symposium, "Psychotherapie in der Schweiz," May 1935. Cf. G. 1935g. TR.—English: CW 10,31.

1935i "Von der Psychologie des Sterbens." *Münchener Neueste Nachrichten,* 269 (2 Oct.), 3. G. 1934b,10 abridged and with title change.

1935j "Geleitwort." *Zbl. Psychotherap.,* VIII:1, 1–5. Repub. as GW 10,28. TR.—English: CW 10,28.

1935k "Vorbemerkung des Herausgebers." *Zbl. Psychotherap.*, VIII:2, 65. Repub. as GW 10,29. TR.—English: CW 10,29.

1935l "Grundsätzliches zur praktischen Psychotherapie." *Zbl. Psychotherap.*, VIII:2, 66–82. Repub. as GW 16,2. Given as lecture to the Medizinische Gesellschaft, Zurich, 1935. TR.—English: CW 16,2.

1936a "Traumsymbole des Individuationsprozesses" *Eran. Jb. 1935.* pp. 13–133. (See G. 1934c.) Pub., rev. and exp., as G. 1944a,3. TR.—English: 1939a,4 / 1959d.

1936b "Psychologische Typologie." *Süddeutsche Monatshefte*, XXXIII:5 (Feb.), 264–72. Repub. as GW 6,7. TR.—English: CW 6,8.

1936c "Wotan." *Neue Schw. R.*, n.s. III:11 (Mar.), 657–69. Repub. as G. 1946a,2. TR.—English: (abridged) 1937c / 1947a,3 / CW 10,10.

1936d Review of Gustav Richard Heyer: *Praktische Seelenheilkunde. Zbl. Psychotherap.*, IX:3, 184–86. GW 18,125. TR.—English: CW 18,125.

1936e "Über den Archetypus, mit besonderer Berücksichtigung des Animabegriffes." *Zbl. Psychotherap.*, IX:5, 259–74. Pub., rev., as G. 1954b,3.

1937a "Die Erlösungsvorstellungen in der Alchemie." *Eran. Jb. 1936.* pp. 13–111. (See G. 1934c.) Pub., rev. and exp., as G. 1944a,4. TR.—English: 1939a,5.

1937b "Zur psychologischen Tatbestandsdiagnostik. Das Tatbestandsexperiment im Schwurgerichtsprozess Näf." *Archiv für Kriminologie*, C (Jan.–Feb.), 123–30. Repub. as GW 2,19. TR.—English: CW 2,19.

1937c "Ueber das 'Rosarium Philosophorum.'" *Aus d. Jhrsb. 1936/37.* pp. 25–29. Printed for private circulation. Summary of 2 lectures to the Psychologischer Club Zürich, given 5 and 16 June 1936. GW 18,126. TR.—English: CW 18,126.

1938a With Richard Wilhelm: *Das Geheimnis der goldenen Blüte. Ein chinesisches Lebensbuch.* "II. Auflage." Zurich: Rascher. pp. 150. Contains the following works by Jung:

1. "Vorrede zur II. Auflage." (v–viii) TR.—English: 1962b,1.
2. "Zum Gedächtnis Richard Wilhelms." (ix–xviii) G. 1930c republb. with title change. TR.—English: 1962b,3.
3. Europäischer Kommentar. (1–66) (Untitled here) G. 1928b,I, 1–6 rev. and exp. TR.—English: 1962b,2.
4. "Beispiele europäischer Mandalas." (67–68 + 10 plates) Plates (excepting #2) incorporated into G. 1950a,5. TR.—English: 1962b,2.

G. 1929b pub. rev. and with addns. Pub. reset and with further addns. as G. 1957b. TR.—English: 1962b.

1938b *Wandlungen und Symbole der Libido. Beiträge zur Entwicklungsgeschichte des Denkens.* Leipzig and Vienna: Franz Deuticke. pp. 428. G. 1925a repub., with addn. of "Vorrede zur dritten Auflage," dated Nov. 1937, on p. v. ("Vorrede zur zweiten Auflage" is on pp. iii–iv.) Repub., greatly rev. and exp., with title change, as G. 1952e.

1938c "Einige Bemerkungen zu den Visionen des Zosimos." *Eran. Jb. 1937.* pp. 15–54 (See G. 1934c.) Pub., rev. and considerably exp., with title change, as G. 1954b,5.

1938d "Begleitwort." Gertrud Gilli: *Der dunkle Bruder.* 2 pp. Zurich/Elgg: Volksverlag. GW 18,116. TR.—English: CW 18,116.

1939a *Über Konflikte der kindlichen Seele.* "Dritte Auflage." Zurich: Rascher. pp. 36. G. 1916b pub. as a pamphlet with a new foreword and supplement. Pub., slightly rev. and exp., as G. 1946b,2.

1939b "Die psychologischen Aspekte des Mutterarchetypus." *Eran. Jb. 1938.* pp. 403–43. (See G. 1934c.) Pub., rev., as G. 1954b,4. TR.—English: 1943a.

1939c "Geleitwort." D. T. Suzuki: *Die grosse Befreiung. Einführung in den Zen-Buddhismus.* pp. 7–37. Leipzig: Curt Weller. Repub. as GW 11,13. TR.—English: 1949d / CW 11,13.

1939d "† Sigmund Freud." *Basl. Nach.,* Sonntagsblatt, XXXIII:40 (1 Oct.), 157–59. Obituary article. Repub. as GW 15,4. TR.—English: CW 15,4.

1939e "Bewusstein, Unbewusstes und Individuation." *Zbl. Psychotherap.,* XI:5, 257–70. Orig. written in English and pub. as E. 1939a,1.

Subsequently rev. considerably and pub. in this German version. Repub. as GW 9,i,10. TR.—English: CW 9,i,10.

1940a *Psychologie und Religion. Die Terry Lectures 1937 gehalten an der Yale University.* Zurich: Rascher. pp. 192. 1962: 4th edn., rev. and reset. ("Rascher Paperback.") pp. 125. Orig. written in English and trans. from E. 1938a by Felicia Froboese and Toni Wolff. Subsequently rev. and exp. and pub. in this version. Contents:
Vorrede. (Oct. 1939.)
1. Die Autonomie des Unbewussten. (9–61)
2. Dogma und natürliche Symbole. (63–116)
3. Geschichte und Psychologie eines natürlichen Symbols. (117–90)
Repub. as GW 11,1. TR.—English: CW 11,1.

1940b "Die verschiedenen Aspekte der Wiedergeburt." *Eran. Jb. 1939.* pp. 399–447. (See G. 1934c.) Pub., rev. and exp., with title change, as G. 1950a,3. TR.—English: 1944a.

1940c "Geleitwort." Jolande [or Jolan] Jacobi: *Die Psychologie von C. G. Jung.* pp. 17–18. Zurich: Rascher. Dated Aug. 1939. Paging varies in successive edns. GW 18,40. TR.—English: 1942c / 1962c / CW 18,40.

1941a With K. Kerényi: *Das göttliche Kind in mythologischer und psychologischer Beleuchtung.* (Albae Vigiliae, 6/7.) Amsterdam: Pantheon Akademische Verlagsanstalt. pp. 124. Contains the following work by Jung:
"Zur Psychologie des Kind-Archetypus." (85–124)
Pub. rev., together with G. 1941b, as G. 1941c.

1941b With K. Kerényi: *Das göttliche Mädchen. Die Hauptgestalt der Mysterien von Eleusis in mythologischer und psychologischer Beleuchtung.* (Albae Vigiliae, 8/9.) Amsterdam: Pantheon Akademische Verlagsanstalt. pp. 109. Contains the following work by Jung:
"Zum psychologischen Aspekt der Korefigur." (85–109)
Pub. rev., together with G. 1941a, as G. 1941c.

1941c With K. Kerényi: *Einführung in das Wesen der Mythologie.* Amsterdam: Pantheon Akademische Verlagsanstalt; Zurich: Rascher. pp. 251. Contains the following works by Jung:
1. "Zur Psychologie des Kind-Archetypus." (105–44)

2. "Zum psychologischen Aspekt der Korefigur." (217–41)
G. 1941a and 1941b rev. and pub. as one vol. Repub. as G. 1951b.
TR.—English: 1949a.

1941d *Die psychologische Diagnose des Tatbestandes.* Zurich: Rascher. pp. 47.
G. 1906k repub. Repub. as GW 2,6. TR.—English: CW 2,6.

1941e "Rückkehr zum einfachen Leben." *Du*, Jhg. I:3 (May), 6–7, 56.
Summation of answers to a questionnaire on the effect of wartime
conditions in Switzerland. TR.—English: (Pts. only) 1945b / CW
18,71.

1941f "Paracelsus als Arzt." *Schweizerische medizinische Wochenschrift*,
LXXI:40 (Oct.), 1153–70. Repub. as G. 1942a,1. Simplified version pub. in *Basler Nachrichten* (21 Sept.). Lecture given at the annual meeting of the Naturforschende Gesellschaft Basel, of the
Schweizerische Gesellschaft zur Geschichte der Medizin und der
Naturwissenschaften, Basel, 7 Sept. 1941 and to the Psychologischer Club Zürich, 21 Feb. 1942.

1942a *Paracelsica. Zwei Vorlesungen über den Arzt und Philosophen Theophras-
tus.* Zurich: Rascher. pp. 188. With 3 plates and 5 text illus.
Contents:
Vorwort. (7–8)
   1. "Paracelsus als Arzt." (9–41) G. 1941f repub. Repub. as GW
   15,2. TR.—English: CW 15,2.
   2. "Paracelsus als geistige Erscheinung." (43–178) Lecture contributed to the Schweizerische Paracelsus Gesellschaft Celebration, Einsiedeln, 5 Oct. 1941. Repub. as GW 13,3. TR.—
   English: CW 13,3.
Two lectures delivered on the occasion of the 400th anniversary
of Paracelsus' death, Autumn 1941.

1942b "Zur Psychologie der Trinitätsidee." *Eran. Jb. 1940/41.* pp. 31–64.
(See G. 1934c.) Pub., rev. and exp. with title change, as G. 1948a,4.
Lecture given also to the Psychologischer Club Zurich, 5 Oct.
1940.

1942c "Das Wandlungssymbol in der Messe." *Eran. Jb. 1940/41.* pp. 67–
155. (See G. 1934c.) Pub., rev. and exp., as G. 1954b,6. Lecture
given also to the Psychologischer Club Zurich, 17 May 1941. TR.—
English: 1955b/ 1955l (Pt. only).

1943a *Über die Psychologie des Unbewussten.* Zurich: Rascher. pp. 213.
1960: reset, "7. vermehrte und verbesserte Auflage." pp. 135.
1966: reset. ("Rascher Paperback.") pp. 148. Contents:
Vorworte. (7–15)
1. Die Psychoanalyse. (17–34)
2. Die Erostheorie. (35–53)
3. Der andere Gesichtspunkt: Der Wille zur Macht. (54–73)
4. Das Problem des Einstellungstypus. (74–115)
5. Das persönliche und das überpersönliche oder kollektive Unbewusste. (116–44)
6. Die synthetische oder konstruktive Methode. (145–60)
7. Die Archetypen des kollektiven Unbewussten. (161–202)
8. Zur Auffassung des Unbewussten: Allgemeines zur Therapie. (203–11)
Schlusswort. (212–13)
G. 1926a rev. and exp. with title change. Repub. as GW 7,1. TR.—
English: CW 7,1.

1943b "Der Geist Mercurius." *Eran. Jb. 1942.* pp. 179–236. (See G. 1934c.) Pub., rev. and exp., as G. 1948a,3.

1943c "Zur Psychologie östlicher Meditation." *Mitteilungen der Schweizerischen Gesellschaft der Freunde ostasiatischer Kultur,* V, 33–53. Repub. as G. 1948a,5. Lecture given to the Psychologischer Club Zurich, 8 May 1943, and to the Schweizerische Gesellschaft der Freunde ostasiatischer Kultur, Zurich/Basel/Bern, Mar.–May 1943. TR.—
English: 1947b.

1943d *"Votum. Zum Thema: Schule und Begabung." Schweizer Erziehungs-Rundschau,* XVI:1 (Apr.), 3–8. Lecture presented as contribution to a meeting of the Basler staatliche Schulsynode, 4 Dec. 1942. Repub. with title change as G. 1946b,3.

1943e "Psychotherapie und Weltanschauung." *Schweizerische Zeitschrift für Psychologie und ihre Anwendungen,* I:3, 157–64. Repub. as G. 1946a,4. Contribution to the Tagung für Psychologie, Zurich, 26 Sept. 1942.

1943f "Ein Gespräch mit C. G. Jung. Über Tiefenpsychologie und Selbsterkenntnis." *Du,* III:9 (Sept.), 15–18. Written in answer to questions from Jolan Jacobi. Repub. as G. 1947c with title change. TR.—English: 1943b.

1944a *Psychologie und Alchemie.* (Psychologische Abhandlungen, 5.) Zurich: Rascher. pp. 696. Contents:
  1. Vorwort. (7–8)
  2. Einleitung in die religionspsychologische Problematik der Alchemie. (11–62) Repub. as G. 1957a,2.
  3. Traumsymbole des Individuationsprozesses. (65–305) G. 1936a rev. and exp.
  4. Die Erlösungsvorstellungen in der Alchemie. (309–631) G. 1937a rev. and exp.
  5. Epilog. (633–46)
  Pub., rev. and with addn. of new foreword, as G. 1952d. TR.—English: CW 12 (1st edn.).

1944b "Vorwort" and essay: "Über den indischen Heiligen." Heinrich Zimmer: *Der Weg zum Selbst.* pp. 5–6, and pp. 11–24. Ed. by C. G. Jung. Zurich: Rascher. Essay repub. as GW 11,15. TR.—English: (essay only) CW 11,15.

1945a *Psychologische Betrachtungen.* A selection from the writings of C. G. Jung, comp. and ed. by Jolan Jacobi. Zurich: Rascher. pp. 455. A collection of short passages from a wide range of writings; contains no new material. Pub., rev. and exp. with title change, as G. 1971b. TR.—English: 1953a.

1945b "Das Rätsel von Bologna." *Festschrift Albert Oeri.* pp. 265–79. Basel: Basler Nachrichten. Cf. G. 1955a,II,3. TR.—English: 1946f.

1945c "Nach der Katastrophe." *Neue Schw. R.,* n.s. XIII:2 (June), 67–88. Repub. as G. 1946a,5. TR.—English: 1946a.

1945d "Vom Wesen der Träume." *Ciba Zeitschrift* (Basel), IX:99 (July), 3546–57. Repub. as G. 1952i. Pub., rev. and exp., as G. 1948b,5. TR.—English: 1948a.

1945e "Medizin und Psychotherapie." *Bulletin der schweizerischen Akademie der medizinischen Wissenschaften,* I:5, 315–28. Repub. as GW 16,8. Lecture delivered to a scientific meeting of the Senate of the Academy, Zurich, 12 May 1945. TR.—English: CW 16,8.

1945f "Die Psychotherapie in der Gegenwart." *Schweizerische Zeitschrift für Psychologie und ihre Anwendungen,* IV:1, 3–18. First pub. in an English trans., E. 1942b. Repub. as G. 1946a,3. Given as the opening address to the Kommission für Psychotherapie, Schweizerische Gesellschaft für Psychiatrie, Zurich, 4th annual meeting, 19 July 1941. TR.—English: 1942b / 1947a,4 / CW 16,9.

1945g "Der philosophische Baum." *Verhandlungen der Naturforschenden Gesellschaft Basel*, LVI:2, 411–23. Pub., greatly rev. and exp., as G. 1954b,7. Written as contribution to a Festschrift for Gustav Senn, professor of botany, which was never published.

1946a *Aufsätze zur Zeitgeschichte.* Zurich: Rascher. pp. 147. Contents:
1. Vorwort. (vii–ix) Repub. as GW 10,9. TR.—English: 1947a,1 / CW 10,9.
2. "Wotan." (1–24) Repub. as GW 10,10. G. 1936c repub. TR.— English: (abridged) 1937c / 1947a,3 / CW 10,10.
3. "Die Psychotherapie in der Gegenwart." (25–55) G. 1945f repub. with slight title change. Repub. as GW 16,9. TR.—English: 1947a,4 / CW 16,9.
4. "Psychotherapie und Weltanschauung." (57–72) G. 1943e repub. Repub. as G. 1954c,3 and GW 16,7. TR.—English: 1947a,5 / CW 16,7.
5. "Nach der Katastrophe." (73–116) G. 1945c repub. Repub. as GW 10,11. TR.—English: 1947a,6 / CW 10,11.
6. "Nachwort." (117–47) Repub. as GW 10,13. TR.—English: 1947a,7 / CW 10,13.

1946b *Psychologie und Erziehung.* Zurich: Rascher. pp. 204. 1963: ("Rascher Paperback.") pp. 135. Contents:
1. "Analytische Psychologie und Erziehung: Drei Vorlesungen." (1–124) G. 1926b rev. and exp., with addn. of new foreword dated June 1945. Repub. as GW 17,4. TR.—English: CW 17,4.
2. "Über Konflikte der kindlichen Seele." (125–81) G. 1939a slightly exp. Repub. as GW 17,1. TR.—English: CW 17,1.
3. "Der Begabte." (183–203) G. 1943d repub. with title change. Repub. as GW 17,5. TR.—English: CW 17,5.

1946c *Die Psychologie der Übertragung. Erläutert anhand einer alchemistischen Bilderserie. Für Ärzte und praktische Psychologen.* Zurich: Rascher. pp. 283. Contents:
Vorrede. (vii–xii) Dated Fall 1945.

I. Einleitende Überlegungen zum Problem der Übertragung. (1–63)
II. Die Bilderserie des Rosarium Philosophorum als Grundlage für die Darstellung der Übertragungsphänomene. (65–253)
  1. Der Mercurbrunnen.
  2. König und Königin.
  3. Die nackte Wahrheit.
  4. Das Eintauchen im Bade.
  5. Die Conjunction.
  6. Der Tod.
  7. Der Aufstieg der Seele.
  8. Die Reinigung.
  9. Die Wiederkehr der Seele.
  10. Die neue Geburt.
Schlusswort. (255–60)
Repub. as GW 16,13. TR.—English: CW 16,13.

1946d "Gérard de Nerval." (Autorreferat.) *Aus d. Jhrsb. 1945/46.* p. 18. Printed for private circulation. Summary of lecture to the Psychologischer Club Zurich, 9 June 1945. GW 18,117. TR.—English: CW 18,117.

1946e "Zur Psychologie des Geistes." *Eran. Jb. 1945.* pp. 385–448. (See G. 1934c.) Pub., rev. and exp., with title change, as G. 1948a,2. TR.—English: 1948d.

1946f Foreword to K. A. Ziegler: "Alchemie II," List no. 17 (May). pp. 1–2. Printed in Bern. Foreword, in both German and English, to a bookseller's catalog. For English version, see E. 1946b.

1946g "Zur Umerziehung des deutschen Volkes." *Basl. Nach.*, No. 486, "Sondernummer . . ." (Centennial edn.) (ca. 16 Nov.), 85. The last 9 paragraphs of an essay, "Randglossen zur Zeitgeschichte," dated 1945, never pub. as a whole in German (until GW 18,73), although trans. and pub. in its entirety in English as CW 18,73. TR.—English: (full text) CW 18,73.

1946h Excerpts of letter (published to anon.) to James Kirsch (26 May 1934), pp. 225–27. Ernest Harms: "Carl Gustav Jung—Defender of Freud and the Jews." *Psychiatric Quarterly*, 20:2 (Apr.), 199–233. Entire letter pub. in G. 1972a and trans. in E. 1973b. TR.—English: 1946d,2.

1947a "Der Geist der Psychologie." *Eran. Jb. 1946.* pp. 385–490. (See G. 1934c.) Pub., rev. and with title change, as G. 1954b,8. TR.—English: 1954b,2 / (sl. abbrev.) 1957e.

1947b "Vorwort." Linda Fierz-David: *Der Liebestraum des Poliphilo; ein Beitrag zur Psychologie der Renaissance und der Moderne.* pp. 5–7. Zurich: Rhein. Dated Feb. 1946. TR.—English: 1950c.

1947c "Über Tiefenpsychologie und Selbsterkenntnis. Ein Gespräch zwischen Prof. C. G. Jung und Dr. Jolande Jacobi." *Hamburger Akademische Rundschau,* II:1 / 2, 11–19. G. 1943f repub. with title change.

1948a *Symbolik des Geistes. Studien über psychische Phänomenologie.* . . . With a contribution by Riwkah Schärf. (Psychologische Abhandlungen, 6.) Zurich: Rascher. pp. 500. 1965: ("Rascher Paperback.") pp. 206. Contains the following works by Jung:

1. Vorwort. (vii–viii) Dated June 1947. GW 18,90. TR.—English: CW 18,90.
2. "Zur Phänomenologie des Geistes im Märchen." (1–67) G. 1946e, rev. and exp., with title change. Repub. as G. 1957a,3 and GW 9,i,8. TR.—English: 1954b,1 / CW 9,i,8.
3. "Der Geist Mercurius." (69–149) G. 1943b rev. and exp. Repub. as GW 13,4. TR.—English: 1953b / CW 13,4.
4. "Versuch zu einer psychologischen Deutung des Trinitätsdogmas." (321–446) G. 1942b, greatly rev. and exp., with title change. Repub. as GW 11,2, with slight title change. TR.—English: CW 11,2.
5. "Zur Psychologie östlicher Meditation." (447–72) G. 1943c repub. Repub. as G. 1957a,4 and GW 11,14. TR.—English: CW 11,14.

1948b *Über psychische Energetik und das Wesen der Träume.* (Psychologische Abhandlungen, 2.) "2., vermehrte und verbesserte Auflage." Zurich: Rascher. pp. 311. 1965: 3d edn., rev. and reset. ("Rascher Paperback.") pp. 206. Contents:

1. Vorwort(e). (1–3) G. 1928b,1 repub. with new foreword (dated May 1947) added for this edn. GW 18,37. TR.—English: CW 18,37.
2. "Über die Energetik der Seele." (5–117) G. 1928b,2 repub. Repub. as GW 8,1. TR.—English: CW 8,1.
3. "Allgemeines zur Komplextheorie." (119–43) G. 1934a, sl.

rev. Repub. as GW 8,3, with reversion to title of G. 1934a.
TR.—English: CW 8,3.

4. "Allgemeine Gesichtspunkte zur Psychologie des Traumes."
(145–225) G. 1928b,3, rev. and exp. Repub. as GW 8,9. TR.—
English: 1956b / CW 8,9.

5. "Vom Wesen der Träume." (227–57) G. 1945d, rev. and exp.
Repub. as G. 1954c,1 and GW 8,10. TR.—English: CW 8,10.

6. "Instinkt und Unbewusstes." (259–76) G. 1928b,4, rev. and
with addn. of brief concluding note. Repub. as GW 8,6. TR.—
English: CW 8,6.

7. "Die psychologischen Grundlagen des Geisterglaubens."
(277–311) G. 1928b,5 rev. Repub. as GW 8,11. TR.—English:
CW 8,11.

G. 1928b exp., with title change. New foreword and items 2. and
4. added.

1948c "De Sulphure." *Nova Acta Paracelsica*, V. pp. 27–40. Pub., exp., as
part of G. 1955a,III,3. TR.—English: ?1947c.

1948d "Vorwort." Esther Harding: *Das Geheimnis der Seele.* pp. 9–10. Zurich: Rhein. Written in German as introduction for the original
English pub. and first pub. in trans. GW 18,42. TR.—English:
1947e.

1948e "Vorwort." Stuart Edward White: *Uneingeschränktes Weltall.* pp. 7–
14. Zurich: Origo. Written in German to accompany the German
trans. of White's *The Unobstructed Universe* (New York, 1940).
Dated July 1948. Also pub. as "Psychologie und Spiritismus." *Neue
Schw. R.,* n.s. XVI:7 (Nov.), 430–35. GW 18,6. TR.—English: CW
18,6.

1948f "Schatten, Animus und Anima." *Wiener Zeitschrift für Nervenheilkunde* ... , I:4 (June), 295–307. Incorporated as part of G.
1951a,II & III. Lecture given to the Schweizerische Gesellschaft
für praktische Psychologie, Zurich, 1948. TR.—English: 1950a.

1949a *Die Bedeutung des Vaters für das Schicksal des Einzelnen.* "Dritte, umgearbeitete Auflage." Zurich: Rascher. pp. 38. G. 1909c rev. and
exp., with addn. of new foreword. Repub. as GW 4,14. TR.—English: CW 4,14 (with addns. from G. 1909c).

1949b "Über das Selbst." *Eran. Jb. 1948.* pp. 285–315. Incorporated into G. 1951a,IV. Lecture given also to the Psychologischer Club Zurich, 22 May 1948. TR.—English: 1951a.

1949c "Vorwort." Robert Crottet: *Mondwald. Lappengeschichten.* pp. 7–9. Zurich: Fretz und Wasmuth. Dated March 1949. GW 18,119. TR.—English: CW 18,119.

1949d "Geleitwort." Esther Harding: *Frauen-Mysterien, einst und jetzt.* pp. viii–xii. Zurich: Rascher. Dated Aug. 1948. GW 18,53. TR.—English: 1955e / CW 18,53.

1949e "Geleitwort zu den 'Studien aus dem C. G. Jung-Institut Zürich'." C. A. Meier: *Antike Inkubation und moderne Psychotherapie.* (Studien aus dem C. G. Jung-Institut Zürich, 1.) Zurich: Rascher. 2 unno.'d pp. after title page. Introduction to the series, of which Jung was the editor. Dated Sept. 1948. GW 18,45. TR.—English: (Pts. only) 1950e / 1967d / CW 18,45.

1949f "Vorwort." Erich Neumann: *Ursprungsgeschichte des Bewusstseins.* pp. 1–2. Zurich: Rascher. Dated 1 March 1949. GW 18,54. / TR.—English: 1954f. CW 18,54.

1949g Letter to the editors on the effect of technology on the psyche. *Zürcher Student,* Jhg. 27:5 (Nov.), 129–30. Written in reply to the eds.' question and dated 14 Sept. 1949. GW 18,76. TR.—English: CW 18,76.

1949h *"Dämonie." (Definition.) *Schweizer Lexikon,* Vol. I. Zurich: Encyclios. Written July 1945 at the request of the publishers. Only the 1st sentence and the references appear here as the definition, which is published without attribution. Full text of Jung's definition pub. as GW 18,89. TR.—English: CW 18,89.

1950a *Gestaltungen des Unbewussten.* With a contribution by Aniela Jaffé. (Psychologische Abhandlungen, 7.) Zurich: Rascher. pp. 616. Contains the following works by Jung:

    1. Vorwort. (1–2) Dated Jan. 1949. GW 18,56. TR.—English: CW 18,56.

    2. "Psychologie und Dichtung." (3–36) G. 1930a, rev. and exp.

Repub. as G. 1954c,2 and GW 15,7. Excerpts pub. as G. 1951f and 1955g. TR.—English: (with addn.) CW 15,7.

3. "Über Wiedergeburt." (37–91) G. 1940b, rev. and exp. with title change. Repub. as GW 9,i,5. TR.—English: CW 9,i,5.

4. "Zur Empirie des Individuationsprozesses." (93–186) G. 1934c, rev. and exp. Repub. as GW 9,i,11. TR.—English: CW 9,i,11.

5. "Über Mandalasymbolik." (187–235) Contains 9 of the plates pub. in G. 1938a,4. Repub. as GW 9,i,12. TR.—English: CW 9,i,12.

1950b "Faust und die Alchemie." (Autorreferat.) *Aus d. Jhrsb. 1949/50.* pp. 29–32. Printed for private circulation. Summary of lecture to the Psychologischer Club Zurich, 8 Oct. 1949. GW 18,105. TR.—English: CW 18,105.

1950d "Geleitwort." Lily Abegg: *Ostasien denkt anders.* pp. 3–4. Zurich: Atlantis. Dated Mar. 1949. GW 18,92. Omitted from pub. of the English trans., *The Mind of East Asia* (London and New York, 1952). TR.—English: 1953f / 1955; / CW 18,92.

1950e "Vorrede" and "Fall von Prof. C. G. Jung." Fanny Moser: *Spuk. Irrglaube oder Wahrglaube.* pp. 9–12 and pp. 253–61. Baden bei Zurich: Gyr. "Vorrede" dated Apr. 1950. "Vorrede" pub. as G. 1956b, with the omission of the first few sentences and the addn. of a title. GW 18,7. TR.—English: CW 18,7.

1950f "Wo leben die Teufel? Zur Psychologie der Ehe." *Welt* (26 July). 1 p.

1950g Contribution to "Rundfrage über ein Referat auf der 66. Wanderversammlung der südwestdeutschen Psychiater und Neurologen in Badenweiler." pp. 464–65. *Psyche,* Jhg. 4:8 (Nov.), 448–80. Answer to questionnaire concerning a report given by Dr. Medard Boss at the above congress and sent out by the editors to Boss's colleagues. GW 18,14. TR.—English: CW 18,14.

1951a *Aion. Untersuchungen zur Symbolgeschichte.* With a contribution by Marie-Louise von Franz. (Psychologische Abhandlungen, 8.) Zurich: Rascher. pp. 561. Contains the following work by Jung:
Vorrede. (1–10)

"Beiträge zur Symbolik des Selbst."

    I. Das Ich. (15–21)

    II. Der Schatten. (22–26) Incorporates G. 1948f.

    III. Die Syzygie: Anima und Animus. (27–43) Incorporates G. 1948f.

    IV. Das Selbst. (44–62) Incorporates G. 1949b.

    V. Christus, ein Symbol des Selbst. (63–110)

    VI. Das Zeichen der Fische. (111–41)

    VII. Die Prophezeiung des Nostradamus. (142–51)

    VIII. Über die geschichtliche Bedeutung des Fisches. (152–71)

    IX. Die Ambivalenz des Fischsymbols. (172–83)

    X. Der Fisch in der Alchemie. (184–224)

    XI. Die alchemistische Deutung des Fisches. (225–50)

    XII. Allgemeines zur Psychologie der christlich-alchemistischen Symbolik. (251–66)

    XIII. Gnostische Symbole des Selbst. (267–320)

    XIV. Die Struktur und Dynamik des Selbst. (321–78)

    XV. Schlusswort. (379–84)

I–IV repub. as G. 1954c,4. Jung's work repub. with rearranged title as GW 9,ii.

On the advice of Dr. von Franz, it is construed that the title *Aion* belongs to Prof. Jung's part of the book rather than to hers. The present entry, however, records the title-page data of the Swiss edn. The CW trans. bears the title *Aion* as well. TR.—English: CW 9,ii.

1951b With K. Kerényi: *Einführung in das Wesen der Mythologie. Das göttliche Kind; Das göttliche Mädchen.* "4. revidierte Auflage." Zurich: Rhein. pp. 260. Contains the following works by Jung:

    1. "Zur Psychologie des Kind-Archetypus." (105–47) Repub. as GW 9,i,6. TR.—English: CW 9,i,6.

    2. "Zum psychologischen Aspekt der Korefigur." (223–50) Repub. as GW 9,i,7. TR.—English: CW 9,i,7.

G. 1941c repub. with the addn. of new foreword Kerényi.

1951c "Tiefenpsychologie." (Definition.) *Lexikon der Pädagogik.* Vol. II, pp. 768–73. Bern: A. Francke. Written in 1948. GW 18,44. TR.—English: CW 18,44.

1951d "Grundfragen der Psychotherapie." *Dialectica*, V:1 (15 Mar.), 8–24. Repub. as GW 16,10. TR.—English: CW 16,10.

1951e "Das Fastenwunder des Bruder Klaus." *Neue Wissenschaft*, Jhg. 1950/51:7 (Apr.), 14. Rev. from letter written 10 Nov. 1948 in response to Fritz Blanke's "Bruder Klaus von der Flüe." *Neue Wissenschaft*, Jhg. 1905/51:4. Orig. text of letter pub. in G. 1972b and trans. in E. 1973b. GW 18,94. TR.—English: CW 18,94.

1951f "Das Geheimnis des Kunstschaffens." *Universitas*, VI:7 (July), 721– 25. G. 1950a,2, sec. 2, repub. abridged.

1952a *Antwort auf Hiob*. Zurich: Rascher. pp. 169. Pub. with addn. as G. 1961a. TR.—English: 1954a/CW 11,9. Note: A paragraph written by Jung describing the book was printed as a blurb on the dust jacket of this edn. Repub. as GW 11,23 and GW 18,95; trans. into English as CW 18,95.

1952b With W. Pauli: *Naturerklärung und Psyche*. (Studien aus dem C. G. Jung-Institut Zürich, 4.) Zurich: Rascher. pp. 194. Contains the following work by Jung:
"Synchronizität als ein Prinzip akausaler Zusammenhänge." (1– 107) Ch. 2 of Jung's article pub. rev. as G. 1958f. Whole article repub. as GW 8,18.
A rev. version with addns. by the author was trans. and pub. as E. 1955a.

1952c **Paracelsus*. (Der Bogen, 25.) St. Gallen: Tschudy. pp. 24. G. 1934b.5 repub. Repub. as GW 15,1. TR.—English: CW 15,1.

1952d *Psychologie und Alchemie*. 2d rev. edn. Zurich: Rascher. pp. 708. G. 1944a pub. rev. and with the addn. of "Vorwort zur 2. Auflage." Repub. as GW 12. TR.—English: CW 12.

1952e *Symbole der Wandlung. Analyse des Vorspiels zu einer Schizophrenie.* With 300 illus., selected and comp. by Jolande Jacobi. "Vierte, umgearbeitete Auflage . . ." Zurich: Rascher, pp. 821. 1971: "Sonderausgabe." Olten: Walter. (Same edn., in boards.) Contents:
Vorreden (vii–xviii)
Part I:
I. Einleitung. (3–8) TR.—English: 1954d.
II. Über die zwei Arten des Denkens. (9–51)
III. Vorgeschichte. (52–58)
IV. Der Schöpferhymnus. (59–129)
V. Das Lied von der Motte. (130–96)

Part II:
  I. Einleitung. (199–217)
  II. Über den Begriff der Libido. (218–33)
  III. Die Wandlung der Libido. (234–83)
  IV. Die Entstehung des Heros. (284–345)
  V. Symbole der Mutter und der Wiedergeburt. (346–468)
  VI. Der Kampf um die Befreiung von der Mutter. (469–528)
  VII. Das Opfer. (529–763)
  VIII. Schlusswort. (764–69)
  G. 1938b, greatly rev. and exp. with title change. Repub. as GW 5.
  TR.—English: CW 5.

1952f "Über Synchronizität." *Eran. Jb. 1951.* pp. 271–84. (See G. 1934c.) Repub. as GW 8,19. Lecture given in 2 pts. also to the Psychologischer Club Zurich, 20 Jan. and 3 Feb. 1951. TR.—English: 1953c / 1957b / CW 8,19.

1952g "Vorwort." Gerhard Adler: *Zur analytischen Psychologie.* pp. 7–9. Zurich: Rascher. Dated May 1949. Not in orig. edn.: London and New York: Norton, 1948. GW 18,55. TR.—English: 1966e / CW 18,55.

1952h "Zu unserer Umfrage 'Leben die Bücher noch?' " [Contribution] *Jungkaufmann; schweizer Monatsschrift für die kaufmännische Jugend,* XXVII:3 (Mar.), 51–52. Jung's reply to Hölderlin's famous question, written as a letter to the editor, A. Galliker (29 Jan. 1952). Text of letter pub. in G. 1972b and trans. in E. 1975b.

1952i * "Vom Wesen der Träume." *Ciba Zeitschrift* (Wehr-Baden), V:55 (May), 1830–37. G. 1945d repub. Pub., rev. and exp., as G. 1948b,5.

1952j "Religion und Psychologie." *Merkur,* VI:5 (May), 467–73. Repub. with title change as GW 11,17. A reply to Prof. Buber. TR.—English: 1957d / 1973e.

1953a Contribution to *Trunken von Gedichten. Eine Anthologie geliebter deutscher Verse.* p. 63. Ed. by Georg Gerster. Zurich: Verlag der Arche. Partial trans. in E. 1975b, p. 193.

1953b "Vorwort." Frances G. Wickes: *Von der inneren Welt des Menschen.* pp. vii–viii. Zurich: Rascher. Dated Sept. 1953. Not included in original English publication: *The Inner World of Man* (New York: Farrar and Rinehart, 1938). GW 18,57. TR.—English: 1954g / CW 18,57.

1954a With Paul Radin and Karl Kerényi: *Der göttliche Schelm. Ein indianischer Mythen-Zyklus.* Zurich: Rhein. pp. 219. Contains the following work by Jung:

"Zur Psychologie der Schelmenfigur." (185–207) Repub. as GW 9,i,9 with title change. TR.—English: 1955d / 1956a.
TR. of entire work—English: 1956a.

1954b *Von den Wurzeln des Bewusstseins. Studien über den Archetypus.* (Psychologische Abhandlungen, 9.) Zurich: Rascher. pp. 681. Contents:

1. Vorrede. (ix–x) Dated May 1953. TR.—English: CW 18,58.
2. "Über die Archetypen des kollektiven Unbewussten." (1–56) G. 1935b rev. Repub. as G. 1957a,1 and GW 9,i,1. TR.—English: CW 9,i,1.
3. "Über den Archetypus mit besonderer Berücksichtigung des Animabegriffes." (57–85) G. 1936e rev. Repub. as GW 9,i,3. TR.—English: CW 9,i,3.
4. "Die psychologischen Aspekte des Mutterarchetypus." (87–135) G. 1939b rev. Repub. as GW 9,i,4. TR.—English: (with pts. of E. 1943a) CW 9,i,4.
5. "Die Visionen des Zosimos." (137–216) G. 1938c, rev. and considerably exp., with title change. Repub. as GW 13,2. TR.—English: CW 13,2.
6. "Das Wandlungssymbol in der Messe." (217–350) G. 1942c, rev. and exp. Repub. as GW 11,3. TR.—English: CW 11,3.
7. "Der philosphische Baum." (351–496) G. 1945g, greatly rev. and exp. Repub. as GW 13,5. TR.—English: CW 13,5.
8. "Theoretische Überlegungen zum Wesen des Psychischen." (497–608) G. 1947a, sl. rev. & with title change. Repub. as GW 8,8. Excerpts repub. as G. 1954c,5. TR.—English: 1954b,2 / CW 8,8.

1954c *Welt der Psyche. Eine Auswahl zur Einführung.* Ed. by A. Jaffé and G. P. Zacharias. Zurich: Rascher. pp. 165. 1965: reset. ("Geist und Psyche.") Munich: Kindler. pp. 149. Contains the following works by Jung:

44

1. "Vom Wesen der Träume." (9–32) G. 1948b,5 repub. Repub. as GW 8,10.
2. "Psychologie und Dichtung." (33–61) G. 1950a,2 repub. Repub. as GW 15,7.
3. "Psychotherapie und Weltanschauung." (63–73) G. 1946a,4 repub. Repub. as GW 16,7.
4. "Beiträge zur Symbolik des Selbst." (75–120) G. 1951a, Chs. I–IV, repub. Repub. as GW 9,ii, chs. I–IV.
5. "Theoretische Überlegungen zum Wesen des Psychischen." (121–59) G. 1954b,8, Section 7 and "Nachwort," repub. Cf. GW 8,8.

1954d Preface to John Custance: *Weisheit und Wahn.* pp. vii–xi. Zurich: Rascher. Written in German in 1951, according to ms. in Jung Library, Küsnacht. First pub., however, in an English trans. GW 18,15. TR.—English: 1952a / CW 18,15.

1954e Two letters to the author. Georg Gerster: "C. G. Jung zu den fliegenden Untertassen." *Weltwoche*, Jhg. 22: 1078 (9 July). Interview request not granted. These letters used in article instead. GW 18,80. TR.—English: 1954h / (Pts. only) 1955i / 1959i,3 / CW 18,80.

1954f "Mach immer alles ganz und richtig." *Weltwoche*, Jhg. 22:1100 (10 Dec.), 31. Answer to question on the rules of life. GW 18,79. TR.—English: CW 18,79.

1955a *Mysterium coniunctionis. Untersuchung über die Trennung und Zusammensetzung der seelischen Gegensätze in der Alchemie.* With the collaboration of M.-L. von Franz. Pt. I. (Psychologische Abhandlungen, 10.) Zurich: Rascher. pp. 284. Contents:
Die Symbolik der Polarität und Einheit.
Vorwort. (ix–xv)
I. Die Komponenten der Coniunctio.
  1. Die Gegensätze. (1–4)
  2. Der Quaternio. (5–15)
  3. Die Waise und die Witwe. (16–37)
  4. Alchemie und Manichäismus. (38–42)
II. Die Paradoxa.
  1. Die Arkansubstanz und der Punkt. (43–50)
  2. Die Scintilla. (50–55)
  3. Das Enigma Bolognese. (56–95) Cf. G. 1945b.

III. Die Personifikationen der Gegensätze.
1. Einleitung. (96–99)
2. Sol. (100–20)
3. Sulphur. (121–40) Includes an exp. G. 1948c.
4. Luna. (141–200)
5. Sal. (200–84)
Repub. as GW 14, vol. I. The 1st of 2 pts. Cf. G. 1956a for Pt. II.
TR.—English: CW 14.

1955b *Versuch einer Darstellung der psychoanalytischen Theorie.* Zurich: Rascher. pp. 195. G. 1913a pub. with the addn. of a foreword. Repub. as GW 4,9. TR.—English: CW 4,9.

1955c "Geleitwort." Gustav Schmaltz: *Komplexe Psychologie und körperliches Symptom.* pp. 7–8. Stuttgart: Hippokrates. GW 18,17. TR.—English: CW 18,17.

1955d "Psychologischer Kommentar." *Das tibetische Buch der grossen Befreiung.* pp. 13–54. Ed. by W. Y. Evans-Wentz. Munich: Barth. "Kommentar" trans. from E. 1954e by M. Niehus-Jung; written in English in 1939. Repub. as GW 11,10.

1955e "Mandalas." *Du*, Jhg. 15:4 (Apr.), 16, 21. Repub. as GW 9,i,13; G. 1977b. TR.—English: 1955g / CW 9,i,13.

1955f Letter to Hans A. Illing (10 Feb. 1955). Hans A. Illing: "Jung und die moderne Tendenz in der Gruppentherapie." *Heilkunst*, no. 7 (July), 233. Full text of letter pub. in G. 1972b and trans. in E. 1975b. Excerpt pub. as G. 1956d,1. TR.—English: (excerpts) 1957i.

1955g "Der Dichter." *Internationale Bodensee-Zeitschrift für Literatur*, IV:6 (July), 88–91. Excerpt from G. 1950a,2.

1956a *Mysterium coniunctionis.* . . . Pt. II. (Psychologische Abhandlungen, 11.) Zurich: Rascher. pp. 418. (See G. 1955a.) Contents:
Die Symbolik der Polarität und Einheit. (cont.)
IV. Rex und Regina.
1. Einleitung. (1–5)
2. Gold und Geist. (5–9)
3. Die königliche Wandlung. (9–19)
4. Die Heilung des Königs. (19–81)

Repub. as GW 14, vol. II. The 2d of 2 pts. Cf. G. 1955a for Pt. I. (A third part was written by M.-L. von Franz. Cf. note under GW 14.) TR.—English: CW 14.

1956b "Die Parapsychologie hat uns mit unerhörten Möglichkeiten bekanntgemacht." *Gibt es Geister? Rundfrage—beantwortet von Psychologen, Schriftstellern, Philosophen* ... pp. 17–22. Bern: Viktoria. G. 1950e ("Vorrede" only) pub. with omission of the 1st few sentences, and addn. of title.

1956c Statement in publisher's brochure (with other statements) announcing publication of Karl Eugen Neumann's translation of *Die Reden Gotamo Buddhos*. 2 pp. Zurich and Stuttgart: Artemis; Vienna: Paul Zsolnay. Typescript dated Jan. 1956. Repub. as GW 11,26. GW 18,101. TR.—English: CW 18,101.

1956d Excerpts of letters to Hans A. Illing. Georg R. Bach and Hans A. Illing: "Historische Perspektive zur Gruppenpsychotherapie." *Zeitschrift für psychosomatische Medizin*, Jhg. 2 (Jan.), 141–42. Contains excerpts from the following letters by Jung:
  1. 10 Feb. 1955 (141) Excerpted from G. 1955f.
  2. 26 Jan. 1955 (141–42)
Full text of letters pub. in G. 1972b and trans. in E. 1975b. TR.—English: 1957i.

1956e "Wotan und der Rattenfänger. Bemerkungen eines Tiefenpsychologen." *Der Monat*, IX:97 (Oct.), 75–76. Letter to the editor, Melvin J. Lasky (Sept. 1956). Text of letter pub. in G. 1973a and trans. in E. 1975b.

1956f Contribution to symposium, "Das geistige Europa und die ungarische Revolution." *Die Kultur*, V:73 (1 Dec.), 8. Ca. 50 words long. GW 18,84a. TR.—English: CW 18,84,i.

1957a *Bewusstes und Unbewusstes. Beiträge zur Psychologie.* Ed. by Aniela Jaffé. ("Bücher des Wissens.") Frankfurt am Main and Hamburg: Fischer. pp. 184. Contents:
  1. "Über die Archetypen des kollektiven Unbewussten." (11–53) G. 1954b,2 repub. Repub. as GW 9,i,1.
  2. "Einleitung in die religionspsychologische Problematik der Alchemie." (54–91) G. 1944a,2 repub. Repub. as GW 12,3,I.
  3. "Zur Phänomenologie des Geistes im Märchen." (92–143) G. 1948a,2 repub. Repub. as GW 9,i,8.
  4. "Zur Psychologie östlicher Meditation." (144–63) G. 1948a, 5 repub. Repub. as GW 11,14.

1957b *With Richard Wilhelm: Das Geheimnis der goldenen Blüte. Ein chinesisches Lebensbuch.* "Fünfte Auflage." Zurich: Rascher. pp. 161. Contains the following works by Jung:
  1. "Vorrede zur II. Auflage. (vii–x) Repub. as part of GW 13,1. TR.—English: CW 13,1.

48

2. "Zum Gedächtnis Richard Wilhelms." (xiii–xxvi) Repub. as GW 15,5. TR.—English: CW 15,5.

3. "Europäischer Kommentar." (1–68 + 10 plates) Repub. as part of GW 13,1. TR.—English: CW 13,1.

G. 1938a reset, with new foreword by Salomé Wilhelm (xi–xii) and the addn. of the text of the *Hui Ming Ging.* (148–67). TR. of entire work—English: 1962b.

1957c *Contribution to symposium: *Aufstand der Freiheit. Dokumente zur Erhebung des ungarischen Volkes.* p. 104. Zurich: Artemis. Ca. 175 words long. GW 18,84b. TR.—English: CW 18,84,ii.

1957d "Vorwort." Eleanor Bertine: *Menschliche Beziehungen; eine psychologische Studie.* pp. 5–7. Zurich: Rhein. Dated Aug. 1956. GW 18,61. TR.—English: 1958e / CW 18,61.

1957e *"Vorrede." Felicia Froboese-Thiele: *Träume—eine Quelle religiöser Erfahrung?* pp. 18–19. Göttingen: Vandenhoeck and Ruprecht. GW 18,102. TR.—English: CW 18,102.

1957f "Vorwort." René J. van Helsdingen: *Beelden uit het onbewuste. Een geval van Jung.* pp. 7–8. Arnhem: Van Loghum Slaterus. Written for this pub. and dated May 1954. Foreword is in German, while the rest of the book is in Dutch. GW 18,59. TR.—English: CW 18,59.

1957g "Vorwort." Jolande Jacobi: *Komplex, Archetypus, Symbol in der Psychologie C. G. Jungs.* pp. ix–xi. Zurich: Rascher. Dated Feb. 1956. GW 18,60. TR.—English: 1959e / CW 18,60.

1957h "Vorwort." Victor White: *Gott und das Unbewusste.* pp. xi–xxvi. Zurich: Rascher. Repub. as GW 11,4. Originally written in German in 1952, but 1st pub. in an English trans. "Anhang" by Gebhard Frei contains extracts of letters written by Jung to Frei, reprinted from *Annalen der Philosophischen Gesellschaften Innerschweiz und Ostschweiz.* TR.—English: 1952c / CW 11,4.

1957i *"Gegenwart und Zukunft." *Schweizer Monatshefte,* Supplement, XXXVI:12 (Mar.), 5–55. Also pub. as paperback: Zurich: Rascher. pp. 55. 1964: reset. ("Rascher Paperback.") pp. 68. Repub. as GW 10,14. TR.—English: 1958b / CW 10,14.

1957j *Contribution *to Flinker Almanac 1958*. pp. 52–53. Paris: Librairie
Française et Etrangère. Ca. 500 words long. Letter to the editor,
Martin Flinker (17 Oct. 1957). Text of letter pub. in G. 1973a and
trans. in E. 1975b.

1958a *Ein moderner Mythus. Von Dingen, die am Himmel gesehen werden.* Zurich: Rascher. pp. 122. 1964: reset. ("Rascher Paperback.") pp.
143. Repub., with addns., as GW 10,15. Contents:
   Vorrede. (7–9)
   1. Das Ufo als Gerücht. (11–25)
   2. Das Ufo im Traum. (26–75)
   3. Das Ufo in der Malerei. (76–93)
   4. Zur Geschichte des Ufophänomens. (94–98)
   5. Zusammenfassung. (99–104)
   6. Das Ufophänomen in nicht-psychologischer Beleuchtung.
   (105–09)
   Epilog. (110–22)
   Dedicated to Walter Niehus. TR.—English: (with addns.) 1959b.

1958b "Die transzendente Funktion." *Geist und Werk. Aus der Werkstatt unserer Autoren. Zum 75. Geburtstag von Dr. Daniel Brody.* pp. 3–33. Zurich: Rhein. A rev. version of the original 1916 ms. first pub. in an
English trans. as E. 1957a. Repub. as GW 8,2. TR.—English: CW
8,2.

1958c "Das Gewissen in psychologischer Sicht." *Das Gewissen.* pp. 185–
207. (Studien aus dem C. G. Jung-Institut, Zurich, 7.) Zurich:
Rascher. Repub. as GW 10,16. Also pub. in *Universitas* (June). Lecture contributed to the series "Das Gewissen," C. G. Jung Institute,
Zurich, Winter Semester 1957/58. TR.—English: CW 10,16.

1958d *Praxis der Psychotherapie.* (GW 16.) See Part II.

1958e "Vorwort." Aniela Jaffé: *Geistererscheinungen und Vorzeichen. Eine
psychologische Deutung.* pp. 9–12. Zurich: Rascher. Dated August
1957. GW 18,8. TR.—English: 1963b / CW 18,8.

1958f "Ein astrologisches Experiment." *Zeitschrift für Parapsychologie und
Grenzgebiete der Psychologie*, I:2/3 (May), 81–92. G. 1952b, ch. 2 extensively rev. and condensed. Prefatory note includes letter to the
editor, Hans Bender (12 Feb. 1958), repub. in G. 1973a and trans.
in E. 1975b. GW 18,48. TR.—English: CW 18,48 (with addns.).

1958g "Drei Fragen an Prof. C. G. Jung." *Zürcher Student,* Jhg. 36:4 (July), 151. Dated 27 June 1958. Answers to questions on psychodiagnostic methods. GW 18,85. TR.—English: CW 18,85.

1958h "Zeichen am Himmel. C. G. Jung und die physische Realität der UFOs." *Badener Tagblatt* (29 Aug.). Ca. 220 words long. Press release to United Press International, probably also pub. in other newspapers. GW 18,81. TR.—English: 1958h / 1958j / 1959i,1 / CW 18,81.

1958i "Die Schizophrenie." *Schweizer Archiv für Neurologie und Psychiatrie,* LXXXI:1/2, 163–77. Repub. as GW 3,9. Paper presented to the II. Internationaler Kongress für Psychiatrie, Zurich, 1957. Brief summary (in German, English, French, Spanish, and Italian) pub. as "Schizophrenia." *Synopses, Lectures to the Full Assemblies and Lectures to the Symposia. [Proceedings] Zurich, II. International Congress for Psychiatry, 1957.* pp. 49–52. [Zurich, ?1958.] TR.—English: CW 3,10.

1958j " 'Nationalcharakter' und Verkehrsverhalten." *Zentralblatt für Verkehrs-Medizin, Verkehrs-Psychologie und angrenzende Gebiete,* IV:3, 131–33. A letter written at the request of the editor, F. v. Tischendorf (19 Apr. 1958). Text of letter pub. in G. 1973a and trans. in E. 1975b. TR.—English: 1959j.

1959a "Über Psychotherapie und Wunderheilungen. Aus einem Brief von C. G. Jung." *Magie und Wunder in der Heilkunde. Ein Tagungsbericht.* pp. 8–9. Ed. by Wilhelm Bitter. (7. Kongressbericht der Stuttgarter Gemeinschaft "Arzt und Seelsorger.") Stuttgart: Klett. Letter (17 Apr. 1959), written at the request of the editor, Wilhelm Bitter, pub. with minor omissions. Entire letter pub. in G. 1973a and trans. in E. 1975b.

1959b "Gut und Böse in der analytischen Psychologie." *Gut und Böse in der Psychotherapie. Ein Tagungsbericht.* pp. 29–42. Ed. by Wilhelm Bitter. (8. Kongressbericht der Stuttgarter Gemeinschaft "Arzt und Seelsorger.") Stuttgart: "Arzt und Seelsorger." Extemporaneous address to the Gemeinschaft, Zurich, Fall 1958. Transcript prepared for pub. by Gebhard Frei, and approved, with corrections, by Jung. Repub. as GW 10,17 and GW 11,19. TR.—English: 1960e / CW 10,17. Also contains on pp. 56–57 the first 2 parags. of a letter to the editor (12 July 1958), the full text of which appears in G. 1973a and is trans. in E. 1975b.

1959c   * Foreword to Frieda Fordham: *Eine Einführung in die Psychologie C. G. Jungs.* pp. 7–8. Zurich: Rascher. Trans. from E. 1953d by Johanna Meier-Fritzsche. CW/GW 18,46.

1959d   *"Geleitwort" and answers to questions. Otto Kankeleit: *Das Unbewusste als Keimstätte des Schöpferischen. Selbstzeugnisse von Gelehrten, Dichtern, und Künstlern.* pp. 9 and 68–69. Munich and Basel: Ernst Reinhardt. GW 18,121. TR.—English: CW 18,121.

1959e   "Vorrede." Toni Wolff: *Studien zu C. G. Jungs Psychologie.* pp. 7–14. Ed. by C. A. Meier. Zurich: Rhein. Dated Aug. 1958. Repub. as GW 10,18. TR.—English: 1960d / CW 10,18.

1959f   "Neuere Betrachtungen zur Schizophrenie." *Universitas,* XIV:1 (Jan.), 31–38. Trans. from the original English text (cf. E. 1957h) by H. Degen. Repub. as GW 3,8. Text of contribution to the "Voice of America" symposium, "The Frontiers of Knowledge and Humanity's Hopes for the Future," broadcast 16 Dec. 1956; written up at the request of the Bollingen Foundation.

1959g   Contribution to "Eine Tat-Umfrage: Das Interview mit dem anonymen Stimmbürger. Psychologen legen das unbewusste Nein des Bürgers bloss." *Tat* (23 Jan.). 1 p. Ca. 350 words long.

1959h   Commentary on Walter Pöldinger: "Zur Bedeutung bildnerischen Gestaltens in der psychiatrischen Diagnostik." *Die Therapie des Monats,* IX:2, 67. GW 18,128. TR.—English: CW 18,128.

1960a   *Psychologische Typen.* (GW, 6.) See Part II.

1961a   *Antwort auf Hiob.* 3d rev. edn. Zurich: Rascher. pp. 122. 1967: reset. ("Rascher Paperback.") pp. 143. 1973: ("Studienausgabe.") Olten: Walter. pp. 143. G. 1952a repub. with the addn. of a "Nachwort" trans. from E. 1956c by Marianne Niehus-Jung. Repub. as GW 11,9; repub. as full letter in G. 1972b, pp. 521–23.

1961b   "Nachwort." Arthur Koestler: *Von Heiligen und Automaten.* pp. 363–68. Zurich: Büchergilde Gutenberg. Bern, Stuttgart, Vienna: Scherz. 1965: Zurich: Buchclub Ex Libris. Trans. from E. 1961c by Hans Flesch-Brunningen. Written in English as a letter to Melvin J. Lasky, editor of *Encounter* (19 Oct. 1960), in response to excerpts of Koestler's book pub. therein, and itself pub. in a subsequent issue. Text of letter trans. into German in G. 1973a.

1961c "Ein Brief zur Frage der Synchronizität." *Zeitschrift für Parapsychologie und Grenzgebiete der Psychologie*, V:1 (Mar.), 1–8. Trans. from the English ms. by H. Bender, with corrections and additions by Jung. Originally written in English as letter to A.D. Cornell (9 Feb. 1960). TR.—English: 1961a.

1962a *Erinnerungen, Träume, Gedanken.* Recorded and ed. by Aniela Jaffé. Zurich: Rascher. pp. 422. 1968: Zurich: Buchclub Ex Libris. pp. 423. 1971: Olten: Walter. pp. 423. Contents:

  1. Prolog. (10–12)
  2. Kindheit. (13–30)
  3. Schuljahre. (31–88)
  4. Studienjahre. (89–120)
  5. Psychiatrische Tätigkeit. (121–50)
  6. Sigmund Freud. (151–73)
  7. Die Auseinandersetzung mit dem Unbewussten. (174–203)
  8. Zur Entstehung des Werkes. (204–26)
  9. Der Turm. (227–41)
 10. Reisen. (242–92)
 11. Visionen. (293–301)
 12. Über das Leben nach dem Tode. (302–29)
 13. Späte Gedanken. (330–56)
 14. Rückblick. (357–61)
 15. Appendix.
    i. Aus den Briefen Jungs an seine Frau aus den USA. 1909. (363–70)
    ii. Aus Briefen von Freud an Jung. 1909–11. (370–73) Cf. G. 1974a.
    iii. Brief an seine Frau aus Sousse, Tunis. 1920. (373–75)
    iv. Aus einem Brief an einen jungen Gelehrten. 1952. (375–76) To Zwi Werblowsky (17 June 1952). Entire letter pub. in G. 1972b and trans. in E. 1975a.
    v. Aus einem Brief an einen Kollegen. 1959. (376–78) To Erich Neumann (10 Mar. 1959). Entire letter pub. as G. 1967a and trans. in E. 1975a.
    vi. "Théodore Flournoy." (378–79)
    vii. "Richard Wilhelm." (380–84) Cf. G. 1930c and G. 1931b.

viii. "Heinrich Zimmer." (385–86)
ix. Nachtrag zum "Roten Buch." (387)
x. "VII Sermones ad Mortuos." (389–98) G. 1916a repub.
Also contains excerpts of letter to Gustav Steiner (30 Dec. 1957),
pp. 3–4. Cf. G. 1964b. TR. (Appendix content abridged)—English:
1962a / 1966a.

1963a "Vorwort." Cornelia Brunner: *Die Anima als Schicksalsproblem des Mannes.* pp. 9–14. (Studien aus dem C. G. Jung-Institut, Zürich, 14.) Zurich: Rascher. Dated April 1959. GW 18,63. TR.—English: CW 18,63.

1963b "Geleitbrief." *Der Mensch als Persönlichkeit und Problem.* Gedenkschrift for Ildefons Betschart on his 60th birthday. pp. 14–15. Ed. by Elisabeth Herbrich. Munich: Anton Pustet. Letter to the editor (30 May 1960). Entire text of letter pub. in G. 1973a and trans. in E. 1975b.

1963c *Zur Psychologie westlicher und östlicher Religion.* (GW, 11.) See Part II.

1964a "Brief von Prof. C. G. Jung an den Verfasser." Josef Rudin: *Psychotherapie und Religion.* pp. 11–13. 2d edn. Olten: Walter. Letter to the author written 30 Apr. 1960 in response to Jung's reading of the 1st edn. of the above, and subsequently included in the 2d. Text of letter pub. in G. 1973a and trans. in E. 1975b. TR.—English: 1968c.

1964b Letter to Gustav Steiner (30 Dec. 1957), pp. 125–28. Gustav Steiner: "Erinnerungen an Carl Gustav Jung. Zur Entstehung der Autobiographie." *Basler Stadtbuch 1965.* Basel: Helbing und Lichtenhahn. A facsimile of the 1st part of the ms. appears on p. 127. Pub. with omissions in G. 1962a, pp. 3–4. Repub. in G. 1973a. TR.—English: (Pt. only) 1962a / 1975b.

1964c *Zwei Schriften über Analytische Psychologie.* (GW 7.) See Part II.

1966a *Psychiatrische Studien.* (GW 1.) See Part II.

1967a Letter to Erich Neumann (10 March 1959). Aniela Jaffé: *Der Mythus vom Sinn im Werk von C. G. Jung.* pp. 182–84. Paperback. Zurich: Rascher. Repub. in G. 1973a. Pub. in abbrev. form as G. 1962a,15,V. TR.—English: 1975b.

1967b *Excerpt of letter to Ernst Hanhart (18 Feb. 1957). *Katalog der Autographen-Auktion* (Marburg), no. 425 (23–24 May). Also pub. in the *Tagesanzeiger für Stadt und Kanton Zürich* (27 May). Full letter pub. in G. 1973a, pp. 74–77. TR.—English: 1975b.

1967c Letters to Richard Evans. Richard I. Evans: *Gespräche mit C. G. Jung und Äusserungen von Ernest Jones.* Zurich: Rhein. pp. 168. Trans. from E. 1964b by Lucy Heyer-Grote. Contains 2 letters dated April 1957 and one dated 30 May 1957. Also contains a lengthy interview, in G. 1986c, 1, and E. 1977b, 4.

1967d *Psychologische Typen.* (GW, 6.) Rev. edn. See Part II.

1967e *Die Dynamik des Unbewussten.* (GW, 8.) See Part II.

1968a "Zugang zum Unbewussten." *Der Mensch und seine Symbole.* pp. 20–103. [Ed. by Carl G. Jung and after his death by M.-L. von Franz; coordinating editor, John Freeman.] Olten: Walter. pp. 320. Trans. from E. 1964a by Klaus Thiele-Dohrmann. Jung's original text pub. with title change as GW 18,2.

1968b Letters to August Forel. August Forel: *Briefe. Correspondance 1864–1927.* Ed. by Hans W. Walser. Bern: Hans Huber. Contains the following letters from Jung:
　　1. 1 Apr. 1906. (381–82)
　　2. 12 Oct. 1909. (403) Repub. in G. 1972a.
　　TR.—English: 1973b.

1968c *Psychogenese der Geisteskrankheiten.* (GW, 3.) See Part II.

1968d *Mysterium Coniunctionis.* (GW, 14.) See Part II.

1969a *Über Grundlagen der Analytischen Psychologie. Die Tavistock Lectures.* Zurich: Rascher. pp. 218. Trans. from E. 1968a by Hilde Binswanger. 1975: ("Studienausgabe.") Olten: Walter. Repub. as GW 18,2.

1969b *Freud und die Psychoanalyse.* (GW, 4.) See Part II.

1971a *Der Einzelne in der Gesellschaft.* ("Studienausgabe.") Olten: Walter. pp. 117. Contents:

1. "Die Bedeutung des Vaters für das Schicksal des Einzelnen."
   (7–31) GW 4,14.
2. "Die Frau in Europa." (33–55) G. 1929a repub. Repub. as
   GW 10,6.
3. "Das Liebesproblem des Studenten." (57–77) First pub. in
   English trans. Repub. as GW 10,5. Lecture to the student
   body, Universität Zürich, in Dec. 1924. TR.—English: 1928a,7
   / CW 10,5.
4. "Die Bedeutung der analytischen Psychologie für die Erziehung." (79–96) GW 17,3 prepub. Orig. German here pub.
   for the first time. Cf. E. 1928a,13, Lecture I, for English version. Lecture given at the Congrès international de Pédagogie, Territet / Montreux, 1923.
5. "Die Bedeutung des Unbewussten für die individuelle Erziehung." (97–115) GW 17,6 prepub. Orig. German here pub.
   for the 1st time. Lecture given at the International Congress
   of Education, Heidelberg, 1925. TR.—English: 1928a,14 /
   CW 17,6.

1971b *Mensch und Seele. Aus dem Gesamtwerk 1905 bis 1961.* Selected and
ed. by Jolande Jacobi. Olten: Walter. pp. 391. "Dritte, erweiterte
Auflage von *Psychologische Betrachtungen.*" G. 1945a, rev. and exp.
Cf. E. 1970b for details. TR. (in effect)—English: 1970b.

1971c *Psychiatrie und Okkultismus.* (Frühe Schriften I; "Studienausgabe.")
Olten: Walter. pp. 155. Contents:
1. "Zur Psychologie und Pathologie sogenannter okkulter Phänomene." (7–102) GW 1,1.
2. "Über hysterisches Verlesen." (103–06) GW 1,2.
3. "Kryptomnesie." (107–19) GW 1,3.
4. "Über manische Verstimmung." (121–49) GW 1,4.

1971d *Psychologie und Religion.* ("Studienausgabe.") Olten: Walter. pp.
280. Contents:
1. "Psychologie und Religion." (7–127) GW 11,1.
2. "Über die Beziehung der Psychotherapie zur Seelsorge."
   (129–52) GW 11,7.
3. "Psychoanalyse und Seelsorge." (153–61) GW 11,8.
4. "Das Wandlungssymbol in der Messe." (163–267) GW 11,3.

1971e   *Über das Phänomen des Geistes in Kunst und Wissenschaft.* (GW, 15.) See Part II.

1972a   *Briefe. Erster Band, 1906–1945.* Ed. by Aniela Jaffé in collaboration with Gerhard Adler. Olten: Walter. pp. 530. English and French letters trans. by Aniela Jaffé. The 1st of 3 vols. Cf. G. 1972b and G. 1973a. Letters arranged chronologically. Contains 381 letters. "With a very few exceptions . . . the selection of letters in the Swiss and American editions is identical." Cf. E. 1973b. TR.—English: 1973b and 1975b.

1972b   *Briefe. Zweiter Band, 1946–1955.* pp. 560. Bibliographical information the same as for G. 1972a. The 2d of 3 vols. Cf. G. 1972a and G. 1973a. Contains 333 letters. TR.—English: 1973b and 1975b.

1972c   *Probleme der Psychotherapie.* ("Studienausgabe.") Olten: Walter. pp. 107. Contents:
   1. "Grundfragen der Psychotherapie." (7–22) GW 16,10.
   2. "Grundsätzliches zur praktischen Psychotherapie." (23–42) GW 16,2.
   3. "Was ist Psychotherapie?" (43–51) GW 16,3.
   4. "Einige Aspekte der modernen Psychotherapie." (52–59) GW 16,4.
   5. "Der therapeutische Wert des Abreagierens." (60–70) GW 16,11.
   6. "Psychotherapie und Weltanschauung." (71–78) GW 16,7.
   7. "Medizin und Psychotherapie." (79–88) GW 16,8. ˙
   8. "Die Psychotherapie in der Gegenwart." (89–106) GW 16,9.

1972d   *Typologie.* ("Studienausgabe.") Olten: Walter. pp. 208. Contents:
   1. "Zur Frage der psychologischen Typen." (7–17) GW 6,4.
   2. "Allgemeine Beschreibung der Typen." (18–104) GW 6,3,10.
   3. "Definitionen." (105–89) GW 6,3,11.
   4. "Psychologische Typen." (190–205) GW 6,5.

1972e   *Zur Psychoanalyse.* (Frühe Schriften III; "Studienausgabe.") Olten: Walter. pp. 121. Contents:
   1. "Die Hysterielehre Freuds. Eine Erwiderung auf die Aschaffenburgsche Kritik." (7–14) GW 4,1.

2. "Die Freudsche Hystèrietheorie." (15–30) GW 4,2.
3. "Die Traumanalyse." (31–40) GW 4,3.
4. "Ein Beitrag zur Psychologie des Gerüchtes." (41–55) GW 4,4.
5. "Ein Beitrag zur Kenntnis des Zahlentraumes." (56–64) GW 4,5.
6. "Morton Prince M.D. *The Mechanism and Interpretation of Dreams*. Eine kritische Besprechung." (65–85) GW 4,6.
7. "Zur Kritik über Psychoanalyse." (86–89) GW 4,7.
8. "Zur Psychoanalyse." (90–93) GW 4,8.
9. "Allgemeine Aspekte der Psychoanalyse." (94–108) GW 4,10.
10. "Über Psychoanalyse." (109–18) GW 4,11.

1972f *Psychologie und Alchemie.* (GW 12.) See Part II.

1972g *Über die Entwicklung der Persönlichkeit.* (GW, 17.) See Part II.

1973a *Briefe. Dritter Band, 1956–61.* pp. 431. Bibliographical information the same as for G. 1972a. The last of 3 vols. Cf. G. 1972a and G. 1972b. Contains 258 letters and a general index to the 3 vols. TR.— English: 1975b.

1973b *Versuch einer Darstellung der psychoanalytischen Theorie.* (Frühe Schriften IV; "Studienausgabe.") Olten: Walter. pp. 209. Contents:
1. "Versuch einer Darstellung der psychoanalytischen Theorie." (9–161) GW 4,9.
2. "Psychotherapeutische Zeitfragen. Ein Briefwechsel zwischen C. G. Jung und R. Loÿ." (163–206) GW 4,12.

1973c *Zum Wesen des Psychischen.* ("Studienausgabe.") Olten: Walter. pp. 149. Contents:
1. "Die transzendente Funktion." (7–36) GW 8,2.
2. "Die Bedeutung von Konstitution und Vererbung für die Psychologie." (37–46) GW 8,4.
3. "Psychologische Determinanten des menschlichen Verhaltens." (47–62) GW 8,5.
4. "Theoretische Überlegungen zum Wesen des Psychischen." (63–145) GW 8,8.

1973d *Zur Psychogenese der Geisteskrankheiten.* ("Studienausgabe.") Olten: Walter. pp. 100. Contents:
  1. "Der Inhalt der Psychose." (7–49) GW 3,2.
  2. "Über das Problem der Psychogenese bei Geisteskrankheiten." (51–66) GW 3,5.
  3. "Über die Bedeutung des Unbewussten in der Psychopathologie." (67–74) GW 3,4.
  4. "Geisteskrankheit und Seele." (75–79) GW 3,6.
  5. "Die Schizophrenie." (81–98) GW 3,9.

1973e *Symbole der Wandlung. Analyse des Vorspiels zu einer Schizophrenie.* (GW, 5.) See Part II.

1974a With Sigmund Freud: *Briefwechsel.* Edited by William McGuire and Wolfgang Sauerländer. Frankfurt a. M.: S. Fischer. pp. 766. Contains 294 letters by Jung, dated 1906–1914 (+ 1 from 1923), of which 8 prev. appeared in G. 1972a. Editorial apparatus translated from E. 1974b by W. Sauerländer. TR.—English: 1974b.

1974b *Zivilisation im Übertragung.* (GW, 10.) See Part II.

1975a Address at the presentation of the Jung Codex and letters to G. Quispel. Gilles Quispel: "Jung en de Gnosis." pp. 85–146. *Jung—een mens voor deze tijd.* Rotterdam: Lemniscaat. Contains the following works by Jung:
  Letters to Quispel:
  1. 18 Feb. 1953. (139)
  2. 21 Apr. 1950. (140–41) Also pub. in G. 1972b. TR.—English: 1973b.
  3. 22 July 1951. (142–43)
  4. [Address at the presentation of the Jung Codex]. (144–46) Given in Zurich, 15 Nov. 1953. Dutch summary included. GW 18,97. TR.—English: CW 18,97.

1975b *100 Briefe. Eine Auswahl.* Selected by Aniela Jaffé. Olten: Walter. pp. 254. Drawn from G. 1972a / 1972b / 1973a.

1976a *Archetypen und das kollektive Unbewusste.* (GW, 9i.) See Part II.

1976b *Aion: Beiträge zur Symbolik des Selbst.* (GW, 9ii.) See Part II.

1977a *C. G. Jung: Bild und Wort.* Edited by Aniela Jaffé. Olten and Freiburg im Breisgau: Walter. pp. 240. Many quotations from Jung's published and unpublished writings, with interconnecting biographical passages, appendixes, illustrations, etc. 1983: special edition, including bibliography. TR.—English: 1979b.

1977b *Mandala. Bilder aus dem Unbewussten.* Olten: Walter. pp. 117. with 24 color and 54 black/white plates. Contents:
   1. "Zur Empirie des individuationsprozesses." G. 1950a,4.
   2. "Über Mandalasymbolik." G. 1950a,5.
   3. "Mandalas." G. 1955e.

1978a *Studien über alchemistische Vorstellungen.* (GW 13.) See Part II.

1979a *Experimentelle Untersuchungen.* (GW, 2.) See Part II.

1981a *Das symbolische Leben.* (GW, 18.) See Part II.

1982a *Die Dynamik des Unbewussten.* (GW, 8.) Rev. edn., repaginated. See Part II.

1983a *Das C. G. Jung Lesebuch.* Selected by Franz Alt. Olten and Freiburg im Breisgau: Walter. pp. 376. Contents:
   1. "Das Grundproblem der gegenwärtigen Psychologie." (13–36) GW 8,13.
   2. C. G. Jung über Sigmund Freud. (37–43) Extract from G. 1962a,6.
   3. "Einige Aspekte der modernen Psychotherapie." (44–52) GW 16,4.
   4. "Vom Wesen der Träume." (53–72) GW 8,10.
   5. "Die praktische Verwendbarkeit der Traumanalyse." (73–100) GW 16,12.
   6. "Die Bedeutung der Analytischen Psychologie für die Erziehung." (101–18) GW 17,3.
   7. "Vom Werden der Persönlichkeit." (119–43) GW 17,7.
   8. "Die Lebenswende." (144–64) GW 8,16.
   9. "Seele und Tod." (165–79) GW 8,17.
   10. "Die Frau in Europa." (180–204) GW 10,6.
   11. "Wotan." (205–20) GW 10,10.
   12. "Nach der Katastrophe." (221–50) GW 10,11.
   13. "Gegenwart und Zukunft." (251–324) GW 10,14.

14. "Techniken für einen dem Weltfrieden dienlichen Einstellungswandel." (325–35) GW 18,75.
15. "Religion und Psychologie. Eine Antwort auf Martin Buber." (336–45) GW 18,96.
16. Letters (each with thematic title) to Niederer, Irminger, Serrano, Oftinger, Westmann, Bruecher, drawn from the *Briefe*, G. 1972a / 1972b / 1973a.

1984a *Grundfragen zur Praxis.* ("Grundwerk C. G. Jung," ed. by Helmut Barz, Ursula Baumgardt, Rudolf Blomeyer, Hans Dieckmann, Helmut Remmler, Theodor Seifert; vol. 1.) Olten: Walter. pp. 339.
Contents:
1. "Grundsätzliches zur praktischen Psychotherapie." (11–30)
2. "Ziele der Psychotherapie." (31–48) GW 16,5.
3. "Psychotherapie und Weltanschauung." (49–56) GW 16,7.
4. "Die Psychotherapie in der Gegenwart." (57–72) GW 16,9.
5. "Grundfragen der Psychotherapie." (73–87) GW 16,10.
6. "Der therapeutische Wert des Abreagierens." (88–98) GW 16,11.
7. "Die praktische Verwendbarkeit der Traumanalyse." (99–121) GW 16,12.
8. "Allgemeine Gesichtspunkte zur Psychologie des Traumes." (122–67) GW 8,9.
9. "Vom Wesen der Träume." (168–84) GW 8,10.
10. "Allgemeines zur Komplextheorie." (185–98) GW 8,3.
11. "Allgemeine Beschreibung der Typen." (199–282) GW 6,10.
12. "Die Schizophrenie." (283–339) GW 3,9.

1984b *Archetyp und Unbewusstes.* ("Grundwerk," 2; cf. G. 1984a.) pp. 443.
Contents:
1. "Theoretische Überlegungen zum Wesen des Psychischen." (1–76) GW 8,8.
2. "Über die Archetypen des kollektiven Unbewussten." (77–113) GW 9i,1.
3. "Der Begriff des kollektiven Unbewussten." (114–25) GW 9i,2.
4. "Über den Archetypus mit besonderer Berücksichtigung des Animabegriffes." (126–42) GW 9i,3.
5. "Die psychologischen Aspekte des Mutterarchetypus." (143–75) GW 9i,4.
6. "Zur Psychologie des Kindarchetypus." (176–205) GW 9i,6.

7. "Zur Phänomenologie des Geistes im Märchen." (206–50) GW 9i,8.
8. "Die transzendente Funktion." (251–78) GW 8,2.
9. "Über Synchronizität." (279–343) GW 8,19.

1984c *Persönlichkeit und Übertragung.* ("Grundwerk," 3; cf. G. 1984a.) pp. 320. Contents:
  1. "Die Beziehungen zwischen dem Ich und dem Unbewussten." (9–125) GW 7,2.
  2. "Die Psychologie der Übertragung." (127–287) GW 16,13.

1984d *Menschenbild und Gottesbild.* ("Grundwerk," 4; cf. G. 1984a.) pp. 361. Contents:
  1. "Psychologie und Religion." (9–109) GW 11,1.
  2. "Das Wandlungssymbol in der Messe." (111–99) GW 11,3.
  3. "Antwort auf Hiob." (201–361) GW 11,9.

1984e *Traumsymbole des Individuationsprozesses. (Psychologie und Alchemie 1.)* ("Grundwerk," 5; cf. G. 1984a.) pp. 267. Contents:
  1. "Einleitung in die religionspsychologische Problematik der Alchemie." (7–44) GW 12,1.
  2. "Traumsymbole des Individuationsprozesses." (45–235) GW 12,11.

1984f *Erlösungsvorstellungen in der Alchemie. (Psychologie und Alchemie 2.)* ("Grundwerk," 6; cf. G. 1984a.) pp. 304. Contents:
  1. "Der Erlösungsvorstellungen in der Alchemie." (9–246) GW 12,111.

1984g With Sigmund Freud: *Briefwechsel.* Edited by William McGuire and Wolfgang Sauerländer. Abridged by Alan McGlashan. (G. 1974a edited [by Ingeborg Meyer-Palmedo] to conform with E. 1979a.) pp. 275. (Paperback.) Frankfurt am Main: Fischer Taschenbuch Verlag.

1984h *Mysterium Coniunctionis.* (GW, 14.) Rev. edn. See Part II.

1985a *Symbol und Libido. (Symbole der Wandlung 1.)* ("Grundwerk," 7; cf. G. 1984a.) pp. 247. GW 5: Vorrede (1950), Erster Teil, Zweiter Teil, 1–111. Vorrede 1924 and 1937 (187–89).

1985b *Heros und Mutterarchetyp. (Symbole der Wandlung 2.)* ("Grundwerk," 8; cf. G. 1984a.) pp. 368. GW 5: Zweite Teil, IV–IX.

1985c *Mensch und Kultur.* ("Grundwerk," 9; cf. G. 1984a.) pp. 303. Contents:
  1. "Vom Werden der Persönlichkeit." (7–26) GW 17,7.
  2. "Die Frau in Europa." (27–47) GW 10,6.
  3. "Die Ehe als psychologische Beziehung." (48–60) GW 17,8.
  4. "Die Lebenswende." (61–77) GW 8,16.
  5. "Seele und Tod." (78–89) GW 8,17.
  6. "Das Gewissen in psychologischer Sicht." (90–109) GW 10,16.
  7. "Gut und Böse in der analytischen Psychologie." (110–23) GW 10,17.
  8. "Psychologie und Dichtung." (124–46) GW 15,7.
  9. "Die träumende Welt Indiens." (147–57) GW 10,23.
  10. "Was Indien uns lehren kann." (158–63) GW 10,24.
  11. "Zur Psychologie östlicher Meditation." (164–81) GW 11,14.
  12. "Vorwort zum I Ging." (182–201) GW 11,16.
  13. "Die Visionen des Zosimos." (202–44) GW 13,2.
  14. "Paracelsus als Arzt." (245–61) GW 15,2.
  15. "Sigmund Freud." (262–70) GW 15,4.

1986a *Von Sinn und Wahn-Sinn.* (Einsichten und Weisheiten.) Selected by Franz Alt. Olten: Walter. pp. 72. Quotations from the published writings, on themes expressed by the titles.

1986b *Von Traum und Selbsterkenntnis.* (Einsichten und Weisheiten.) pp. 104. (Cf. G. 1986a.)

1986c *C. G. Jung im Gespräch. Interviews, Reden, Begegnungen.* Zürich: Daimon. pp. 340. Based on E. 1977a, with omissions and additions. The contents are memoirs, notes (sometimes stenographic), and journalistic articles, therefore not considered to have been written *by* Jung, except for the following, which were transcribed from electronic recordings or, if recorded in another way, were approved by Jung:
  1. "Houston Filme" (1957). (94–178) Tr. from E. 1977a, pp. 276–352.
  2. "Gut und Böse in der Analytischen Psychologie" (1958). (208–24) GW 10,17.

3. "Diskussion mit der Psychologischen Gesellschaft Basel" (1958). (225–48)
4. "Das 'Face to Face' Interview von John Freeman und C. G. Jung" (1959). (264–280) Tr. from E. 1977a, pp. 424–39.
5. "Interview von Dr. Georg Gerster mit C. G. Jung anlässlich seines 85. Geburtstag, Radio DRS" (1960) (308–22)

1986d "Briefe von Carl Gustav Jung an Sabina Spielrein (1908–1919)." In: *Tagebuch einer heimlichen Symmetrie. Sabina Spielrein zwischen Jung und Freud.* pp. 187–225. Edited by Aldo Carotenuto. [Vol. I of a 2-vol. set; Vol. II: Collected writings of Spielrein.] Freiburg i. Br.: "Kore," Traute Hensch. Vol. I is based on Carotenuto, *Diario di una segreta simmetria*, Rome: Astrolabio, 1980. The following writings by Jung, in addition to his letters to Spielrein, are added in the "Kore" edition:
1. "Sabina Spielrein in dem Briefwechsel zwischen Sigmund Freud und Carl Gustav Jung (1906–1912)." pp. 227–49. Contains passages relating to Spielrein in Jung's letters to Freud of 23 Oct 1906; 6 Jul 1907; 7 Mar, 11 Mar, 4 Jun, 12 Jun, 21 Jun, 10/13 Jul 1909; 12 Jun, 14 Nov, 11 Dec 1911; 10 Mar, 1 Apr 1912. From G. 1974a.
2. "Sabina Spielrein in dem Vortrag Carl Gustav Jungs über die Freudsche Hysterietheorie (1907)." pp. 250–54. Extract from GW 4,2, retitled.

1987a *Von Religion und Christentum.* (Einsichten und Weisheiten.) pp. 106. (Cf. G. 1986a.)

1987b *Kinderträume.* Seminare. See Part III, [1987] (p. 202).

1988a *Lexikon Jungscher Grundbegriffe.* Mit Originaltexten von C. G. Jung. Ed. by Helmut Hark. Olten: Walter. pp. 197.

1988b *Von Sexualität und Liebe.* (Einsichten und Weisheiten.) pp. 146. (Cf. G. 1986a.)

1988c *Zur Psychologie westlicher und östlicher Religion.* (GW 11.) Rev edn., repaginated, without Anhang (appendix).

1989a *Von Vater, Mutter und Kind.* (Einsichten und Weisheiten.) pp. 132. (Cf. G. 1986a.)

1989b *Von Mensch und Gott.* Ein Lesebuch. Selected by Franz Alt. Olten and Freiburg i. Br.: Walter. pp. 326. [Each selection is followed by letters quoted from the *Briefe*, G. 1972a, 1972b, 1973a.]
Contents:

1. "Einleitung in die religionspsychologische Problematik." (11–32) Excerpt from GW 12,3. Letters to Boltze and Lang. (33–36)
2. "Psychotherapie und Weltanschauung." (37–45) GW 16,7. Letters to Wittwer, Eickhoff, and Rolfe. (46–50)
3. "Über die Beziehung der Psychotherapie zur Seelsorge." (51–73) GW 11,7. Letters to David, Hoch, and Sinclair. (74–85)
4. "Das persönliche und das kollektive Unbewusste." (86–98) Excerpt from GW 7,1. Letters to Cogo and Serrano. (99–108)
5. "Die Individuation." (109–54) Excerpt from GW 7,2. Letters to White and Uhsadel. (155–62)
6. "Was indien uns lehren kann." (163–68) GW 10,24. Letters to Anon. and White. (169–77)
7. "Zur Psychologie östliche Meditation [Yoga]." (178–98) GW 11,14. Letters to Magor and Anon. (199–200)
8. "Zur Phänomenologie des Geistes im Märchen." (201–40) GW 9i,8. Letters to Werblowsky and Buri. (241–45)
9. "Gut und Böse in der analytischen Psychologie." (246–60) GW 10,17. Letters to Wegmann and Kelsey. (261–66)
10. "Das Gewissen in psychologischer Sicht." (267–89) GW 10,16. Letters to Kinney and Leonhard. (290–92)
11. "Über das Leben nach dem Tod." (293–323) G. 1962a,12.

1989c *Zwei Schriften über Analytische Psychologie.* (GW, 7.) Rev. ed., repaginated. See Part II.

1990a *Von Schein und Sein.* (Einsichten und Weisheiten.) pp. 119. (Cf. G. 1986a.)

1990b *Von Gut und Böse.* (Einsichten und Weisheiten.) pp. 154. (Cf. G. 1986a.)

1990c *Die Beziehungen zwischen dem Ich und dem Unbewussten.* Ed. by Lorenz Jung. Munich: Deutscher Taschenbuch Verlag. pp. 129. GW 7,2. (First vol. of a paperback ed. in 11 vols.)

1990d *Antwort auf Hiob.* pp. 117. (Taschenbuch. Cf. G. 1990c.) GW 11,9.

1990e *Typologie.* pp. 206. (Taschenbuch. Cf. G. 1990c.) Contents:
1. "Einleitung." (7–11) GW 6,3,1.
2. "Psychologische Typologie" (1936). (13–25) GW 6, Anhang, 7.
3. "Allgemeine Beschreibung der Typen." (27–104) GW 6,3,X.
4. "Psychologische Typen" (1923). (105–18) GW 6, Anhang, 5.
5. "Definitionen." (119–94) GW 6,3,XI.
6. Schlusswort." (195–202) GW 6,3.

1990f *Traum und Traumdeutung.* pp. 366. (Taschenbuch. Cf. G. 1990c.) Contents:
1. "Symbole und Traumdeutung." (7–87) GW 18,2.
2. "Allgemeine Gesichtspunkte zur Psychologie des Traumes." (89–131) GW 8,9.
3. "Vom Wesen der Träume." (133–48) GW 8,10.
4. "Die praktische Verwendbarkeit der Traumanalyse." (149–69) GW 16,12.
5. "Traumsymbole des Individuationsprozesses." (171–279, including 93 figs.) Extract from GW 12,3.

1990g *Synchronizität, Akausalität und Okkultismus.* pp. 259. (Taschenbuch. Cf. G. 1990c.) Contents:
1. "Synchronizität als ein Prinzip akausaler Zusammenhänge." (9–97) GW 8,18.
2. "Briefe über Synchronizität." (99–106) GW 18,49.
3. "Die psychologischen Grundlagen des Geisterglaubens." (109–26) GW 8,11.
4. "Über spiritistische Erscheinungen." (127–43) GW 18,4.
5. Drei Vorreden (White, Moser, Jaffé). (145–64) GW 18,6–8.
6. "Zur Psychologie und Pathologie sogenannter okkulter Phänomene." (165–249) GW 1,1.

1990h *Archetypen.* pp. 176. (Taschenbuch. Cf. G. 1990c.) Contents:
1. Über die Archetypen des kollektiven Unbewussten." (1–44) GW 9i,1.
2. "Der Begriff des kollektiven Unbewussten." (45–56) GW 9i,2.

3. "Über den Archetypus mit besonderer Berücksichtigung des Animabegriffes." (57–74) GW 9i,3.
4. "Die psychologischen Aspekte des Mutterarchetypus." (75–106) GW 9i,4.
5. "Zur Psychologie des Kindarchetypus." (107–44) GW 9i,6.
6. "Zum psychologischen Aspekt der Korefigur." (145–58) GW 9i,7.
7. "Zur Psychologie der Tricksterfigur." (159–76) GW 9i,9.

1990i *Wirklichkeit der Seele.* pp. 138. (Taschenbuch. Cf. G. 1990c; also G. 1934b.) Contents:
1. "Vorwort" [to G. 1934b, abridged]. (7–8) (GW 18,133)
2. "Das Grundproblem der gegenwärtigen Psychologie." (9–26) GW 8,13.
3. "Die Bedeutung der Psychologie für die Gegenwart." (27–48) GW 10,7.
4. "Paracelsus." (49–58) GW 15,1.
5. "Sigmund Freud als kulturhistorische Erscheinung." (59–66) GW 15,3.
6. " 'Ulysses'; Ein Monolog." (67–90) GW 15,8.
7. "Picasso." (91–96) GW 15,9.
8. "Vom Werden der Persönlichkeit." (97–116) GW 17,7.
9. "Seele und Tod." (117–28) GW 8,17.

1991a *Traumanalyse.* Seminare. See Part III, [1991] (p. 196).

1991b *Die Psychologie der Übertragung.* pp. 166. (Taschenbuch. Cf. G. 1990c.) GW 16,13.

1991c *Psychologie und Religion.* pp. 236. (Taschenbuch. Cf. G. 1990c.) Contents:
1. "Psychologie und Religion." (7–116) GW 11,1.
2. "Über die Beziehung der Psychotherapie zur Seelsorge." (117–32) GW 11,7.
3. "Psychoanalyse und Seelsorge." (133–38) GW 11,8.
4. "Die Wandlungssymbol in der Messe." (139–228) GW 11,3.

1991d *Vom Leiden und Heilen.* (Einsichten und Weisheiten.) pp. 144. (Cf. G. 1986a.)

1991e *Vom Abenteuer Wachsen und Erwachsenwerden.* Ein Lesebuch. Selected by Franz Alt. pp. 336. (Cf. G. 1989b.)
1. "Die Struktur der Seele." (9–32) GW 8,7. Letters to Illing and Isaac. (32–39)
2. "Über Konflikte der kindlichen Seele." (40–70) GW 17,1.
3. "Das Liebesproblem des Studenten." (71–91) GW 10,5. Letter to Bovet. (91–92)
4. "Die Ehe als psychologische Beziehung." (93–107) GW 17,9.
5. "Die Bedeutung des Vaters für das Schicksal des Einzelnen." (108–29) Excerpt from GW 4,14. Letter to Corti. (129–30)
6. "Über den Archetypus mit besonderer Berücksichtigung des Animabegriffes." (131–51) GW 9i,3. Letters to Lewino, Rolfe, Evans, and Anon. (151–57)
7. "Die psychologischen Aspekte des Mutterarchetypus." (158–96) GW 9i,4. Letters to Vetter, Keyserling, and McCullen. (196–201)
8. "Allgemeines zur Komplextheorie." (202–17) GW 8,3. Letters to Anon. (3), Meyer, Verzár, and Rolfe. (217–26)
9. "Die Bedeutung des Unbewussten für die individuelle Erziehung." (227–45) GW 17,6. Letters to Anon., England, Thompson, and van Lier-Schmidt Ernsthausen. (245–57)
10. "Analytische Psychologie und Erziehung." (258–321) Extract from GW 17,4. Letters to Frei and Lasky. (321–29)

1991f *Seelenprobleme der Gegenwart.* pp. 258. (Taschenbuch. Cf. G. 1990c.)
Contents:
Vorwort zur ersten Auflage (1931) (7) GW 18,67.
Vorwort zur zweiten Auflage (1933) (8) GW 18,67.
1. "Die Probleme der modernen Psychotherapie" (1929) (9–30) GW 16,6.
2. "Über die Beziehungen der analytischen Psychologie zum dichterischen Kunstwerk" (1922) (31–50) GW 15,6.
3. "Der Gegensatz Freud und Jung" (1929) (51–58) GW 4,16.
4. "Ziele der Psychotherapie" (1929) (59–76) GW 16,5.
5. "Psychologische Typologie" (1928) (77–94) GW 6,6.
6. "Die Struktur der Seele" (1927) (95–114) GW 8,7.
7. "Seele und Erde" (1927) (115–34) GW 10,2.
8. "Der archaische Mensch" (1930) (135–56) GW 10,3.
9. "Die Lebenswende" (1930) (157–72) GW 8,16.
10. "Die Ehe als psychologische Beziehung" (1925) (173–84) GW 17,8.

11. "Analytische Psychologie und Weltanschauung" (1927) (185–208) GW 8,14.
12. "Geist und Leben" (1926) (209–28) GW 8,12.
13. "Das Seelenproblem des modernen Menschen" (1928) (229–48) GW 10,4.

1991g *Wandlungen und Symbole der Libido. Beiträge zur Entwicklungsgeschichte des Denkens.* pp. 446. G. 1938b repub. with corrs. of citations according to GW 5, transls. of foreign quots., bibliography, foreword by Lutz Niehus. (Taschenbuch. Cf. G. 1990c.) Contents:

1. Vorrede zur vierten Auflage (7).
2. Vorrede zur zweiten Auflage (12).
3. Vorrede zur dritten Auflage (13).

Erster Teil:

1. Einleitung (17–20).
2. Über die zwei Arten des Denkens (21–47).
3. Vorbereitende Materialien zur Analyse der Millerschen Phantasien (48–53).
4. Der Schöpferhymnus (54–84).
5. Das Lied von der Motte (85–121).

Zweiter Teil:

1. Einleitung (123–32).
2. Über den Begriff und die genetische Theorie der Libido (133–46).
3. Die Verlagerung der Libido als mögliche Quelle der primitiven menschlichen Erfindungen (147–74).
4. Die unbewusste Entstehung des Heros (175–207).
5. Symbole der Mutter und der Wiedergeburt (208–66).
6. Der Kampf um die Befreiung von der Mutter (267–94).
7. Das Opfer (295–411).

Anhang: Miss Frank Miller: Phänomene vorübergehender Suggestion oder momentaner Autosuggestion (415–26).

ENGLISH

1907a   "On Psychophysical Relations of the Associative Experiment." *J. abnorm. Psychol.*, 1:6 (Feb.), 247–55. Repub., slightly rev., with slight title change as CW 2,12. TR.—GW 2,12.

1907b   With F. Peterson: "Psycho-physical Investigations with the Galvanometer and Pneumograph in Normal and Insane Individuals." *Brain*, XXX:2 (pt. 118) (July), 153–218. Repub., slightly rev., as CW 2,13. TR.—GW 2,13.

1908a   With Charles Ricksher: "Further Investigations on the Galvanic Phenomenon and Respiration in Normal and Insane Individuals." *J. abnorm. Psychol.*, II:5 (Dec. 1907–Jan. 1908), 189–217. Repub., slightly rev., as CW 2,14. TR.—GW 2,14.

1909a   *The Psychology of Dementia Praecox.* (Nervous and Mental Disease Monograph Series No. 3.) New York: The Journal of Nervous and Mental Disease Publishing Co. pp. 153. 1971: facsimile edn. New York: Johnson Reprint Corp. pp. 150. Trans. from G. 1907a by Frederick W. Peterson and A. A. Brill. Contents:
     Author's Preface. (xix–xx) Dated July 1906.
         I. Critical Presentation of Theoretical Views on the Psychology of Dementia Praecox.
        II. The Emotional Complex and Its General Action on the Psyche.
       III. The Influence of the Emotional Complex on Association.
       IV. Dementia Praecox and Hysteria, a Parallel.
        V. Analysis of a Case of Paranoid Dementia as a Paradigm.
Pub. in dif. trans.'s as E. 1936b and CW 3,1.

1910a   "The Association Method." *American Journal of Psychology*, XXI:2 (Apr.), 219–69. Trans. from a largely unpub. German text by A. A. Brill. Contents:
     1. Lecture I. (Untitled) (219–40) Pub. in a dif. trans. as CW 2,10. Partially incorporates It. 1908a.

2. Lecture II. "Familial [printed as "Familiar"] Constellations. (240–51) Pub. in a dif. trans. as CW 2,11. Cf. Fr. 1907a.

3. Lecture III. "Experiences Concerning the Psychic Life of the Child." (251–69) German version pub. as G. 1910k. Cf. CW 17,1.

Repub. in *Lectures and Addresses Delivered before the Departments of Psychology and Pedagogy in Celebration of the Twentieth Anniversary of the Opening of Clark University—September, 1909.* Worcester, Mass.: The University. pp. 39–89. Pub. with stylistic alterations as E. 1916a,3.

1913a "On the Doctrine of Complexes." *Australasian Medical Congress, Transactions of the 9th Session,* II, 835–39. Sydney: Wm. Applegate Gullick, Government Printer, under the direction of the Literary Committee. Repub., slightly rev., as CW 2,18. Paper contributed to the Congress, Sydney, Australia, Sept. 1911. TR.—GW 2,18.

1913b "The Theory of Psychoanalysis." [1st section: Introduction and Chs. I–III.] *Psychoanal. Rev.,* I:1 (Nov.), 1–40. Trans. from G. 1913a by Edith and M. D. Eder and Mary Moltzer. The 1st of 5 sections. Repub., with E. 1914a and 1915b, as E. 1915a. Pub., together with E. 1914a and 1915b, with addns., in a dif. trans. as CW 4,9. First part of a series of 9 lectures given in English as an Extension Course at Fordham University, New York City, Sept. 1912.

1913c "Letter from Dr. Jung." (To *The Psychoanalytic Review,* Nov. 1913.) *Psychoanal. Rev.,* I:1 (Nov.), 117–18. Repub. in E. 1973b. TR.—German: 1972a.

1913d "Psycho-Analysis." *Transactions of the Psycho-Medical Society,* IV:2, pp. 19. Trans. (by ?) from the orig. German ms., a version of which was ultimately pub. as GW 4,10. Repub. with slight title change as E. 1915d. Read before the Psycho-Medical Society, London, 5 Aug. 1913.

1914a "The Theory of Psychoanalysis." *Psychoanal. Rev.* [2d–4th sections: Chs. IV–VII: 1:2 (Feb.), 153–77; Ch. VIII: I:3 (July), 260–84; Ch. IX: 1:4 (Oct.), 415–30.] Trans. from G. 1913a by Edith and M. D. Eder and Mary Moltzer. The 2d, 3d, and 4th of 5 sections. Cf. E. 1913b and E. 1915b. Repub., with E. 1913b and 1915b, as E.

1915a. Pub., with E. 1913b and 1915b, with addns., in a dif. trans. as CW 4,9. The middle portion of a series of 9 lectures. Cf. E. 1913b.

1914b "On the Importance of the Unconscious in Psychopathology." *British Medical Journal*, II (5 Dec.), 964–66. Repub. as E. 1916a,11. Paper read in the Section of Neurology and Psychological Medicine, 82d Annual Meeting of the British Medical Association, Aberdeen, 29–31 July 1914. (Discussion with Ernest Jones follows ?) Summary appeared in *The Lancet*, II (1914) (5 Sept.), 650.

1915a *The Theory of Psychoanalysis.* (Nervous and Mental Disease Monograph Series No. 19.) New York: Journal of Nervous and Mental Disease Publishing Co. pp. 135. 1971: Facsimile edn. New York: Johnson Reprint Corp. Contents:
Introduction. (1–3)
    I. Consideration of Early Hypotheses. (4–16)
    II. The Infantile Sexuality. (17–26)
    III. The Conception of Libido. (27–44)
    IV. The Etiological Significance of the Infantile Sexuality. (45–54)
    V. The Unconscious. (55–59)
    VI. The Dream. (60–66)
    VII. The Content of the Unconscious. (67–71)
    VIII. The Etiology of the Neuroses. (72–95)
    IX. The Therapeutical Principles of Psychoanalysis. (96–110)
    X. Some General Remarks on Psychoanalysis. (111–33)
E. 1913b, 1914a, and 1915b repub. as a monograph. Pub. in a dif. trans. as CW 4,9.

1915b "The Theory of Psychoanalysis." [5th section: Ch. X.] *Psychoanal. Rev.*, II:1 (Jan.), 29–51. Trans. from G. 1913a by Edith and M. D. Eder and Mary Moltzer. The last of 5 sections. Cf. E. 1913b and 1914a. Repub., with E. 1913b and 1914a, as E. 1915a. Pub., with E. 1913b and 1914a, with addns., in a dif. trans. as CW 4,9. The last of a series of lectures. Cf. E. 1913b.

1915c "On Psychological Understanding." *J. abnorm. Psychol.*, IX:6 (Feb.–Mar.), 385–99. German version, rev. and slightly exp., pub. as supplement in G. 1914a. ?Incorporated in E. 1916a,14. English version read before the Psycho-Medical Society, London, 24 July 1914.

1915d "Psychoanalysis." *Psychoanal. Rev.*, II:3 (July), 241–59. E. 1913d repub. with slight title change. Repub. as E. 1916a,8. Pub. in a dif. trans., with title change, as CW 4,10.

1916a *Collected Papers on Analytical Psychology*. Ed. by Constance E. Long. New York: Moffat, Yard; London: Baillére, Tindall & Cox. pp. 392. Some copies bear the title: *Analytical Psychology*. Contents:

1. Author's Preface. (vii–x) Probably trans. from a German ms. by Constance E. Long. Dated Jan. 1916. Repub. as E. 1917a, 1, and in a dif. trans. as CW 4,13. "First Edition." TR.—German: GW 4,13,a.

2. "On the Psychology and Pathology of So-called Occult Phenomena." (1–93) Trans. from G. 1902a by M. D. Eder. Repub. as E. 1917a,2, and, in a dif. trans., as CW 1,1.

3. "The Association Method." (94–155) E. 1910a pub. with stylistic alterations. Consists of 3 lectures, the 1st 2 pub. in a dif. trans. as CW 2,10 and 11. In regard to the 3d, cf. CW 17,1. Repub. as E. 1917a,3.

4. "The Significance of the Father in the Destiny of the Individual." (156–75) Trans. from G. 1909c by M. D. Eder. Repub. as E. 1917a,4. Cf. CW 4,14.

5. "A Contribution to the Psychology of Rumour." (176–90) Trans. from G. 1910q. Repub. as E. 1917a,5. Pub. in a dif. trans. as CW 4,4.

6. "On the Significance of Number-Dreams." (191–99) Trans. from G. 1911e by M. D. Eder. Repub. as E. 1917a,6. Pub. in a dif. trans. as CW 4,5.

7. "A Criticism of Bleuler's 'Theory of Schizophrenic Negativism'." (200–05) Trans. from G. 1911c by M. D. Eder. Repub. as E. 1917a,7. Pub. in a dif. trans. as CW 3,4.

8. "Psychoanalysis." (206–25) E. 1915d repub. Repub. as E. 1917a,8. Pub. in a dif. trans., with title change, as CW 4,10.

9. "On Psychoanalysis." (226–35) Repub. as E. 1917a,9, and with minor revs. and title change as CW 4,11. Read in English before the New York Academy of Medicine, 8 Oct. 1912, and to the 17th International Medical Congress, London, 1913.

10. "On Some Crucial Points in Psychoanalysis." (236–77)

Trans. from G. 1914b by Edith Eder. Repub. as E. 1917a,10. Pub. in a dif. trans. with minor title change as CW 4,12.

11. "On the Importance of the Unconscious in Psychopathology." (278–86) E. 1914b repub. Repub. as E. 1917a,11. Pub., slightly rev., as CW 3,5.

12. "A Contribution to the Study of Psychological Types." (287–98) Trans. from Fr. 1913a by Constance E. Long. Repub. as E. 1917a,12. Pub. in a dif. trans. as CW 6,5.

13. "The Psychology of Dreams." (299–311) Trans. from an unpub. ms. (greatly exp. and pub. as G. 1928b,2) by Dora Hecht. Repub. as E. 1917a,13. Cf. E. 1956b and CW 8,9 for dif. trans.'s of an exp. version.

14. "The Content of the Psychoses." (312–51) Trans. from G. 1914a by M. D. Eder. Repub. as E. 1917a,14. Pub. in a dif. trans. as CW 3,2. ?Incorporates E. 1915c.

15. "New Paths in Psychology." (352–77) Trans. from G. 1912d by Dora Hecht. Pub., rev. and exp., with title change, as E. 1917a,15. Pub. in a dif. trans. as CW 7,3.

1916b *Psychology of the Unconscious. A Study of the Transformations and Symbolisms of the Libido. A Contribution to the History of the Evolution of Thought.* New York: Moffat, Yard; London: Kegan Paul, Trench, Trubner. pp. lvi + 566. (Lengthy front matter contains intro. by the translator.) Trans. from G. 1912a by Beatrice M. Hinkle. The American edn. was imported, presumably as sheets, into Great Britain by Kegan Paul, who substituted their title page. Publication date for the London edn. is considered to be 1917, although copies bear only the 1916 copyright date by Moffat Yard. In 1919, Moffat Yard issued a "new edn.," xxxvi + 339 pp. Kegan Paul reprinted this last version in 1921, continuing to do so through the 6th impression, 1951. (In 1947, the imprint became Routledge & Kegan Paul.) Dodd Mead (New York) acquired the book from Moffat Yard in 1925, reprinting the 1916 edn. which was in print until 1972. Contents (the first pagination given is that of the 1916 edn., the second, that of the 1919 edn.):

1. Author's Note. (xlvii) (xxix) Cf. CW 5, 2d edn., 2d pr.
Part I.
2. Introduction. (3–7) (1–3)
3. Concerning the Two Kinds of Thinking. (8–41) (4–21)
4. The Miller Phantasies. (42–48) (22–25)

5. The Hymn of Creation. (49–86) (26–46)
6. The Song of the Moth. (87–126) (47–69)

Part II.

7. Aspects of the Libido. (127–38) (70–76)
8. The Conception and the Genetic Theory of Libido. (139–56) (77–86)
9. The Transformation of the Libido. A Possible Source of Primitive Human Discoveries. (157–90) (87–105)
10. The Unconscious Origin of the Hero. (191–232) (106–28)
11. Symbolism of the Mother and of Rebirth. (233–306) (129–168)
12. The Battle for Deliverance from the Mother. (307–40) (169–87)
13. The Dual Mother Role. (341–427) (188–236)
14. The Sacrifice. (428–83) (237–67)

Entire work pub., rev. and expanded, in a dif. trans. with change of title, as CW 5. For reissue of the 1916 work, see Part II, Supplementary Vol. B.

1917a *Collected Papers on Analytical Psychology.* Ed. by Constance E. Long. 2d edn. New York: Moffat, Yard; London: Baillière, Tindall & Cox. pp. 492. Contents conform to those of the 1st edn. (cf. E. 1916a) with the following addns. and substitution:

1a. Author's Preface to the Second Edition. (ix–xii) Probably trans. from the German ms. by Constance E. Long. Dated June 1917. Repub. in a dif. trans. as CW 4,13,b.
15. "The Psychology of the Unconscious Processes." (352–444) Trans. from G. 1917a by Dora Hecht. Replaces E. 1916a,15, of which this is a rev. and exp. version. Cf. E. 1928b,1 and CW 7,1 for trans.'s of further rev. versions.
16. "The Conception of the Unconscious." (445–74) Trans. from a German ms. subsequently lost, a French trans. of which was pub. as Fr. 1916a. The orig. ms. was found posthumously and a dif. trans. pub. as CW 7,4 (2d edn.). Cf. E. 1928b,2 and CW 7,2 for trans. of further rev. versions. Delivered as a lecture to the Zurich School of Analytical Psychology, 1916.

1918a *Studies in Word-Association. Experiments in the Diagnosis of Psychopathological Conditions Carried Out at the Psychiatric Clinic of the University of Zurich, under the direction of C. G. Jung.* New York: Moffat, Yard; London: Heinemann, 1919. pp. 575. 1969: New York: Russell & Russell; London: Routledge & Kegan Paul. Trans. by M. D. Eder. Contains the following works by Jung:

1. With F. Riklin: "The Associations of Normal Subjects." (8–172) Trans. from G. 1906a,1. Pub. in a dif. trans. as CW 2,1.
2. "Analysis of the Associations of an Epileptic." (206–26) Trans. from G. 1906a,2. Pub. in a dif. trans. as CW 2,2.
3. "Reaction-Time in Association Experiments." (227–65) Trans. from G. 1906a,3. Pub. in a dif. trans. as CW 2,3.
4. "Psycho-Analysis and Association Experiments." (297–321) Trans. from G. 1906a,4. Pub. in a dif. trans. with slight title change as CW 2,5.
5. "Association, Dream, and Hysterical Symptoms." (354–95) Trans. from G. 1909a,1. Pub. in a dif. trans. with slight title change as CW 2,7.
6. "On Disturbances in Reproduction in Association Experiments." (396–406) Trans. from G. 1909a,2. Pub. in a dif. trans. with slight title change as CW 2,9.

1919a "On the Problem of Psychogenesis in Mental Diseases." *Proceedings of the Royal Society of Medicine* (Section of Psychiatry), XII:9 (Aug.), 63–76. Repub., slightly rev., as CW 3,6. Written in English and read to the Section of Psychiatry, The Society, Annual Meeting, London, 11 July 1919.

1919b "Instinct and the Unconscious." *British Journal of Psychology*, X:1 (Nov.), 15–26. Trans. by H. G. Baynes from a German ms. subsequently pub. as G. 1928b,4. Repub. as E. 1928a,10. *Also issued as a pamphlet including other authors' papers, Cambridge, England: Cambridge University Press. Pub. in a dif. trans. as CW 8,6. A contribution to the Symposium of the same name, presented at the joint meeting of the British Psychological Society, the Aristotelian Society, and the Mind Association, London, 12 July 1919.

1920a "Introduction." Elida Evans: *The Problem of the Nervous Child.* pp. v–viii. New York: Dodd Mead; London: Kegan Paul [1921]. Dated Oct. 1919. Repub. as CW 18,129.

1920b "The Psychological Foundations of Belief in Spirits." *Proceedings of the Society for Psychical Research*, XXXI:79 (May), 75–93. Trans. by H. G. Baynes from a German ms. subsequently pub. as G. 1928b,

5. Repub. as E. 1928a,9. Pub. in a dif. trans. as CW 8,11. Read before a general meeting of the Society, London, 4 July 1919.

1921a "The Question of the Therapeutic Value of 'Abreaction'." *British Journal of Psychology* (Medical Section), II:1 (Oct.), 13–22. Pub., slightly rev., as E. 1928a,11. TR.—German: GW 16,11.

1923a *Psychological Types, or, The Psychology of Individuation.* New York: Harcourt Brace; London: Kegan Paul, Trench, Trubner. pp. 654. 1959: New York: Pantheon; London: Routledge & Kegan Paul. Trans. from G. 1921a by H. G. Baynes. Contents:
1. Introduction. (9–14)
2. The Problem of Types in the History of Classical and Medieval Thought. (15–86)
3. Schiller's Ideas upon the Type Problem. (87–169)
4. The Apollonian and the Dionysian. (170–83)
5. The Type Problem in the Discernment of Human Character. (184–206)
6. The Problem of Types in Poetry. (207–336)
7. The Type Problem in Psychiatry. (337–57)
8. The Problem of Typical Attitudes in Aesthetics. (358–71)
9. The Problem of Types in Modern Philosophy. (372–400)
10. The Type Problem in Biography. (401–11)
11. General Description of the Types. (412–517)
12. Definitions. (518–617)
13. Conclusion. (618–28)
Repub., trans. rev., as CW 6. Items 1, 11, 12 pub. as E. 1959a,4.

1923b "On the Relation of Analytical Psychology to Poetic Art." *British Journal of Medical Psychology*, III:3, 213–31. Trans. from G. 1922a by H. G. Baynes. Repub. as E. 1928a,8. Pub. in a dif. trans. as CW 8,11.

1925a *VII Sermones ad Mortuos. The Seven Sermons to the Dead Written by Basilides in Alexandria, the City Where the East Toucheth the West.* Edinburgh: Neill. pp. 28. Trans. from G. 1916a by H. G. Baynes. Printed for private circulation. Repub. as E. 1966a,19 and E. 1967b. Cf. E. 1967a. Presentation copy examined inscribed "To R. F. C. Hull. C. G. Jung. June 1959. Translation by H. G. Baynes."

1925b "Psychological Types." *Problems of Personality. Studies Presented to Morton Prince, Pioneer in American Psychopathology.* pp. 289–302. Ed. by C. MacFie Campbell, et al. New York: Harcourt Brace; London: Kegan Paul, Trench, Trubner. Trans. from G. 1925c by H. G. Baynes. Pub. in dif. trans.'s as E. 1928a,12 and CW 6,6. Lecture delivered at the International Congress of Education, Territet, 1923.

1926a "Marriage as a Psychological Relationship." *The Book of Marriage.* pp. 348–62. Ed. by Hermann Keyserling. New York: Harcourt Brace. Trans. from G. 1925b by Therese Duerr. Pub. in dif. trans.'s as E. 1928a,6 and CW 17,8.

1927a "Introduction." Frances G. Wickes: *The Inner World of Childhood.* pp. xiii–xiv. New York: D. Appleton. Trans. from a ms. subsequently expanded into G. 1931e, of which the above comprises the 1st 3 1/2 pars. Entire text of G. 1931e trans. and pub. as E. 1966c. Cf. CW 17,2.

1928a *Contributions to Analytical Psychology.* New York: Harcourt Brace; London: Kegan Paul, Trench, Trubner. pp. 410. Trans. by H. G. and Cary F. Baynes. Contents:
1. "On Psychical Energy." (1–76) Trans. from G. 1928b,2. Pub. in a dif. trans. with slight title change as CW 8,1.
2. "Spirit and Life." (77–98) Trans. from G. 1926c. Pub. in a dif. trans. as CW 8,12.
3. "Mind and the Earth." (99–140) Trans. from a German ms. subsequently pub. as G. 1931a,8. Pub. in a dif. trans. with minor title change as CW 10,2.
4. "Analytical Psychology and Weltanschauung." (141–63) Trans. from a German ms. subsequently rev. and exp. into G. 1931a,12. Cf. CW 8,14.
5. "Woman in Europe." (164–88) Trans. from G. 1927b. Pre-pub. as E. 1928c. Excerpt pub. as E. 1930d. Pub. in a dif. trans. as CW 10,6.
6. "Marriage as a Psychological Relationship." (189–203) Trans. from G. 1925b. Pub. in dif. trans.'s as E. 1926a and CW 17,8.
7. "The Love Problem of the Student." (204–24) Trans. from a German ms. subsequently pub. as G. 1971a,3. Pub. in a

dif. trans. with minor title change as CW 10,5. Lecture delivered to the student body, University of Zurich, 1924.

8. "On the Relation of Analytical Psychology to Poetic Art." (225–49) E. 1923b repub. Pub. in a dif. trans. with minor title change as CW 15,6.

9. "The Psychological Foundations of Belief in Spirits." (250–69) E. 1920b repub. Pub. in a dif. trans. as CW 8,11.

10. "Instinct and the Unconscious." (270–81) E. 1919b repub. Pub. in a dif. trans. as CW 8,6.

11. "The Question of the Therapeutic Value of 'Abreaction'." (282–94) E. 1921a, slightly rev. Repub., slightly rev. and with minor title change, as CW 16,11.

12. "Psychological Types." (295–312) Trans. from G. 1925c. Pub. in dif. trans.'s as E. 1925b and CW 6,6.

13. "Analytical Psychology and Education." (313–82) Consists of 4 lectures. Lecture I trans. from the unpub. German ms. subsequently pub. as G. 1971a,4. Repub., slightly rev., as CW 17,3. Delivered to the International Congress of Education, Territet, 1923. Lectures II–IV drafted in English and rev. by Roberts Aldrich. Cf. CW 17,4. Delivered to the International Congress of Education, London, May 1924.

14. "The Significance of the Unconscious in Individual Education." (383–402) Trans. from a German ms. subsequently pub. as G. 1971a,5. Delivered as a lecture to the International Congress of Education, Heidelberg, 1925. Pub. in a dif. trans. as CW 17,6. Excerpt pub. as "Analysis of Two Homosexual Dreams." pp. 286–93. *The Homosexuals as Seen by Themselves and Thirty Authorities.* Ed. by A. M. Krich. New York: Citadel Press, 1957.

1928b *Two Essays on Analytical Psychology.* New York: Dodd, Mead; London: Baillière, Tindall & Cox. pp. 280. Trans. by H. G. and C. F. Baynes. Contents:

1. "The Unconscious in the Normal and Pathological Mind." (1–121) Trans. from G. 1926a. Cf. E. 1917a,15 and CW 7,1 for trans.'s of earlier and later versions. Extracts (Chs. V & VII; pt. of last par. omitted) pub. in *Classics in Psychology.* pp. 715–55. Ed. by Thorne Shipley. New York: Philosophical Library, 1961.

2. "The Relation of the Ego to the Unconscious." (125–269)

Trans. from G. 1928a. Pub. in a dif. trans. with slight title change as CW 7,2.

1928c "Woman in Europe." *New Adelphi*, n.s. II:1 (Sept.), 19–35. E. 1928a,5 prepub.

1930a "Your Negroid and Indian Behavior." *Forum*, LXXXIII:4 (Apr.), 193–99. Repub., slightly rev. and with title change, as CW 10,22. Written in English.

1930b "Some Aspects of Modern Psychotherapy." *Journal of State Medicine*, XXXVIII:6 (June), 348–54. Repub. as CW 16,3. Written in English and delivered before the Congress of the Society of Public Health, Zurich, 1929. TR.—German: GW 16,4.

1930c "Psychology and Poetry." *transition*, no. 19/20 (June), 23–45. Trans. from G. 1930a by Eugene Jolas. Pub. in a dif. trans. with title change as E. 1933a,8. Cf. CW 15,7.

1930d "The Plight of Woman in Europe." *The 1930 European Scrap Book.* pp. 213–16. New York: Forum Press. Excerpted from E. 1928a,5.

1931a With Richard Wilhelm: *The Secret of the Golden Flower.* New York: Harcourt Brace; London: Kegan Paul, Trench, Trubner. pp. 151. 1955: New York: Wehman Bros. pp. 151. Trans. by Cary F. Baynes. Pub., rev. and augmented, as E. 1962b. Contains the following works by Jung:
   1. "Commentary." (77–137) Trans. from G. 1929b,I,1–6. Cf. CW 13,1.
   2. "Examples of European Mandalas." (137–38 + 10 plates) Trans. from G. 1929b,I,7. Cf. CW 13,1, pp. 56 ff and CW 9,i,12.
   3. "In Memory of Richard Wilhelm." (139–51) Trans. from G. 1930c. Cf. E. 1958a,9 and CW 15,5.

1931b "Foreword." Charles Roberts Aldrich: *The Primitive Mind and Modern Civilization.* pp. xv–xvii. New York: Harcourt Brace; London: Kegan Paul, Trench, Trubner. Trans. by Aldrich from the German ms. (Cf. GW 18,69.) Repub., trans. slightly rev., as CW 18,69.

1931c "The Spiritual Problem of Modern Man." *Prabuddha Bharata*, 36:8 (Aug.), 377–84; 36:9 (Sept.), 435–43. Trans. from G. 1928f by? Also pub. as monograph: Mayavati Almora, Himalayas: Advaiti Ashrama. pp. 15. Cf. E. 1933a,10 and CW 10,4 for trans.'s of rev. version.

1931d "Problems of Modern Psychotherapy." *Schweizerische Medizinische Wochenschrift*, LXI:35 (29 Aug.) 810–32. Trans. from G. 1929d by Carl [F.] Baynes. Repub. as E. 1933a,2. Pub. in a dif. trans. as CW 16,6.

1932a "Introduction." W. M. Kranefeldt: *Secret Ways of the Mind*. pp. xxv–xl. New York: Henry Holt; London: Kegan Paul, Trench, Trubner, 1934. Trans. from G. 1930b by Ralph M. Eaton. Pub. in a dif. trans. as CW 4,15.

1932b "Sigmund Freud in His Historical Setting." *Character and Personality*, I:1 (Sept.), 48–55. Trans. from G. 1932f by Cary F. Baynes. English trans. issued simultaneously with the orig. German (cf. G. 1932f) which was pub. in the German edn. of this journal. Pub. in a dif. trans. as CW 15,3.

1932c "Crime and the Soul. The Mystery of Dual Personality in the Law-breaker. Inoffensive People Who Become Criminals." *Sunday Referee* (London) (11 Dec.). For German version, see G. 1933a. Pub., with minor rev. in accordance with G. 1933a, as CW 18,13.

1933a *Modern Man in Search of a Soul*. New York: Harcourt Brace; London: Kegan Paul, Trench, Trubner. pp. 282. 1955: Paperback edn. (Harvest Books) New York: Harcourt Brace Jovanovich. pp. 244. 1961: London: Routledge & Kegan Paul. pp. 282. Trans. by W. S. Dell and Cary F. Baynes. Contents:

    1. "Dream Analysis in Its Practical Application." (1–31) Trans. from G. 1931c. Pub. in a dif. trans. with title change as CW 16,12.

    2. "Problems of Modern Psychotherapy." (32–62) E. 1931d repub. Pub. in a dif. trans. as CW 16,6.

    3. "The Aims of Psychotherapy." (63–84) Trans. from G. 1931a, 5. Pub. in a dif. trans. as CW 16,5.

    4. "A Psychological Theory of Types." (85–108) Trans. from G. 1931a,6. Repub., trans. slightly rev., as CW 6,7.

5. "The Stages of Life." (109–31) Trans. from G. 1931a,10. Pub. in a dif. trans. as CW 8,16.
6. "Freud and Jung: Contrasts." (132–42) Trans. from G. 1931a, 4. Pub. in a dif. trans. as CW 4,16.
7. "Archaic Man." (143–74) Trans. from G. 1931a,9. Pub. in a dif. trans. as CW 10,3.
8. "Psychology and Literature." (175–99) Trans. from G. 1930a. Pub. in a dif. trans. with title change as E. 1930c. Cf. CW 15,7.
9. "The Basic Postulates of Analytical Psychology." (200–25) Trans. from G. 1931g. Pub., trans. slightly rev., as CW 8,13.
10. "The Spiritual Problem of Modern Man." (226–54) Trans. from G. 1931a,14. Pub. in a dif. trans. as CW 10,4. Cf. E. 1931c for a trans. of earlier version.
11. "Psychotherapists or the Clergy." (255–82) Trans. from G. 1932a. Repub. as E. 1956d. Pub. in a dif. trans. as CW 11,7.

1933b "Introduction." M. E. Harding: *The Way of All Women.* pp. ix–xiii. London: Longmans, Green. 1970: Rev. edn. New York: G. P. Putnam's Sons for the C. G. Jung Foundation for Analytical Psychology. pp. xv–xviii. Trans. by Cary F. Baynes from the German ms. subsequently pub. as G. 1935c. Repub., somewhat rev., as CW 18,130. Dated Feb. 1932.

1936a *The Concept of the Collective Unconscious.* (Papers of the Analytical Psychology Club of New York.) New York: Analytical Psychology Club. pp. 20. Mimeographed for private circulation, Dec. 1936. Reissued in 2 pts. as E. 1936d and 1937b. Cf. CW 9,i,2. Text of lecture delivered to the Analytical Psychology Club, Plaza Hotel, New York, 2 Oct. 1936, and in London (cf. E. 1936d).

1936b *The Psychology of Dementia Praecox.* (Nervous and Mental Disease Monograph Series No. ?3.) New York and Washington: Journal of Nervous and Mental Disease Pub. Co. pp. 150. Trans. from G. 1907a by A. A. Brill. Pub. in dif. trans.'s as E. 1909a and CW 3,1. For contents, see E. 1909a.

1936c "Yoga and the West." *Prabuddha Bharata*, Section III, Sri Ramakrishna Centenary Number (Feb.), 170–77. Trans. from a German ms. by Cary F. Baynes. Pub. in a dif. trans. (based on this one) as CW 11,12. For German version, see GW 11,12.

1936d "The Concept of the Collective Unconscious." (Pt. I.) *St. Bartholomew's Hospital Journal*, XLIV:3 (Dec.), 46–49. The 1st part of E. 1936a repub. The 1st of 2 pts. Cf. E. 1937b. Repub., slightly rev., with E. 1937b, as CW 9,i,2. Text of lecture previously delivered in New York (cf. E. 1936a) given before the Abernethian Society, St. Bartholomew's Hospital, London, 19 Oct. 1936.

1936e See 1968a.

1937a "Psychological Factors Determining Human Behavior." *Factors Determining Human Behavior*. pp. 49–63. (Harvard Tercentenary Publications.) Cambridge, Mass.: Harvard U. P.; London: Humphrey Milford/Oxford U. P. Pub., with slight alterations and title change, as E. 1942a, and with above title and slight alterations as CW 8,5. For German version based on the orig. ms., cf. GW 8,5. Paper delivered in English as contribution to the Harvard Tercentenary Conference of Arts and Sciences, Sept. 1936. Author given as Charles Gustav Jung. 1937: Pub. as a pamphlet by Harvard U. P. pp. 15.

1937aa Letter to the author (24 Sept. 1926). Louis London: *Mental Therapy: studies in fifty cases*. Vol. 2, p. 637. New York: Covici, Friede. Excerpts only. Written in English. Full text pub. in E. 1973b and trans. in G. 1972a.

1937b "The Concept of the Collective Unconscious." (Pt. II.) *St. Bartholomew's Hospital Journal*, XLIV:4 (Jan.), 64–66. The 2d pt. of E. 1936a repub. The 2d of 2 pts. Cf. E. 1936b. Repub., slightly rev., with E. 1936b, as CW 9,i,2.

1937c "Wotan." *Saturday Review of Literature*, XVI:25 (16 Oct.), 3–4, 18, 20. Trans. from G. 1936c by Barbara Hannah and altered by the editors. Pub. unaltered in dif. trans.'s, as E. 1947a,3 and CW 10,10.

1938a *Psychology and Religion.* (The Terry Lectures.) New Haven, Conn.: Yale U. P.; London: Oxford U. P. pp. 131. 1960: Paperback edn. (Yale Paperbound), New Haven: Yale U. P. Contents:
   1. The Autonomy of the Unconscious Mind. (1–39)
   2. Dogma and Natural Symbols. (40–77)
   3. The History and Psychology of a Natural Symbol. (78–114)

Cf. CW 11,1. Written in English and delivered as the 15th series of "Lectures on Religion in the Light of Science and Philosophy," Yale University, New Haven, Connecticut, 1937. Subsequently trans. into German, rev. by Toni Wolff and exp. by Jung, to form G. 1940a.

1938b "Presidential Address. Views Held in Common by the Different Schools of Psychotherapy Represented at the Congress, July, 1938." *Journal of Mental Science*, LXXXIV:353 (Nov.), 1055. Summary of Jung's address delivered to the Tenth International Medical Congress for Psychotherapy, Oxford, 29 July–2 Aug. 1938. Cf. CW 10,33.

1939a *The Integration of the Personality*. New York: Farrar and Rinehart; London: Kegan Paul, 1940. pp. 313. Trans. by Stanley M. (i.e., W. Stanley) Dell. Contents:
   1. "The Meaning of Individuation." (3–29) Written in English for this volume, and pub. here with some addns. of material from other of Jung's writings by the translator. Subsequently rewritten in German, considerably rev., and pub., with the deletion of Dell's addns., as G. 1939e. Cf. CW 9,i,10, for a trans. of the rev. version.
   2. "A Study in the Process of Individuation." (30–51) Trans. from G. 1934c. Cf. CW 9,i,11 for a trans. of the rev. version.
   3. "Archetypes of the Collective Unconscious." (52–95) Trans. from G. 1935b. Cf. CW 9,i,1 for a trans. of the rev. version.
   4. "Dream Symbols of the Process of Individuation." (96–204) Trans. from G. 1936a. Pub. in a dif. trans., with slight title change, as E. 1959d. Cf. CW 12,3, pt. II (2d edn.) for a trans. of the rev. version.
   5. "The Idea of Redemption in Alchemy." (205–80) Trans. from G. 1937a. Cf. CW 12,3, pt. III (2d edn.) for a trans. of the rev. version.
   6. "The Development of the Personality." (281–305) Trans. from G. 1934b,9. Pub. in a dif. trans. with slight title change as CW 17,7.

1939b "The Dreamlike World of India." *Asia*, XXXIX:1 (Jan.), 5–8. Repub. as CW 10,23. Written in English. TR.—German: GW 10,23.

1939c "What India Can Teach Us." *Asia*, XXXIX:2 (Feb.), 97–8. Repub. as CW 10,24. Written in English. TR.—German: GW 10,24.

1939d "On the Psychogenesis of Schizophrenia." *Journal of Mental Science*, LXXXV:358 (Sept.), 999–1011. Repub. as E. 1959a,8. Written in English and read at a meeting of the Section of Psychiatry, Royal Society of Medicine, London, 4 April 1939. TR.—German: GW 3,7.

1940a *Picasso*. (Papers of the Analytical Psychology Club.) New York: Analytical Psychology Club. pp. 8. Trans. from G. 1934b,8 by Alda F. Oertly. Printed for private circulation. Pub. in dif. trans.'s as E. 1953i and CW 15,9.

1942a "Human Behaviour." *Science and Man. Twenty-Four Original Essays.* ... pp. 423–35. Ed. by Ruth Nanda Anshen. New York: Harcourt Brace. E. 1937a pub. with minor alterations, omission of last par., and title change. Pub. with slight alterations and reversion to title of E. 1937a as CW 8,5. Author given as "Charles Gustav Jung."

1942b "Psychotherapy Today." *Spring 1942*. pp. 1–12. New York: Analytical Psychology Club. Trans. by Hildegard Nagel from a German ms. pub. as G. 1945f. Printed for private circulation. Pub. in dif. trans.'s as E. 1947a,4 and CW 16,9.

1942c "Foreword." Jolande Jacobi: *The Psychology of C. G. Jung*. pp. vii–viii. London: Kegan Paul, Trench, Trubner. 1943: New Haven, Conn.: Yale U. P.; London: Kegan Paul, Trench, Trubner. pp. v–vi. Trans. from G. 1940c by K. W. Bash. Dated Aug. 1939. Pub. in a dif. trans. as E. 1962c. Repub., trans. rev., as CW 18,40.

1943a "The Psychological Aspects of the Mother Archetype." *Spring 1943*. pp. 1–31. New York: Analytical Psychology Club. Trans. from G. 1939b by Cary F. Baynes and Ximena de Angulo. Printed for private circulation. Cf. CW 9,i,4 for a trans. of a rev. version, which incorporates parts of the above.

1943b "An Interview with C. G. Jung." *Horizon*, VIII:48 (Dec.), 372–81. Trans. from G. 1943f by an unknown hand. Repub., trans. rev. and with title change, as E. 1969f and CW 18,131. Answers written by Jung to questions from Jolande Jacobi.

1944a "The Different Aspects of Rebirth." *Spring 1944*. pp. 1–25. New York: Analytical Psychology Club. Trans. from G. 1940b by Theodor Lorenz and Ximena de Angulo. Printed for private circulation. Cf. CW 9,i,5 for a trans. of the rev. version.

1944b "Introduction." Julius Spier: *The Hands of Children; An Introduction to Psychochirology.* pp. xv–xvi. London: Kegan Paul, Trench, Trubner. 1955: 2d edn. London: Routledge & Kegan Paul. Trans. from the German ms. by Victor Grove (who trans. the entire book). (Cf. GW 18,132.) Repub., trans. rev., as CW 18,132.

1945a "The Soul and Death." *Spring 1945.* pp. 1–9. New York: Analytical Psychology Club. Trans. from G. 1934b,10 by Eugene H. Henley. Printed for private circulation. Repub., trans. slightly rev., as E. 1959c. Cf. CW 8,17.

1945b "Return to the Simple Life. Excerpts from a Swiss Newspaper Article." *Bull. APC*, 7:1 (Jan.), Supplement, 1–6. Excerpts of G. 1941e trans. by Eugene H. Henley. Printed for private circulation. Full text pub. in a dif. trans. as CW 18,72.

1946a "After the Catastrophe." *Spring 1946.* pp. 4–23. New York: Analytical Psychology Club. Trans. from G. 1945c by Elizabeth Welsh. Printed for private circulation. Repub. as E. 1947a,6. Pub. in a dif. trans. as CW 10,11.

1946b Foreword to K. A. Ziegler: "Alchemie II," List No. 17 (May). pp. 1–2. Bern. Written both in English and in German as a foreword to a bookseller's catalog. English text repub. as E. 1968d, and, slightly rev., as CW 18,104. Cf. G. 1946f for the German version.

1946c Contribution entitled "Jung's Commentary." pp. 372–77. Horace Gray: "Brother Klaus, With a Translation of Jung's Commentary." *Journal of Nervous and Mental Diseases*, CIII:4 (Apr.), 359–77. Trans. from G. 1933c by Horace Gray; title omitted. Pub. in a dif. trans. with inclusion of title as CW 11,6.

1946d Two letters. (1 Dec., and 26 May 1934) Ernest Harms: "Carl Gustav Jung—Defender of Freud and the Jews." *Psychiatric Quarterly*, 20:2 (Apr.), 199–233. Trans. by Ernest Harms.
   1. Circular letter to *Zentralblatt* subscribers (1 Dec. 1934). (222–23) Trans. from G. 1934j. Pub. in a dif. trans. as CW 10,27.
   2. Excerpts from letter "to a Jewish pupil and friend" (James

Kirsch, 26 May 1934) (227–30) Trans. from the German ms., parts of which are included here on pp. 225–27. Cf. G. 1946h. Repub. as E. 1972c,7, and, in a dif. trans., in E. 1973b. Cf. G. 1972a for text of the original letter.

1946e "The Fight with the Shadow." *Listener*, 37:930 (7 Nov.), 615–16, 641. Repub. with title change as E. 1947f and 1947a,2. Repub. slightly rev. and with reversion to above title as CW 10,12. Text of talk broadcast in the Third Programme, British Broadcasting Corp., 3 Nov. 1946.

1946f "The Bologna Enigma." *Ambix*, II:3/4 (Dec.), 182–91. Trans. from G. 1945b by Miss Marmorstein. Incorporated, in a dif. trans., into CW 14,II,3.

1947a *Essays on Contemporary Events.* London: Kegan Paul, Trench, Trubner. pp. 90. Contents:
1. Preface. (vii–viii) Trans. from G. 1946a,1 by Elizabeth Welsh. Pub. in a dif. trans. as CW 10,9.
2. Introduction: "Individual and Mass Psychology." (ix–xviii) E. 1946e repub. with title change. Repub. with title above as E. 1947f, and, slightly rev. and with reversion to title of E. 1946e, as CW 10,12.
3. "Wotan." (1-16) Trans. from G. 1946a,2 by Barbara Hannah. Pub. in dif. trans.'s as E. 1937c and CW 10,10.
4. "Psychotherapy Today." (17–35) Trans. from G. 1946a,3 by Mary Briner. Pub. in dif. trans.'s as E. 1942b and CW 16,9.
5. "Psychotherapy and a Philosophy of Life." (36–44) Trans. from G. 1946a,4 by Mary Briner. Pub. in a dif. trans. as CW 16,7.
6. "After the Catastrophe." (45–72) E. 1946a repub. Pub. in a dif. trans. as CW 10,11.
7. "Epilogue." (73–90) Trans. from G. 1946a,6 by Elizabeth Welsh. Pub. in a dif. trans. as CW 10,13.

1947b "On the Psychology of Eastern Meditation." *Art and Thought.* (Issued in honor of Dr. Ananda K. Coomaraswamy.) pp. 169–79. Ed. by K. Bharatha Iyer. London: Luzac. Trans. from G. 1943c by Carol Baumann. Reprint issued, dated Feb. 1948. Repub. as E. 1949b. Pub. in a dif. trans. with slight title change as CW 11,14.

1947c "An Alchemistic Text Interpreted As If It Were a Dream." *Spring 1947.* pp. 3–10. New York: Analytical Psychology Club. Trans. and slightly condensed from G. 1955a,III,3 by Carol Baumann. Printed for private circulation.

1947d "Jungian Method of Dream Analysis." *World of Dreams. An Anthology.* pp. 634–59. Ed. by Ralph L. Woods. New York: Random House. Extracts compiled from E. 1916a,8&13; E. 1939a,3; E. 1928b,2 and E. 1933a,1.

1947e "Foreword." M. Esther Harding: *Psychic Energy: Its Source and Goal.* pp. xi–xii. (B. S. 10.) New York: Pantheon. 1963: 2d edn., rev. & enl. pp. xix–xx. Retitled *Psychic Energy: Its Source and Its Transformation.* pp. xix–xx. 1973: (Princeton/Bollingen Paperback.) Princeton University Press. Trans. by Hildegard Nagel from a German ms. pub. as G. 1948d. Dated 8 July 1947. Repub., trans. sl. rev., as CW 18,42.

1947f "Individual and Mass Psychology." *Chimera,* V:3 (Spring), 3–11. E. 1946e repub. Repub. with title change as E. 1947a,2.

1948a "On the Nature of Dreams." *Spring 1948.* pp. 1–12. New York: Analytical Psychology Club. Trans. from G. 1945d by Ethel Kirkham. Also issued separately for private circulation as mimeographed pamphlet: (Papers of the Analytical Psychology Club of New York, 6.) The Club. 12 pp. Cf. CW 8,10 for trans. of rev. & exp. version.

1948b "Address Given at the Opening Meeting of the C. G. Jung Institute of Zurich, April 24, 1948." *Bull. APC,* 10:7 (Oct.), Suppl., 1–7. Trans. by Hildegard Nagel from the unpub. German ms. Pub. in a dif. trans. as CW 18,43.

1948c "Letter to Miss Pinckney." *Bull. APC,* 10:7 (Oct.), 3. Written in English at the request of the editor, Sally M. Pinckney; dated 30 Sept. 1948. Repub. in E. 1973b. TR.—German: 1972b.

1948d *On the Psychology of the Spirit.* (Papers of the Analytical Psychology Club of New York, 6.) New York: The Club. 43 pp. Trans. from G. 1946e by Hildegard Nagel. Printed for private circulation.

1949a With C. Kerényi: *Essays on a Science of Mythology. The Myth of the Divine Child and the Mysteries of Eleusis.* (B. S. 22.) New York: Pantheon. pp. 289. 1950: British edn. *Introduction to a Science of Mythology.* London: Routledge & Kegan Paul. pp. 289. Trans. from G. 1941c by R.F.C. Hull. Repub., trans. rev., as E. 1963a. Contains the following works by Jung:

    1. "The Psychology of the Child Archetype." (95–138) Repub. as E. 1958a,4, and, trans. rev., as CW 9,i,6.
    2. "The Psychological Aspects of the Kore." (215–56) Repub., trans. rev., as CW 9,i,7.

1949b *On the Psychology of Eastern Meditation.* New York: Analytical Psychology Club. pp. 19. E. 1947b repub. Printed for private circulation. Pub. in a dif. trans. with slight title change as CW 11,14.

1949c "Ulysses, a Monologue." *Spring 1949.* pp. 1–20. New York: Analytical Psychology Club. Trans. from G. 1934b,7 by W. Stanley Dell. Printed for private circulation. Repub. as E. 1953h. Pub. in a dif. trans. as CW 15,8. Unauthorized facsimile of this edn. without indication of source pub. 1972: Folcroft, Pa.: Folcroft Library Editions. pp. 22.

1949d "Foreword." Daisetz Teitaro Suzuki: *An Introduction to Zen Buddhism.* pp. 9–29. New York: Philosophical Library; London: Rider. *1959: Paperback edn. London: Arrow Books. 1964: Paperback edn. (Evergreen Black Cat) New York: Grove Press. Trans. from G. 1939c by Constance Rolfe. Pub. in a dif. trans. as CW 11,13. (1st edn.—Kyoto, 1934—lacks Foreword.)

1950a "Shadow, Animus and Anima." *Spring 1950.* pp. 1–11. New York: Analytical Psychology Club. Trans. from G. 1948f by William H. Kennedy. Incorporated, in a dif. trans., into CW 9,ii, Chs. II–III.

1950b "Foreword." H. G. Baynes: *Analytical Psychology and the English Mind and Other Papers.* p. v. London: Methuen. Written in English. Repub. as CW 18,78.

1950c "Foreword." Linda Fierz-David: *The Dream of Poliphilo.* pp. xiii–xv. (B. S. 25.) New York: Pantheon. Trans. from G. 1947b by Mary Hottinger. Repub., trans. rev., as CW 18,118.

1950d "Foreword." *The I Ching, or Book of Changes.* The Richard Wilhelm translation . . . pp. i–xx. New York: Pantheon (B. S. 19); London: Routledge & Kegan Paul. (In 2 vols.) 1961: 2d edn. (In 1 vol.) pp. i–xx. 1967: 3d edn. (In 1 vol.) Princeton University Press. pp. xxi–xxxix. Trans. from the German ms. by Cary F. Baynes. Written for the English edn. and dated 1949. Repub. as E. 1958a,6 and, trans. slightly rev., as CW 11,16. Cf. GW 11,16 for original German version.

1950e "Introductions by C. G. Jung." *Bull. APC,* 12:5 (May), 10–13. Excerpts from G. 1935e and G. 1949e trans. by Hildegard Nagel. Entire text of G. 1935e pub. in dif. trans.'s as E. 1967d and CW 18,45. Entire text of G. 1949e pub. in a dif. trans. as CW 18,45.

1951a "Concerning the Self." *Spring 1951.* pp. 1–20. New York: Analytical Psychology Club. Trans. from G. 1949b by Hildegard Nagel. Also issued for private circulation as mimeographed pamphlet. (Papers of the APC of NY, 7.) 20 pp. Cf. CW 9,ii, Chs. IV–V for trans. of exp. version.

1951b "Foreword to the English Edition." *Paracelsus: Selected Writings.* pp. 23–24. Ed. by Jolande Jacobi. (B. S. 28.) New York: Pantheon. 1958: 2d edn. pp. xxi–xxii. Trans. from the German ms. by Norbert Guterman. Dated May 1949. Repub., slightly rev., as CW 18,120. (Cf. GW 18,120.)

1952a "Preface." John Custance: *Wisdom, Madness and Folly. The Philosophy of a Lunatic.* pp. [1–4]. New York: Pellegrini and Cudahy. Trans. by an unknown hand from a German ms. pub. as G. 1954d. Written in 1951. Repub., trans. rev., as CW 18,15. (British edn., 1951, lacks this Preface.)

1952b "Introduction." R. J. Zwi Werblowsky: *Lucifer and Prometheus. A Study of Milton's Satan.* pp. ix–xii. London: Routledge & Kegan Paul. Trans. from a German ms. pub. as GW 11,5 by R.F.C. Hull Dated March 1951. Repub., trans. slightly rev., as CW 11,5.

1952c "Foreword." Victor White: *God and the Unconscious.* pp. xiii–xxv. London: Harvill Press; Chicago: Henry Regnery, 1953. Trans. by Victor White from a German ms. pub. as G. 1957h. Dated May 1952. Pub. slightly rev. as CW 11,4. Also contains extracts from letters to Gebhard Frei (13 Jan. 1948 and 17 Jan. 1949), Appendix, pp. 235–62, the full texts of which appear in G. 1972b and are trans. in E. 1973b.

1953a *Psychological Reflections. An Anthology of the Writings of C. G. Jung.* Selected and ed. by Jolande Jacobi. New York: Pantheon (B. S. 31); London: Routledge & Kegan Paul. pp. 342. 1961: Paperback edn. (Harper Torchbooks: The Bollingen Library.) New York: Harper. pp. 340. In effect, a trans. of G. 1945a: "R.F.C. Hull's translations for the *Collected Works* have been drawn upon insofar as possible . . . (supplemented by those of S. Dell, H. G. and C. F. Baynes and others; see p. xxi). . . . The passages for which no English translation is cited have been translated especially . . . by J. Verzar and revised by Elizabeth Welsh." Pub., rev. and exp., as E. 1970b.

1953b *The Spirit Mercury.* New York: Analytical Psychology Club. pp. 63. Trans. from G. 1948a,3 by Gladys Phelan and Hildegard Nagel. Printed for private circulation. Pub. in a dif. trans. with slight title change as CW 13,4.

1953c "Concerning Synchronicity." *Spring 1953.* pp. 1–10. New York: Analytical Psychology Club. Trans. from G. 1952f by Alice H. Dunn. Printed for private circulation. Pub. in a dif. trans. with title change as E. 1957b.

1953d "Foreword." Frieda Fordham: *An Introduction to Jung's Psychology.* p. 10. Harmondsworth, England and Baltimore, Md.: Penguin. 1966: 3d edn. p. 11. Written in English and dated Sept. 1952. Repub. as CW 18,46. TR.—German: 1959c / GW 18,46.

1953e "Foreword." John Weir Perry: *The Self in Psychotic Process; Its Symbolization in Schizophrenia.* pp. v–viii. Berkeley and Los Angeles: University of California Press; London: Cambridge University Press. Written in English. Repub. as CW 18,16. TR.—German: GW 18,16.

1953f "Preface by C. G. Jung. *Ostasien denkt anders.* . . ." *Bull. APC,* 15:3 (Mar.), Supplement, 1–3. Trans. from G. 1950d by Hildegard Nagel and Ellen Thayer. Printed for private circulation. Repub. with title change as E. 1955j.

1953g "The Challenge of the Christian Enigma. A Letter . . . to Upton Sinclair." (3 Nov. 1952) *New Repub.*, 128:17 (27 Apr.), 18–19. Repub., with omission of some minor changes, in E. 1975b. Written in English. TR.—German: 1972b.

1953h "Ulysses: A Monologue." *Nimbus*, II:1 (June–Aug.), 7–20. E. 1949c repub. Pub. in a dif. trans. as CW 15,8.

1953i "Picasso." *Nimbus*, II:2 (Autumn), 25–27. Trans. from G. 1932g by Ivo Jarosy. Pub. in dif. trans.'s as E. 1940a and CW 15,9.

1953j *Psychology and Alchemy.* (CW, 12.) See Part II.

1953k *Two Essays on Analytical Psychology.* (CW, 7.) See Part II.

1954a *Answer to Job.* London: Routledge & Kegan Paul; Great Neck, N.Y.: Pastoral Psychology Book Club, 1955. pp. 194. Trans. from G. 1952a by R.F.C. Hull. Repub. with the addn. of E. 1956c sl. rev. and titled "Prefatory Note," as CW 11,9. 1979: (Paperback edn.) Routledge & Kegan Paul.

1954b *Spirit and Nature.* (Papers from the Eranos Yearbooks, 1.) New York: Pantheon (B. S. 30); London: Routledge & Kegan Paul, 1955. Trans. by R.F.C. Hull. 1982: (Princeton/Bollingen Paperback.) Contains the following works by Jung:
   1. "The Phenomenology of the Spirit in Fairy Tales." (3–48) Trans. from G. 1948a,2. Repub. as E. 1958a,3, and, trans. slightly rev., as CW 9,i,8.
   2. "The Spirit of Psychology." (371–444) Trans. from G. 1947a. Pub., slightly abbreviated, as E. 1957e. Cf. CW 8,8 for trans. of the rev. and exp. version.

1954c *The Symbolic Life.* (Guild Lecture No. 80.) London: Guild of Pastoral Psychology. pp. 30. Pub. in abbrev. form as E. 1961d. Printed for private circulation. Repub., sl. rev., as CW 18,3. Transcript from the shorthand notes of Derek Kitchin of a seminar talk given to the Guild, London, 5 April 1939. TR.—GW 18,3.

1954d "Foreword to *Symbols of Transformation.*" *Spring 1954.* pp. 13–15. New York: Analytical Psychology Club. Trans. from G. 1952e, Pt. I,I by R.F.C. Hull. Repub. as CW 5,4,I.I.

1954e "Psychological Commentary." *The Tibetan Book of the Great Liberation.* . . . pp. xxix–lxiv. Ed. by W. Y. Evans-Wentz. London, New
York: Oxford University Press. Repub., slightly rev., as CW 11,10.
1st 21 pp. of the commentary pub., very slightly rev. and with title
change, as E. 1955k. Written in English in 1939. TR.—German:
1955d.

1954f "Foreword." Erich Neumann: *The Origins and History of Consciousness.* pp. xiii–xiv. New York: Pantheon (B. S. 42.); London: Routledge & Kegan Paul. 1955. 1962: Paperback edn. (Harper Torchbooks: The Bollingen Library.) New York: Harper. 2 vols. Trans.
from G. 1949f by R.F.C. Hull. Repub. as CW 18,54.

1954g "Preface by C. G. Jung." *Bull. APC*, 16:2 (Feb.), 7–8. Trans. from
G. 1953b by Ethel D. Kirkham. Printed for private circulation.
Pub. in a dif. trans. as CW 18,57.

1954h "C. G. Jung on Flying Saucers." *Bull. APC*, 16:7 (Oct.), 7–14. Trans.
from G. 1954e by Ellen Thayer with the help of Hildegard Nagel.
Printed for private circulation. Pub. in dif. trans.'s as E. 1959i,3
and CW 18,80. Extracts pub. in a dif. trans. as E. 1955i.

1954i *The Practice of Psychotherapy.* (CW, 16.) See Part II.

1954j *The Development of Personality.* (CW, 17.) See Part II.

1955a With W. Pauli: *The Interpretation of Nature and the Psyche.* New York:
Pantheon (B. S. 51.); London: Routledge & Kegan Paul. pp. 247.
Contains the following work by Jung:
"Synchronicity: An Acausal Connecting Principle." (5–146) G.
1952b, rev. and exp. by the author, and trans. by R.F.C. Hull.
Dated August 1950. Repub., trans. slightly rev., as CW 8,18.
1972: (Paperback edn.) Routledge & Kegan Paul.

1955b "Transformation Symbolism in the Mass." *The Mysteries.* (Papers
from the Eranos Yearbooks, 2.) pp. 274–336. New York: Pantheon
(B. S. 30.); London: Routledge & Kegan Paul, 1956. 1978: (Prince-
ton/Bollingen Paperback.) Trans. from G. 1942c by R.F.C. Hull.
Includes certain of the rev.'s of G. 1954b,6. Repub. as E. 1958a,5
and in a slightly dif. trans. as CW 11,3. Cf. E. 1955l.

1955c "Memorial to J. S." *Spring 1955.* p. 63. New York: Analytical Psychology Club. Written in English and delivered in 1927. (J. S. = Jerome Schloss.—Ed. note.) Repub. as CW 18,107. (Cf. GW 18,107.)

1955d "On the Psychology of the Trickster." *Spring 1955.* pp. 1–14. New York: Analytical Psychology Club. Trans. from G. 1954a by Hildegard Nagel. Pub. in a dif. trans., with slight title change, as E. 1956a. Cf. CW 9,i,9.

1955e "Introduction." M. Esther Harding: *Woman's Mysteries.* pp. ix–xii. New and rev. edn. New York: Pantheon. Trans. from G. 1949d by Edward Whitmont. Repub., trans. rev., as CW 18,53. (1st edn.— London, 1935—pub. without this introduction, which was written for the Swiss edn.)

1955f "The Christian Legend. An Interpretation." (Letter to Upton Sinclair, 7 Jan. 1955.) *New Repub.*, 132:8 (21 Feb.), 30–31. Written in English. Letter pub. with minor changes and some omissions. Full text pub. in E. 1975b. Title appears thus on cover only. Titled "A Communication." on p. 30. TR.—German: 1972b.

1955g "Mandalas." *Du*, Jhg. XV:4 (Apr.), 1 p. Trans. from G. 1955e by E. W. [Elizabeth Welsh]. This English trans. accompanied the pub. of the German original in the same issue. Pub. in a dif. trans. as CW 9,i,13.

1955h "Human Nature Does Not Yield Easily to Idealistic Advice." *New Repub.*, 132:20 (16 May), 18–19. Written in English as an invited comment on a previous article. Repub. as CW 18,83.

1955i *"C. G. Jung on the Question of Flying Saucers." *Flying Saucer Review*, May–June. Extracts trans. from G. 1954e. (Extracts selected give misleading impression of Jung's views.) Repub. as E. 1958f. Entire text pub. in dif. trans.'s as E. 1954h, E. 1959i,3 and CW 18,81.

1955j "The Mind of East and West." *Inward Light*, no. 49 (Fall), 3–4. E. 1953f repub. with title change. Repub. with title change as CW 18,92.

1955k "Psychology, East and West." *Tomorrow*, IV:1 (Autumn), 5–23. The 1st 21 pp. of E. 1954e pub., very slightly rev. and with title change.

1955l "The Mass and the Individuation Process." *The Black Mountain Review* (Bañalbufar, Mallorca), no. 5 (Summer), 90–147. Trans. from G. 1942c, last part, by Elizabeth Welsh. Cf. E. 1955b.

1956a "On the Psychology of the Trickster Figure." Paul Radin and Karl Kerényi: *The Trickster. A Study of American Indian Mythology*. pp. 193–211. New York: Philosophical Library; London: Routledge & Kegan Paul. Trans. from G. 1954a by R.F.C. Hull. Repub., trans. slightly rev., as CW 9,i,9, and in a dif. trans. with slight title change as E. 1955d.

1956aa *Answer to Job*. Great Neck, N.Y.: Pastoral Psychology Book Club. pp. ?194. E. 1954a pub. with new title page. Repub. as CW 11,9.

1956b "General Aspects of the Psychology of the Dream." *Spring 1956*. pp. 1–25. New York: Analytical Psychology Club. Trans. from G. 1948b,4 by Robert A. Clark. Pub. in a dif. trans. with slight title change as CW 8,9. Cf. E. 1916a,13 for trans. of an earlier version.

1956c "Why and How I Wrote My 'Answer to Job'." *Pastoral Psychology*, VI:60 (Jan.), 80–81. Written in English as a letter to the ed., Simon Doniger (Nov. 1955). Repub. in *Bull. APC*, 18:4 (Apr.), 1–3. Included as "Prefatory Note," with minor stylistic rev., in CW 11,9. Pub. with the restoration of "an important phrase" in E. 1973a. Original letter pub. in E. 1975b. TR.—German: 1961a ("Nachwort") / 1972b (text of letter).

1956d "Psychotherapists or the Clergy." *Pastoral Psychology*, VII:63 (Apr.), 27–42. E. 1933a,11 repub. Pub. in a dif. trans. as CW 11,7.

1956e "Preface." *Psychotherapy*, I:1 (Apr.), 1 p. Typescript written in English and dated 7 Sept. 1955. Inaugural issue of Calcutta journal devoted to Analytical Psychology. Repub. as CW 18,127.

1956f *Symbols of Transformation*. (CW, 5.) See Part II.

1957a *The Transcendent Function*. Zurich: Students' Association, C. G. Jung-Institut. pp. 23. Trans. by A. R. Pope from a German ms.

written in 1916 and pub., rev. and exp., as G. 1958b. Printed for private circulation. Cf. CW 8,2 for a trans. of the rev. version.

1957b "On Synchronicity." *Man and Time.* (Papers from the Eranos Yearbooks, 3.) pp. 201–11. New York: Pantheon (B. S. 30); London: Routledge & Kegan Paul, 1958. Trans. from G. 1952f by R.F.C. Hull. Repub., trans. slightly rev., as CW 8,19. Pub. in a dif. trans. with title change as E. 1953c.

1957c "The Mind of Man Reaches Out." *New Frontiers of Knowledge: A Symposium.* pp. 53–55. Ed. by M. B. Schnapper. Washington: Public Affairs Press. E. 1957h condensed and re-edited, with title change.

1957d "Answer to Buber." *Spring 1957.* pp. 1–9. New York: Analytical Psychology Club. Trans. from G. 1952j by Robert A. Clark. Printed for private circulation. Pub. in a dif. trans. with title change as E. 1973e.

1957e "The Spirit of Psychology." *This Is My Philosophy.* pp. 115–67. Ed. by Whit Burnett. New York: Harper; London: Allen and Unwin. E. 1954b,2, slightly abbreviated.

1957f "Psychological Commentary." *The Tibetan Book of the Dead* ... pp. xxxv–lii. Ed. by W. Y. Evans–Wentz. 3d edn. London: Oxford University Press. Trans. from G. 1935f by R.F.C. Hull. Repub. with slight title change as E. 1958a,8, and, with minor alterations, as CW 11,11. (1st and 2d edn.'s lack commentary.)

1957g "Foreword." Michael Fordham: *New Developments in Analytical Psychology.* pp. xi–xiv. London: Routledge & Kegan Paul. Trans. from a German ms. dated June 1957. Repub. as CW 18,47.

1957h "Dr. Jung's Contribution to the Voice of American Symposium 'The Frontiers of Knowledge and Humanity's Hopes for the Future'." *Bull. APC,* 19:4 (Apr.), Supplement, 1–8. Text of contribution, written in English, to the United States Information Agency broadcast in 30 languages the week of the 16th Dec. 1956. Printed for private circulation. Repub. as E. 1959f. Pub., slightly rev. in accordance with the German version (G. 1959f) and with title change, as CW 3,9. Pub., condensed and re-edited, with title change, as E. 1957c. TR.—German: 1959f.

1957i Letters to the author (26 Jan. and 10 Feb. 1955). Hans A. Illing: "C. G. Jung on the Present Trends in Group Psychotherapy." *Human Relations*, X:1, 78ff. Trans. from the orig. German mss. by Hans A. Illing. Letter of 10 Feb. repub., with slight deletions, on p. 394, in Illing's "Jung's Theory of the Group as a Tool in Psychotherapy." *International Journal of Group Psychotherapy*, VII:4 (Oct.), 392–97. Letters pub. in a dif. trans. in E. 1975b. German originals pub. in full in G. 1972b, and with deletions as G. 1956d (both letters), and G. 1955f (letter of 10 Feb. only).

1957j Excerpt of letter to the author. Patricia Hutchins: *James Joyce's World*. pp. 184–85, ftnote i. London: Methuen. Written in English to Patricia Graecen (Hutchins) (29 June 1955). Repub. as E. 1959l,2. Entire letter pub. in E. 1976a.

1957k *Psychiatric Studies.* (CW, 1.) See Part II.

1958a *Psyche and Symbol. A Selection from the Writings of C. G. Jung.* Ed. by Violet S. de Laszlo. Paperback. (Anchor Books.) Garden City, N.Y.: Doubleday. pp. 363. Contents:
1. "Preface." (xi–xvii) Dated August 1957. Repub., slightly rev., as CW 18,62.
2. "Five Chapters from: *Aion.*" (1–60) CW 9,ii, Chs. I–V prepub.
3. "The Phenomenology of the Spirit in Fairy Tales." (61–112) E. 1954b,1 repub. Repub., trans. slightly rev., as CW 9,i,8.
4. "The Psychology of the Child Archetype." (113–47) E. 1949a, 1 repub. Repub., trans. rev., as CW 9,i,6 (1st edn.).
5. "Transformation Symbolism in the Mass." (148–224) E. 1955b repub. Repub., trans. slightly rev., as CW 11,3.
6. "Foreword to the *I Ching.*" (225–44) E. 1950d repub. Repub., trans. slightly rev., as CW 11,16.
7. "Two Chapters from: *The Interpretation of Nature and the Psyche.*" (245–82) E. 1955a, Chs. III–IV repub. Repub., along with rest of text, trans. slightly rev., as CW 8,18.
8. "Psychological Commentary on *The Tibetan Book of the Dead.*" (283–301) E. 1957f repub. Repub., trans. slightly rev., as CW 11,11.

9. "Commentary on The Secret of the Golden Flower." (302–51) E. 1962b,2 prepub. Pub. in a dif. trans. as CW 13,1. Repub. as E. 1991b.

1958b *The Undiscovered Self.* (Atlantic Monthly Press Book.) Boston: Little, Brown; London: Routledge & Kegan Paul. pp. 113. 1959: Paperback edn. New York: Mentor Books/New American Library. pp. 125. 1971: (Atlantic Monthly Press Book.) Boston: Little, Brown. pp. 113. 1974: (Paperback edn.) Routledge & Kegan Paul. Trans. from G. 1957i by R.F.C. Hull, and rev. by the American editors. Repub., trans. further rev., as CW 10,14 and E. 1990a. Extract prepub. as "God, the Devil, and the Human Soul." *Atlantic Monthly*, CC:5 (Nov. 1957), 57–63. ". . . prompted by conversations between Dr. Jung and Dr. Carleton Smith, Director of the National Arts Foundation, which brought it to the attention of the editors of the Atlantic Monthly Press."

1958c Answers to questions of, and correspondence with, the author and David Cox. Howard L. Philp: *Jung and the Problem of Evil.* pp. 5–21, 209–54. London: Rockliff. Repub., with minor stylistic rev. and addn. of title, as CW 18,103. Letter of 11 June 1957 repub. in E. 1976a.

1958d "Message of the Honorary President." *Chemical Concepts of Psychosis.* p. xxi. Ed. by Max Rinkel with Herman C. B. Denber. New York: McDowell/Obolensky. Letter to Max Rinkel (Apr. 1957), chairman of a Symposium on Chemical Concepts of Psychosis, pub. in the volume above, which comprises the "Proceedings of the Symposium . . . held at the Second International Congress of Psychiatry in Zurich . . . 1 to 7 September 1957." Repub. with title change as CW 3,11. TR.—German: 1973a.

1958e "Foreword." Eleanor Bertine: *Human Relationships: In the Family, in Friendship, in Love.* pp. v–vii. New York, London: Longmans, Green. 1963: New York: David MacKay. Trans. from G. 1957d by Barbara Hannah. Repub., trans. slightly rev., as CW 18,61.

1958f "Dr. Carl Jung on Unconventional Aerial Objects." *A.P.R.O. Bulletin* (July), 1,5. E. 1955i repub. Repub. in E. 1959i,3. Cf. E. 1954h and CW 18,81.

1958g "Dr. Jung Sets the Record Straight." *UFO Investigator,* I:5 (Aug.–Sept.), 1 p. Letter written (in English) to Major Keyhoe (NICAP) (16 Aug. 1958). Repub. with title change as E. 1959g. Pub. condensed as E. 1959i,2.

1958h "Released to United Press from Dr. Jung." *Bull. APC,* 20:6 (Oct.), 10. Trans. from G. 1958h by Henry Carioba. Pub. in dif. trans.'s as E. 1958j, 1959i,1 and CW 18,81. Repudiates statement attributed to him in an *A.P.R.O. Bulletin* article. Cf. E. 1955i.

1958i "Banalized beyond Endurance." Contribution to symposium, "If Christ Walked the Earth Today." *Cosmopolitan,* CXLV:6 (Dec.), 30. Title added by editors. Repub. under title of the symposium as CW 18,86.

1958j Statement to United Press International. *A.P.R.O. Bulletin* (Sept.), 7. Trans. from G. 1958h. Repub. in dif. trans.'s as E. 1958h, 1959i,1 and CW 18,81.

1958k *Psychology and Religion: West and East.* (CW, 11.) See Part II.

1959a *The Basic Writings of C. G. Jung.* Ed. by Violet Staub de Laszlo. New York: Modern Library (Div. of Random House). pp. 552. Contents:

1. from *Symbols of Transformation.* (3–36) CW 5,1&4, Pt. I, Ch. I–II repub.
2. from "On the Nature of the Psyche." (37–104) CW 8,8 repub. with some omissions.
3. from "The Relations between the Ego and the Unconscious." (105–82) CW 7,2: Preface to 2d edn.; Pt. I, Chs. 1–3; Pt. II, Chs. 1–2, repub.
4. from *Psychological Types.* (183–285) E. 1923a: Introduction, and Chs. 10–11 (abridged), repub. Cf. CW 6.
5. "Archetypes of the Collective Unconscious." (286–326) CW 9,i,1 repub.
6. "Psychological Aspects of the Mother Archetype." (327–60) CW 9,i,4 repub.
7. "On the Nature of Dreams." (363–79) CW 8,10 prepub.
8. "On the Psychogenesis of Schizophrenia." (380–97) E. 1939d repub. Repub. as CW 3,8.

9. from "The Psychology of the Transference." (398–429) CW 16,13 (1st edn.): Introduction, repub.
10. "Introduction to the Religious and Psychological Problems of Alchemy." (433–68) CW 12,2, Pt. I (1st edn.) repub.
11. "Psychology and Religion." (469–528) CW 11,1 repub.
12. "Marriage as a Psychological Relationship." (531–44) CW 17,8 repub.

Repub. as E. 1991c.

1959b *Flying Saucers. A Modern Myth of Things Seen in the Skies.* New York: Harcourt Brace: London: Routledge & Kegan Paul. pp. 184. 1969: Paperback edn. New York: Signet Books/New American Library. pp. 144. Trans. from G. 1958a by R.F.C. Hull. Pts. 1 & 9 below not included in the text of G. 1958a. Repub., trans. slightly rev., as CW 10,15. Much abbreviated version pub. with title change as E. 1959h. 1977: (Paperback edn.) Routledge & Kegan Paul. Cf. E. 1978a. 1987: (Ark Paperback.) Contents:
1. Preface to the English Edition. (ix–x) Dated Sept. 1958. TR.— German: GW 10,15.
2. Introductory. (xi–xiv)
3. Ufos as Rumours. (1–24)
4. Ufos in Dreams. (25–101)
5. Ufos in Modern Painting. (102–27)
6. Previous History of the Ufo Phenomenon. (128–45)
7. Ufos Considered in a Non-Psychological Light. (146–53)
8. Epilogue. (154–74)
9. Supplement. (174–76) Added to the English edition. TR.— German: GW 10,15. pp. 471–73.

Repub. in E. 1978a.

1959c "The Soul and Death." *The Meaning of Death.* pp. 3–15. Ed. by Herman Feifel. New York: McGraw-Hill, Blakiston Division. E. 1945a repub., trans. slightly rev. by R.F.C. Hull. Repub. as CW 8,17.

1959d "Dream Symbols of the Individuation Process." *Spiritual Disciplines.* (Papers from the Eranos Yearbooks, 4.) pp. 341–423. New York: Pantheon (B. S. 30); London: Routledge & Kegan Paul. Trans. from G. 1936a by R.F.C. Hull. Pub. in a dif. trans. with slight title change as E. 1939a,4. Cf. CW 12,3. Pt. II (2d edn.) for a trans. of the rev. version.

1959e "Foreword." Jolande Jacobi: *Complex/Archetype/Symbol in the Psychology of C. G. Jung.* pp. ix–xi. New York: Pantheon (B. S. 57); London: Routledge & Kegan Paul. 1971: Paperback edn. (Princeton/ Bollingen Paperback.) Princeton University Press. Trans. from G. 1957g by R.F.C. Hull. Repub. as CW 18,60.

1959f "New Thoughts on Schizophrenia." *Universitas,* III:1 (Jan.), 53–58. E. 1957h repub. with title change. Repub., slightly rev., with title change, as CW 3,9. Cf. E. 1957c for condensed version. Pub. simultaneously with the German trans. Cf. G. 1959f.

1959g "UFO." *Bull. APC,* 21:2 (Feb.), 6–8. E. 1958g repub. with title change. Printed for private circulation. Repub. with title change as CW 18,83. Pub. condensed as E. 1959i,2.

1959h "A Visionary Rumour." *Journal of Analytical Psychology,* IV:1 (Apr.), 5–19. E. 1959b much abbreviated.

1959i "Jung on the UFO . . ." *CSI of New York,* No. 27 (July), var. pp. Contains the following works by Jung:
    1. Statement on UFO's to UPI (13 Aug. 1958). (4) Trans. from G. 1958h by "CSI." Pub. in dif. trans.'s as E. 1958h, 1958j and CW 18,81.
    2. Letter to Maj. Donald Keyhoe (NICAP), (16 Aug. 1958). (5) E. 1959g pub. condensed. Full text pub. as E. 1958g, 1959g and CW 18,82.
    3. "C. G. Jung on the Question of Flying Saucers." (Appendix 1: 1–5) Consists of a trans. by "CSI" of G. 1954e together with E. 1955i repub. for purpose of comparison. Includes in brackets "material omitted [from E. 1955i]. When [these translations] differ appreciably, the CSI version appears [on left, the other] in the right-hand column." Pub. in dif. trans.'s as E. 1954h and CW 18,80.
  Repub. in E. 1978a.

1959j " 'National Character' and Behavior in Traffic. A Letter from Dr. Jung." *Bull. APC,* 21:8 (Dec.), Supplement, 1–4. Trans. from G. 1958j by Hildegard Nagel. Printed for private circulation. Letter to F. von Tischendorf (19 April 1958). Pub. in a dif. trans. in E. 1975b.

ENGLISH

1959k "The Swiss National Character." *Adam*, 275 (27th year), 13–16. Trans. from G. 1928e by Gwen Mountford and Miron Grindea. Pub. in a dif. trans. with title change as CW 10,19. A retort to Keyserling's *Das Spektrum Europas*.

1959l Two letters. Richard Ellmann: *James Joyce*. New York: Oxford University Press. Contains the following letters from Jung:
1. To James Joyce (27 Sept. 1932) (642) Repub. as E. 1966d.
2. To Patricia Graecen (Hutchins) (29 June 1955) (692) E. 1957 repub. Entire letter pub. in E. 1975b and trans. in G. 1972b.

1959m *The Archetypes and the Collective Unconscious.* (CW, 9i.) See Part II.

1959n *Aion.* (CW, 9ii.) See Part II.

1960a *Answer to Job.* Paperback edn. New York: Meridian. pp. 223. CW 11,9 repub. (reset) with omission of "Prefatory Note."

1960b "Foreword." Miguel Serrano: *The Visits of the Queen of Sheba.* 2 pp. Bombay: Asia Publishing House. 1972: London: Routledge & Kegan Paul. Paperback edn. New York: Harper. Written in English as letter to Serrano (14 Jan. 1960) and pub. here slightly rev. Repub., somewhat rev., as CW 18,122. Entire letter pub. in full as E. 1966b,1.

1960c Letter to the Editor (Jan. 1960). *Listener*, XLIII:1608 (21 Jan.), 133. Written in English in response to reaction to his interview on the B.B.C. program "Face to Face," 22 Oct. 1959. Cf. E. 1975b, letters to Hugh Burnett (5 Dec. 1959) and M. Leonard (5 Dec. 1959). TR.—German: GW 11,25/1973a.

1960d "Preface by Dr. Jung." *Bull. APC*, 22:5 (May), 20–28. Trans. from G. 1959e by Edith Wallace. Pub. in a dif. trans. with title change as CW 10,18.

1960e "Good and Evil in Analytical Psychology." *Journal of Analytical Psychology*, V:2 (July), 91–99. Trans. from G. 1959b by R.F.C. Hull. Repub., trans. rev., as CW 10,17.

1960f *The Psychogenesis of Mental Disease.* (CW, 3.) See Part II.

1960g *The Structure and Dynamics of the Psyche.* (CW 8.) See Part II.

1961a "A Letter on Parapsychology and Synchronicity. Dr. Jung's Response to an Inquiry." *Spring 1961.* pp. 50–57. New York: Analytical Psychology Club. Trans. from G. 1961b by Hildegard Nagel. Written in English to A. D. Cornell (9 Feb. 1960) and trans., with addns. and corrections by Jung, as G. 1961c, from which the above has been trans. in turn. Repub., slightly rev., in E. 1975b. (In lieu of the orig. English ms., which had been lost.) *Spring 1961* reissued, photocopied and bound as one with *Spring 1960* and *Spring 1962,* in 1973.

1961b "Foreword." *Hugh Crichton-Miller, 1877–1959, A Personal Memoir by His Friends and Family.* pp. 1–2. Dorchester (England): Longmans Ltd. Written in English and dated Jan. 1960. Repub., slightly rev., as CW 18,87.

1961c "Yoga, Zen, and Koestler." *Encounter,* XVI:2 (Feb.), 56–58. Letter written in English to the editor, Melvin J. Lasky (19 Oct. 1960) in response to 2 articles by Koestler. Repub. as E. 1963f. TR.—German: 1961b / 1973a.

1961d "The Symbolic Life." *Darshana,* I:3 (Aug.) (C. G. Jung memorial issue.) 11–22. E. 1954c abbrev. Cf. CW 18,3.

1961e *Freud and Psychoanalysis.* (CW, 4.) See Part II.

1962a *Memories, Dreams, Reflections.* Recorded and ed. by Aniela Jaffé. New York: Pantheon (Div. of Random House). pp. 398. London: Collins and Routledge & Kegan Paul, 1963. pp. 383. 1965: Paperback edn. New York: Vintage (Div. of Random House). pp. 398 (index added). 1973: Rev. edn., with corrections. Trans. from G. 1962a by Richard and Clara Winston. Pub. with addn. as E. 1966a. 1983: (Paperback edn.) London: Flamingo. Contents (2d pagination refers to London edn.):
  1. Prologue. (3–5) (17–19) Extracts prepub. as pt. of "Jung on Freud." *Atlantic Monthly,* CCX:5 (Nov.), 47–56. Cf. no. 6 below.
  2. First Years. (6–23) (21–36)
  3. School Years. (24–83) (37–89)

4. Student Years. (84–113) (90–115)
5. Psychiatric Activities. (114–45) (116–43)
6. Sigmund Freud. (146–69) (144–64) Extracts pub. as pt. of "Jung on Freud." Cf. no. 1 above.
7. Confrontation with the Unconscious. (170–99) (165–91)
8. The Work. (200–22) (192–211)
9. The Tower. (223–37) (212–24)
10. Travels. (238–88) (224–69)
11. Visions. (289–98) (270–77)
12. On Life after Death. (299–326) (278–301) Extracts pub. as "Jung on Life after Death." *Atlantic Monthly*, CCX:6 (Dec.), 39–44.
13. Late Thoughts. (327–54) (302–26) 1st par. and Pt. I pub. as "Jung's View of Christianity." *Atlantic Monthly*, CCXI:1 (Jan. 1963), 61–66.
14. Retrospect. (355–59) (327–30)

Appendixes (contents differ somewhat from Anhang of G. 1962a):

15. Freud to Jung. (Letters: 16 Apr. 1909; 12 May 1911; 15 June 1911) (361–64) (333–35) Cf. E. 1974b.
16. Letters to Emma Jung from America (1909). (365–70) (336–40)
17. Letters to Emma Jung from North Africa (1920). (371–72) (340–41)
18. "Richard Wilhelm." (373–77) (342–45)

Also contains pts. of letter to Gustav Steiner (30 Dec. 1957). (viii–ix) (11–12) Cf. E. 1975a.

1962b With Richard Wilhelm: *The Secret of the Golden Flower. A Chinese Book of Life.* New York: Harcourt Brace. pp. 149. 1962: Paperback edn. New York: Harvest Books. Trans. from G. 1938a by Cary F. Baynes. E. 1931a, rev. and augmented by the addn. of "part of the Chinese meditation text 'The Book of Consciousness and Life' with a Foreword by Salomé Wilhelm." Cf. G. 1957b. Contains the following works by Jung:

1. "Foreword to the Second German Edition." (xiii–xiv) Trans. from G. 1938a,1. Pub. in a dif. trans. as pp. 3–5, CW 13,1.
2. "Commentary." (81–137) Trans. from G. 1938a,3&4, here combined. Pub. in a dif. trans. as CW 13,1. Prepub. as E. 1958a,9.

3. "In Memory of Richard Wilhelm." (138–49) Trans. from G. 1938a,2. Pub. in a dif. trans. with title change as CW 15,5.

1962c "Foreword." Jolande Jacobi: *The Psychology of C. G. Jung.* p. vii. New Haven: Yale University Press. Trans. from G. 1940c by Ralph Manheim. Repub., trans. rev., as CW 18,40. Pub. in a dif. trans. as E. 1942c.

1963a With C. Kerényi: *Essays on a Science of Mythology: The Myth of the Divine Child and The Mysteries of Eleusis.* Paperback edn. (Harper Torchbooks/Bollingen Library.) New York: Harper & Row. pp. 200. E. 1949a, trans. rev. Cf. E. 1969a. Contains the following works by Jung:

   1. "The Psychology of the Child Archetype." (70–100) CW 9,i,6 (1st edn.) repub. Repub., trans. further slightly rev., as CW 9,i,6 (2d edn.).
   2. "The Psychological Aspects of the Kore." (156–77) CW 9,i,7 (1st edn.) repub. Repub., trans. further slightly rev., as CW 9,i,7 (2d edn.).

1963b "Foreword." Aniela Jaffé: *Apparitions and Precognition; A Study from the Point of View of C. G. Jung's Analytical Psychology.* pp. v–viii. New Hyde Park, N.Y.: University Books. Trans. from G. 1958e by R.F.C. Hull. Repub., trans. sl. rev., as CW 18,8.

1963c Letter to Emanuel Maier (24 March 1950). Benjamin Nelson: "Hesse and Jung. Two Newly Recovered Letters." p. 15. *Psychoanal. Rev.*, 50:3 (Fall), 11–16. Repub. in E. 1973b. TR.—German: 1972b.

1963d Letter to Wm. G. Wilson (30 Jan. 1961), pp. 6–7, "The Bill W.-Carl Jung Letters." *AA Grapevine*, XIX:8 (Jan.), 2–7. Also pub. in *Bull. APC*, 25:3 (Mar.), 6–13. Repub. as E. 1968e. TR.—German: 1973a.

1963e Answers to questionnaire, "The Future of Parapsychology," added as "Appendix," pp. 450–51, to Martin Ebon, "The Second Soul of C. G. Jung." *International Journal of Parapsychology*, V:4 (Autumn), 427–58. Dated 23 June 1960. Repub. with addn. of title as CW 18,50.

1963f Letter to Melvin Lasky, editor of *Encounter, Bull. APC*, 25:6 (Oct.), 16–20. Dated 19 Oct. 1960. E. 1961c repub. without title. Repub. in *Bull. APC*, 25:6 (Oct.), 16–20, and in E. 1975b.

1963g *Mysterium Coniunctionis.* (CW, 14.) See Part II.

1964a "Approaching the Unconscious." *Man and His Symbols.* pp. 18–103. Ed. by Carl G. Jung and after his death M.-L. von Franz. Co-ordinating ed., John Freeman. London: Aldus Books; Garden City, N.Y.: Doubleday. 1968: Paperback edn. New York: Dell. pp. 1–94. 1978: (Paperback edn.) London: Picador Books. Written in English in 1961 and extensively rev. and rearranged under the supervision of John Freeman in collaboration with Marie-Louise von Franz. Jung's original text pub. with title change as CW 18,2. "The remaining chapters were written by the various authors to Jung's direction and under his supervision." TR.—German: 1968a.

1964b Letters to Richard Evans. Richard I. Evans: *Conversations with Carl Jung and Reactions from Ernest Jones.* Princeton, N.J.: D. Van Nostrand. pp. 173. Contains the following letters:
1. April 1957. (7)
2. April 1957. (9)
3. 30 May 1957. (10)
Also contains a lengthy interview from cinema film, rev. by Evans. Repub. 1976: *Jung on Elementary Psychology: A Discussion between Carl Jung and Richard Evans.* New York: Dutton. A verbatim transcript of the interview added in appendix. Cf. E. 1977b,4. TR.—German: 1967c.

1964c Abridgement of interview with Jung by John Freeman, in: *Face to Face.* Ed. by Hugh Burnett. London: Jonathan Cape. pp. 48–51. Cf. E. 1977b,6 for complete interview.

1964d *Civilization in Transition.* (CW, 10.) See Part II.

1965aa *Answer to Job.* Paperback edn. London: Hodder and Stoughton. pp. 192. E. 1954a repub. (offset). Repub. with the addn. of "Prefatory Note" as E. 1971a,15.

1965a Letter to the author (7 July 1958), pp. 141–42. Edward Thornton: "Jungian Psychology and the Vedanta." pp. 131–42. *Spectrum Psy-*

chologiae. Eine Freundesgabe. Festschrift zum 60. Geburtstag C. A. Meier. Ed. by C. T. Frey-Wehrlin. Zurich: Rascher. Written in English.

1966a *Memories, Dreams, Reflections.* Recorded and ed. by Aniela Jaffé. Paperback edn. New York: Vintage Books (Div. of Random House). pp. 430. E. 1962a (New York edn., 1965 paperback) repub. with the following addn.:

19. "Septem Sermones ad Mortuos." (378–90) E. 1925a repub. Cf. hardcover, E. 1967a.

1966b Letters to the author. Miguel Serrano: *C. G. Jung and Hermann Hesse. A Record of Two Friendships.* London: Routledge & Kegan Paul. pp. 112. 1968: Paperback edn. New York: Schocken. pp. 112. Written in English. Letters orig. pub. with Spanish trans. in Serrano, *El circulo hermetico, de Hermann Hesse a C. G. Jung,* Santiago (Chile): Zig Zag, 1965. 1966: (Paperback edn.) Routledge & Kegan Paul. Contains the following letters by Jung:

1. 14 January 1960. (68) Pub. with minor deletions and alteration as E. 1960b.
2. 16 June 1960. (69–70)
3. 31 March 1960. (74–75) Repub. in E. 1975b. TR.—German: 1973a.
4. 14 September 1960. (83–88) Repub. in E. 1975b. TR.—German: 1973a.

1966c "Introduction." Frances G. Wickes: *The Inner World of Childhood. A Study in Analytical Psychology.* pp. xvii–xxv. Rev. edn. New York: Appleton-Century. 1968: Paperback edn. (Signet) New York: New American Library. pp. 304. CW 17,2 repub. Original brief version pub. as E. 1927a.

1966d Letter to James Joyce (27 Sept. 1932).† *Letters of James Joyce.* Ed. by Richard Ellmann. Vol. 3, pp. 253–54. New York: Viking. E. 1959l,1 repub. Repub. in CW 15,8, pp. 133–34 and E. 1973b.
† Date given as "? August 1932."

1966e "Foreword." Gerhard Adler: *Studies in Analytical Psychology.* pp. 3–5. New edn. London: Hodder & Stoughton. 1967: New York: G. P. Putnam's Sons for the C. G. Jung Foundation for Analytical Psychology. 1969: Paperback edn. New York: Capricorn. Trans.

from G. 1952g by R.F.C. Hull. Repub. as CW 18,55. (1st edn.—London & New York, 1948—lacks Foreword.)

1966f *The Spirit in Man, Art, and Literature.* (CW 15.) See Part II.

1966g *The Practice of Psychotherapy.* (CW, 16.) 2d edn., partially reset, with new appendix. See Part II.

1967a *Memories, Dreams, Reflections.* Recorded and ed. by Aniela Jaffé. 4th ptg. New York: Pantheon (Div. of Random House). pp. 430. E. 1962a repub. with same addn. as E. 1966a.

1967b *VII Sermones ad Mortuos. The Seven Sermons to the Dead Written by Basilides in Alexandria.* . . . London: Stuart & Watkins. pp. 34. E. 1925a repub. Cf. 1966a,19.

1967c *Symbols of Transformation.* (CW, 5.) 2d edn. See Part II.

1967d "Foreword to Studies from the C. G. Jung Institute, Zurich." *Evil.* pp. xi–xii. Ed. by the Curatorium of the C. G. Jung Institute, Zurich. (Studies in Jungian Thought.) Evanston, Ill.: Northwestern University Press. Trans. from G. 1949e by Ralph Manheim. Also pub. in C. A. Meier: *Ancient Incubation and Modern Psychotherapy.* pp. ix–x. (Studies in Jungian Thought.) Evanston, Ill.: Northwestern University Press. Pub. in a dif. trans. with slight title change as CW 18,45. Excerpt pub. in a dif. trans. as pt. of E. 1950e.

1967e "Preface." John Trinick: *The Fire-Tried Stone.* pp. [8–11]. Marazion, Cornwall: Wordens of Cornwall, in association with London: Stuart & Watkins. Two letters to the author, written in English (13 Oct. 1956 and 15 Oct. 1957), pub. as Preface. Letter of 15 Oct. 1957 repub. in E. 1975b.

1967f Letter to the author (1 Dec. 1960). Edward Thornton: *Diary of a Mystic.* p. 14. London: George Allen & Unwin. Written in English. Repub. in E. 1975b. TR.—German: 1973a.

1967g *Alchemical Studies.* (CW, 13.) See Part II.

1968a *Analytical Psychology; Its Theory and Practice. The Tavistock Lectures.* New York: Pantheon (Div. of Random House); London: Routledge & Kegan Paul. pp. 224. 1970: Paperback edn. New York: Vintage Books (Div. of Random House). pp. 224. 1976: (Paperback edn.) Routledge & Kegan Paul. 1986: (Ark Paperback.) Routledge & Kegan Paul. 5 lectures, each with transcript of ensuing discussion, given for the Institute of Medical Psychology, London, 30 Sept.–4 Oct. 1935. Stenographic transcript ed. by Mary Barker and Margaret Game, mimeographed for private circulation by the Analytical Psychology Club of London, 1936, entitled *Fundamental Psychological Conceptions: A Report of Five Lectures* ... and here slightly rev. by R.F.C. Hull. Repub. as CW 18,1. TR.—German: 1969a.

1968b Letter to the author (27 April 1959). Joseph F. Rychlak: *A Philosophy of Science for Personality Theory.* pp. 342–43. Boston: Houghton Mifflin. Written in English. Repub. in E. 1975b. TR.—German: 1973a.

1968c "Letter of Professor C. G. Jung to the Author." Josef Rudin: *Psychotherapy and Religion.* pp. xi–xiii. Notre Dame, Ind.: Notre Dame University Press. Trans. from G. 1964a by Elisabeth Reinecke and Paul C. Bailey. Dated 30 Apr. 1960. Pub. in a dif. trans. in E. 1975b.

1968d Prefatory note. *Alchemy and the Occult. A Catalogue of Books and Manuscripts from the Collection of Paul and Mary Mellon Given to Yale University Library.* Vol. I, 1 p. Compiled by Ian MacPhail. New Haven, Conn.: Yale University Library. (In 2 vols.) E. 1946b repub. Repub., slightly rev. and with addn. of title, as CW 18,104.

1968e Letter to Wm. G. Wilson (30 Jan. 1961), pp. 20–21, "The Bill W.-Carl Jung Letters." *AA Grapevine,* XXIV:8 (Jan.), 16–21. E. 1963d repub. Repub. in E. 1975b.

1968f "Answers to Questions on Freud." *Spring 1968.* pp. 46–48. New York: Analytical Psychology Club. Written in English in reply to questions sent by Michael L. Hoffman, Geneva representative of the *New York Times,* and dated 7 Aug. 1953. Repub. as CW 18,32.

1968g "A 1937 Letter from C. G. Jung." *Journal of Religion and Health,* V:3 (July), 275. Written in English to the Rev. Kendig Cully (25 Sept. 1937). Repub. in E. 1973b. TR.—German: 1972a.

1968h *Psychology and Alchemy.* (CW, 12.) 2d edn., reset. See Part II.

1968i *The Archetypes and the Collective Unconscious.* (CW, 9i.) 2d edn. See Part II.

1968j *Aion.* (CW, 9ii.) 2d edn. See Part II.

1968k *Psychology and Religion: West and East.* (CW, 11.) 2d edn. See Part II.

1969a With C. Kerényi: *Essays on a Science of Mythology* . . . Rev. edn. (Princeton/Bollingen Paperback.) Princeton University Press. pp. 200. CW 9,i,6 and 7 (2d edn.) repub.

1969b *On the Nature of the Psyche.* (Princeton/Bollingen Paperback.) Princeton University Press. 1982: (Paperback edn.) Routledge & Kegan Paul. 1989: (Ark Paperback.) Routledge. pp. 175. Contents:
   1. "On Psychic Energy." (3–66) CW 8,1 repub.
   2. "On the Nature of the Psyche." (67–144) CW 8,8 repub.

1969c *Psychology and Education.* (Princeton/Bollingen Paperback.) Princeton University Press. pp. 161. Contents:
   1. "Psychic Conflicts in a Child." (1–35) CW 17,1 repub.
   2. "Child Development and Education." (37–52) CW 17,3 repub.
   3. "Analytical Psychology and Education." (53–122) CW 17,4 repub.
   4. "The Gifted Child." (123–35) CW 17,5 repub.

1969d *The Psychology of the Transference.* (Princeton/Bollingen Paperback.) Princeton University Press. pp. 207. CW 16,13 (2d edn.) repub. 1983: (Ark Paperback.) Routledge.

1969e "Foreword." Erich Neumann: *Depth Psychology and a New Ethic.* pp. 11–18. New York: G. P. Putnam's Sons for the C. G. Jung Foundation for Analytical Psychology. Trans. from the German ms. by R.F.C. Hull. Written for a proposed English edn. not pub. until 1969. Dated March 1949. Repub., trans. slightly rev., as CW 18,77. German edn. lacks this Foreword.

1969f "Depth Psychology and Self-Knowledge. Dr. Jung's Answers to Questions Asked by Dr. Jolande Jacobi." *Spring 1969.* pp. 129–39. New York: Analytical Psychology Club. E. 1943b repub. with title change; trans. rev. by R.F.C. Hull. Repub. as CW 18,131.

1969g *The Structure and Dynamics of the Psyche.* (CW, 8.) 2d edn., extensive revs. See Part II.

1970a *Four Archetypes: Mother, Rebirth, Spirit, Trickster.* (Princeton/Bollingen Paperback.) Princeton University Press. pp. 173. 1972: London: Routledge & Kegan Paul. 1986: (Ark Paperback.) Routledge & Kegan Paul. Contents:
    1. "Psychological Aspects of the Mother Archetype." (7–44) CW 9,i,4 repub.
    2. "Concerning Rebirth." (45–81) CW 9,i,5 repub.
    3. "The Phenomenology of the Spirit in Fairytales." (83–132) CW 9,i,8 repub.
    4. "On the Psychology of the Trickster-Figure." (133–52) CW 9,i,9 repub.

1970b *Psychological Reflections. A New Anthology of His Writings 1905–1961.* Selected and ed. by Jolande Jacobi in collaboration with R.F.C. Hull. Princeton University Press (B. S. 31); London: Routledge & Kegan Paul. pp. 391. 1971: (Paperback edn.) Routledge & Kegan Paul. 1986: (Ark Paperback.) Routledge. 1973: (Princeton/Bollingen Paperback.) Princeton University Press. pp. 379. Trans. by R.F.C. Hull. (". . . all but relatively few of the quotations are taken from the Collected Works. . . ." This revision, prepared in English, adds passages from 1945–61 and omits some older material. The Swiss edn. [G. 1971b] is based on this one.) E. 1953a rev. and exp. Extracts pub. as E. 1972e.

1970c "Two Posthumous Papers. 1916." *Spring 1970.* pp. 170–76. Zurich: Analytical Psychology Club of New York. Trans. by R.F.C. Hull from the unpub. German typescripts found posthumously. Dated Oct. 1916. Contents:
    1. "Adaptation." (170–73)
    2. "Individuation and Collectivity." (174–76)
Repub. as CW 18,35.

1970d *Letter to André Barbault (26 May 1954). *Aquarian Agent*, I:13 (Dec.). Trans. from Fr. 1954b by an unknown hand. Pub. in a dif. trans. in E. 1976a.

1970e *Psychiatric Studies.* (CW, 1.) 2d edn. See Part II.

1970f *Civilization in Transition.* (CW, 10.) 2d edn. See Part II.

1970g *Mysterium Coniunctionis.* (CW, 14.) 2d edn. See Part II.

1971a *The Portable Jung.* Ed. with an intro. by Joseph Campbell. New York: Viking. pp. 650. (Published simultaneously in paperback.) Trans. by R.F.C. Hull. Contents:

Part I.
1. "The Stages of Life." (3–22) CW 8,16 repub.
2. "The Structure of the Psyche." (23–46) CW 8,7 repub.
3. "Instinct and the Unconscious." (47–58) CW 8,6 repub.
4. "The Concept of the Collective Unconscious." (59–69) CW 9,i,2 repub.
5. "The Relations between the Ego and the Unconscious." (70–138) CW 7,2 repub.
6. "Aion: Phenomenology of the Self." (139–62) CW 9,ii, Chs. I–III, repub.
7. "Marriage as a Psychological Relationship." (163–77) CW 17,8 repub.
8. "Psychological Types." (178–269) CW 6, Ch. X, repub.

Part II.
9. "The Transcendent Function." (273–300) CW 8,2 repub.
10. "On the Relation of Analytical Psychology to Poetry." (301–22) CW 15,6 repub.
11. "Individual Dream Symbolism in Relation to Alchemy." (323–455) CW 12,3, Pt. II (2d edn.) repub.
12. "The Spiritual Problem of Modern Man." (456–79) CW 10,4 repub.
13. "The Difference between Eastern and Western Thinking." (480–502) CW 11,10, pars. 759–87, repub.

Part III.
14. "On Synchronicity." (505–18) CW 8,19 repub.
15. "Answer to Job." (519–650) CW 11,9 repub. Cf. E. 1973a.

1971b "Excerpts from Selected Letters." *Spring 1971.* pp. 121–35. Zurich: Analytical Psychology Club of New York. Excerpts from E. 1973b and 1976a prepub. Contents:

    †1. ". . . to a little daughter." (1 July 1919) To Marianne Jung.
    †2. "to a solicitous colleague." (6 Nov. 1926) To Frances G. Wickes.
    †3. ". . . to Freud." (5 Oct. 1906) Also prepub. from E. 1974b.
    †4. "Recollections of . . . the U. S." (23 July 1949) To Virginia Payne.
    ‡5. "On Einstein and Synchronicity." (25 Feb. 1953) To Carl Seelig.
    ‡6. "On Mescalin." (15 Feb. 1955) To A. M. Hubbard.
    ‡7. "On the Shadow and Protestantism." (9 Nov. 1955) To Theodor Bovet.
    †8. "To a Colleague on Suicide." (25 July 1946) To Eleanor Bertine.
    ‡9. "On Suicide." (19 Nov. 1955) To an anonymous recipient.
    ‡10. "In Old Age." (10 Aug. 1960) To the Earl of Sandwich.

    † Prepub. from E. 1973b.   ‡ Prepub. from E. 1975b.

1971c *Psychological Types.* (CW, 6.) See Part II.

1972a *Mandala Symbolism.* (Princeton/Bollingen Paperback.) Princeton University Press. pp. 121. Contents:

    1. "Mandalas." (3–5) CW 9,i,13 repub.
    2. "A Study in the Process of Individuation." (6–70) CW 9,i,11 repub.
    3. "Concerning Mandala Symbolism." (71–100) CW 9,i,12 repub.

1972b Letters to the author (4 Mar. and 3 Dec. 1957). Frederic Spiegelberg: *Images from Tibetan Art.* pp. [4–5]. A folio collection of eight reproductions for coloring and meditation with an essay and commentaries by Frederic Spiegelberg and additional commentaries by C. G. Jung. San Francisco: Lodestar Press. Trans. by Frederic Spiegelberg from the German letters.

1972c "Letters to a Friend: Part I." *Psychological Perspectives*, III:1 (Spring), 9–18. To James Kirsch. Trans. by James Kirsch from the

German mss. except as otherwise noted. The 1st of 2 pts. Cf. E.
1972d. Contents:

1. 19 Aug. 1929. Pub. in a dif. trans. in E. 1976a. German letter pub. in G. 1973a.
2. 15 Aug. 1930.
3. 12 Aug. 1931.
4. 12 Mar. 1932.
5. 20 Jan. 1933.
6. 20 Feb. 1934.
7. 26 May 1934. E. 1946d,2 repub. Trans. by Ernest Harms.
   Pub. in a dif. trans. in E. 1973b. German letter pub. in G.
   1972a.
8. 16 Aug. 1934.
9. 29 Sept. 1934. Last par. only. Entire letter pub. in a dif.
   trans. in E. 1973b. German letter pub. in G. 1972a.
10. 17 Feb. 1935.
11. 25 July 1946. Written in English.
12. 12 July 1951.
13. 18 Nov. 1952. Written in English. Repub. in E. 1975b. TR.—
    German: 1972b.
14. 23 Nov. 1952.
15. 28 Nov. 1952. Written in English.

1972d "Letters to a Friend: Part II." *Psychological Perspectives*, III:2 (Fall),
167–78. To James Kirsch, except no. 15 below, to Hildegard
Kirsch. Trans. by James Kirsch from the German mss. except as
otherwise noted. The last of 2 pts. Cf. E. 1972c. Contents:

1. 29 Jan. 1953. Pub. in a dif. trans. in E. 1975b. German letter
   pub. in G. 1972b.
2. 28 May 1953. Pub. in a dif. trans. in E. 1975b. German letter
   pub. in G. 1972b.
3. 6 Aug. 1953.
4. 2 Oct. 1953.
5. 16 Feb. 1954. Pub. in a dif. trans. in E. 1975b. German letter
   pub. in G. 1972b.
6. 5 Mar. 1954. Pub. in a dif. trans. in E. 1975b. German letter
   pub. in G. 1972b.
7. 23 June 1954.
8. 11 Sept. 1954.
9. Summer 1957.

10. 29 Apr. 1958. Pub. in a dif. trans. in E. 1975b. German letter pub. in G. 1973a.
11. 3 Nov. 1958.
12. 10 Dec. 1958. Pub. in a dif. trans. in E. 1975b. German letter pub. in G. 1973a.
13. 12 Nov. 1959. Pub. in a dif. trans. in E. 1975b. German letter pub. in G. 1973a.
14. 10 Jan. 1960.
15. 2 Nov. 1960. To Hildegard Kirsch.

1972e " 'Psychological Reflections' on Youth and Age." *University*, 51 (Winter), 18–22. Extracts of E. 1970b.

1972f *Two Essays on Analytical Psychology.* (CW, 7.) 2d edn., rev. See Part II.

1973a *Answer to Job.* (Princeton/Bollingen Paperback.) Princeton University Press. pp. 121. CW 11,9, 2d edn., 2d ptg. (1973) repub.

1973b *Letters. I: 1906–1950.* Selected and ed. by Gerhard Adler in collaboration with Aniela Jaffé. Princeton University Press (B. S. 95); London: Routledge & Kegan Paul. pp. 596. German letters trans. by R.F.C. Hull, French letters by Jane A. Pratt. The 1st of 2 vols. Cf. E. 1976a. Contains 522 letters, of which 152 are in the orig. English. Contents arranged chronologically. "With a very few exceptions . . . the selection of letters in the Swiss and American editions is identical." Cf. G. 1972a and 1972b for the German version; E. 1984a for abridged edn. TR.—(English originals) German: 1972a/1972b.

1973c *Synchronicity: An Acausal Connecting Principle.* (Princeton/Bollingen Paperback.) Princeton University Press; London: Routledge & Kegan Paul. pp. 135. 1985: (Paperback edn.) Routledge & Kegan Paul. Contents:
1. "Synchronicity: An Acausal Connecting Principle." (1–103) CW 8,18 repub.
2. "On Synchronicity." (104–15) E. 1971a,14 repub.

1973d "Three Early Papers." *Spring 1973.* pp. 171–87. Zurich: Analytical Psychology Club of New York. Trans. by R.F.C. Hull. Contents:

1. "Sigmund Freud: *On Dreams* (1901)." (171–79) Trans. from a typescript apparently of a report given at Burghölzli and dated 25 Jan. 1901. CW 18,18 prepub.
2. "Marginal Note on F. Wittels: *Die sexuelle Not.* (1910)." (179–82) Trans. from G. 1910l. CW 18,24 prepub.
3. "A Comment on Tausk's Criticism of Nelken (1913)." (182–87) Trans. from G. 1913d. CW 18,31 prepub.

1973e "Religion and Psychology: A Reply to Martin Buber." *Spring 1973.* pp. 196–203. Zurich: Analytical Psychology Club of New York. Trans. from G. 1952j by R.F.C. Hull. Repub. as CW 18,96. Pub. in a dif. trans. with title change as E. 1957d.

1973f *Experimental Researches.* (CW, 2.) See Part II.

1974a *Dreams.* (Princeton/Bollingen Paperback.) Princeton University Press. 1982: (Paperback edn.) Routledge & Kegan Paul. 1985: (Ark Paperback.) Routledge & Kegan Paul. pp. 337. Contents:
    Part I: Dreams and Psychoanalysis.
        1. "The Analysis of Dreams." (3–12) CW 4,3 repub.
        2. "On the Significance of Number Dreams." (13–20) CW 4,5 repub.
    Part II: Dreams and Psychic Energy.
        3. "General Aspects of Dream Psychology." (23–66) CW 8,9 repub.
        4. "On the Nature of Dreams." (67–83) CW 8,10 repub.
    Part III: The Practical Use of Dream–Analysis.
        5. "The Practical Use of Dream-Analysis." (87–109) CW 16,12 repub.
    Part IV: Individual Dream Symbolism in Relation to Alchemy.
        6. "Individual Dream Symbolism in Relation to Alchemy." (111–297) CW 12,3, Part II (2d edn.) repub.

1974b With Sigmund Freud: *The Freud/Jung Letters. The Correspondence between Sigmund Freud and C. G. Jung.* Ed. by William McGuire. Princeton University Press (B. S. 94); London: Hogarth Press and Routledge & Kegan Paul. pp. 650. Freud letters trans. by Ralph Manheim, Jung letters trans. by R.F.C. Hull, from the German mss. (pub. simultaneously as G. 1974a). Contains 196 letters by Jung to Freud written 1906–1914 (+ 1 from 1923); 8 were prepub. in E. 1973b, 8 in E. 1974d, and 1 as E. 1971b,3. Intro. includes 2 letters to Ernest Jones (22 Feb. 1952) p. xxi and (19 Dec. 1953) p. xxiii, and 1 to K. R. Eissler (20 July 1958) pp. xxvii–xxviii, the full texts of which appear in E. 1975b. 1975: Princeton/Bollingen Paperback (bound sheets from 2nd, unaltered, printing). 1977: Paperback (bound sheets), Routledge & Kegan Paul. 1979: Princeton/Bollingen Paperback. "Third Printing, with corrections and additions (in the notes)." Princeton University Press. Cf. E. 1979a and E. 1988a.

1974c *The Psychology of Dementia Praecox.* (Princeton/Bollingen Paperback.) Princeton University Press. pp. 222. CW 3,1 repub.

1974d Letters to Freud. pp. 40–42, 86–94. "The Freud/Jung Letters." Ed. by William McGuire. *Psychology Today*, VII:9 (Feb.), 37–42, 86–94. Extracts of E. 1974b prepub. 8 letters dated 18 Jan. 1911–6 Jan. 1913, selected and ed. by Elizabeth Hall, with an introduction by William McGuire.

1974e Letters to Mary Foote. pp. 259–66. Edward Foote: "Who Was Mary Foote?" *Spring 1974.* pp. 256–68. Zurich: Analytical Psychology Club of New York. Contents:
1. 19 Mar. 1927. Prepub. from E. 1975b.
2. 12 Dec. 1929.
3. 18 Dec. 1929. Prepub. from E. 1975b.
4. 29 Mar. 1933. Prepub. from E. 1975b.
5. 12 July 1937. Prepub. from E. 1975b.
6. 22 July 1939.
7. 28 July 1942.
8. 11 May 1944.

1974f *The Psychoanalytic Years.* (Princeton/Bollingen Paperback.) Princeton University Press. pp. 168. Contents:
1. "Psychoanalysis and Association Experiments." (3–32) CW 2,5.
2. "Freud's Theory of Hysteria: A Reply to Aschaffenburg." (33–39) CW 4,1.
3. "The Freudian Theory of Hysteria." (40–54) CW 4,2.
4. "A Contribution to the Psychology of Rumour." (55–67) CW 4,4.
5. "Morton Prince, *The Mechanism and Interpretation of Dreams:* A Critical Review." (68–85) CW 4,6.

6. "On the Criticism of Psychoanalysis." (86–89) CW 4,7.
7. "Concerning Psychoanalysis." (90–93) CW 4,8.
8. "The Significance of the Father in the Destiny of the Individual." (94–116) CW 4,14.
9. "Psychic Conflicts in a Child." (117–51) CW 17,1b.

1974g *Symbols of Transformation.* (CW, 5.) 2d edn., 2d printing. See Part II.

1975a "To Oskar Schmitz (1921–1931)" *Psychological Perspectives*, 6:1 (Spring), 79–95. Trans. from the German, with the aid of an anon. trans., by James Kirsch, except as noted below. Contains the following letters from Jung to Schmitz:

1. 15 Mar. 1921 (80)
2. 26 May 1923 (80–83) †Repub. from E. 1973b. For orig. German, see G. 1972a.
3. 2 Nov. 1926 (83–84)
4. 13 Nov. 1926 (84–85)
5. 7 Jan. 1927 (85–86) †Prepub. from E. 1975b.
6. 21 July 1927 (86–87) †Prepub. from E. 1975b.
7. 3 Mar. 1928 (87)
8. 20 Sept. 1928 (89–90) †Repub. from E. 1973b.
9. 5 Apr. 1929 (91)
10. 5 Apr. 1929 (92)
11. 8 Sept. 1929 (92)
12. 24 Sept. 1929 (93)

Also contains a letter from Jung to Keyserling (25 Aug. 1928), pp. 87–88,† repub. from E. 1973b, as well as letters to Schmitz from Emma Jung, pp. 90–91, 93–95.

† Trans. by R.F.C. Hull.

1975b *Letters. 2: 1951–1961.* Selected and ed. by Gerhard Adler in collaboration with Aniela Jaffé. Princeton University Press (B. S. 95); London: Routledge & Kegan Paul. pp. 716. German letters trans. by R.F.C. Hull (8 trans. by Hildegard Nagel), French letters by Jane A. Pratt. The 2d of 2 vols. Cf. E. 1973b. Contains 463 letters, of which 214 are in the orig. English. In addition, the 1914–50 Addenda consist of 16 letters, of which 9 are in the orig. English. Contents arranged chronologically. Cf. G. 1972b and 1973a for the German version; E. 1984a for abridged edn. TR.—(English originals) G. 1972b/1973a.

1975c *Critique of Psychoanalysis.* (Princeton/Bollingen Paperback.) Princeton University Press. pp. 259. Contents:
 1. "The Theory of Psychoanalysis." (1–144) CW 4,9.
 2. "General Aspects of Psychoanalysis." (147–60) CW 4,10.
 3. "Psychoanalysis and Neurosis." (161–69) CW 4,11.
 4. "Some Crucial Points in Psychoanalysis: . . . Jung and Loÿ." (170–207) CW 4,12.
 5. "Prefaces to *Collected Papers on Analytical Psychology.*" (208–15) CW 4,13.
 6. "*Introduction to Kranefeldt's Secret Ways of the Mind.*" (216–24) CW 4,15b.
 7. "Freud and Jung: Contrasts." (225–32) CW 4,16.
 Appendix:
 8. "Answers to Questions on Freud." (235–37) CW 18,32.

1976a *The Symbolic Life.* (CW, 18.) See Part II.

1977a *Psychology and the Occult.* (Princeton/Bollingen Paperback.) Princeton University Press. pp. 167. 1982: (Paperback.) London: Routledge & Kegan Paul. 1987: (Ark Paperback.) London: Routledge & Kegan Paul. Contents:
 1. "Foreword to Jung: *Phénomènes occultes.*" (3–5) CW 18,5.
 2. "On the Psychology and Pathology of So-Called Occult Phenomena." (6–91) CW 1,1.
 3. "On Spiritualistic Phenomena." (92–107) CW 18,4.
 4. "The Psychological Foundations of Belief in Spirits." (108–25) CW 8,11.
 5. "The Soul and Death." (126–37) CW 8,17.
 6. "Psychology and Spiritualism." (138–42) CW 18,6.
 7. "On Spooks: Heresy or Truth?" (143–52) CW 18,7. with change of title.
 8. "Foreword to Jaffé: *Apparitions and Precognition.*" (153–55) CW 18,8.
 9. "The Future of Parapsychology." (156–57) CW 18,50.

1977b *C. G. Jung Speaking: Interviews and Encounters.* Ed. by William McGuire and R.F.C. Hull. Princeton University Press. pp. 416.

London: Thames & Hudson. pp. 447. (Latter ed. omits, for reasons of copyright, two articles by Miguel Serrano.) Cf. G. 1986c 1980: Picador Paperback (reset) of London ed. London: Pan Books. pp. 413. 1986: Paperback ed. with corrections. Princeton University Press. The contents are memoirs, notes (sometimes stenographic), and journalistic articles, therefore not considered to be *by* Jung, except for the following, which were transcribed from electronic recording or, if recorded in another way, were approved by Jung:

1. "An Interview on Radio Berlin" (1933; with Rudolf Weizsäcker). Trans. by R.F.C. Hull from the transcript of a stenogram in the unpublished *Bericht über das Berliner Seminar.* Cf. Part III, 1933 (p. 198). (59–66)
2. "Questions and Answers at the Oxford Congress, 1938." Transcript from stenogram. (99–114)
3. "The Stephen Black Interviews" (1955). Transcript from cinema film. (252–67)
4. "The Houston Films" (1957; with Richard I. Evans). Transcript (corrected by R.F.C. Hull, Aniela Jaffé, William McGuire, et al.) from cinema film. Cf. E. 1964b. (276–352)
5. "At the Basel Psychological Club" (1958). Trans. by R.F.C. Hull from transcript of tape recording. (370–91)
6. "The 'Face to Face' Interview" (1959; with John Freeman). Transcript from television film. Cf. E. 1964c. (424–39)
7. "An Eighty-fifth Birthday Interview for Switzerland" (1960; with Georg Gerster). Transcript from radio. (453–61)

1978a *Flying Saucers: A Modern Myth of Things Seen in the Skies.* (Princeton/ Bollingen Paperback.) Princeton University Press. pp. 138. (Paperback.) London: Routledge & Kegan Paul. pp. 198. 1987: (Ark Paperback.) London: Routledge. pp. 208. Contents (P.U.P. ed.):
1. "Flying Saucers." (1–127) CW 10,15.
2. "On Flying Saucers." (131–38) CW 18,80–82.

1978b *Psychology and the East.* (Princeton/Bollingen Paperback.) Princeton University Press. pp. 211. 1982: (Paperback.) London: Routledge & Kegan Paul. 1986: (Ark Paperback.) London: Routledge & Kegan Paul. Contents:
1. "Commentary on *The Secret of the Golden Flower.*" (3–57) CW 13,1.

2. "Psychological Commentary on *The Tibetan Book of the Dead*." (59–76) CW 11,11.
3. "Yoga and the West." (77–85) CW 11,12.
4. "The Dreamlike World of India." (87–96) CW 10,23.
5. "What India Can Teach Us." (97–102) CW 10,24.
6. "Psychological Commentary on *The Tibetan Book of the Great Liberation*." (103–37) CW 11,10.
7. "Foreword to Suzuki's *Introduction to Zen Buddhism*." (138–57) CW 11,13.
8. "The Psychology of Eastern Meditation." (158–75) CW 11,14.
9. "The Holy Men of India." (176–86) CW 11,15.
10. "Foreword to Abegg, *Ostasien denkt anders*." (187–88) CW 18,92.
11. "Foreword to the *I Ching*." (189–208) CW 11,16.
12. "On the Discourses of the Buddha." (209–11) CW 18,101.

1979a With Sigmund Freud: *The Freud/Jung Letters*. . . . Abridged by Alan McGlashan from E. 1974b. London: Picador (Paperback), Pan Books. pp. 320. Includes pref. by McGlashan and intro. by William McGuire. Cf. G. 1984g.

1979b *C. G. Jung: Word and Image.* Ed. by Aniela Jaffé. Princeton University Press (B.S. 97:2). pp. 238. 1983: Paperback (from sheets). Princeton University Press. Trans. from G. 1977a by Krishna Winston (i.e., text and editorial material not previously published in English). Subsequently reprinted. Many quotations from Jung's published and unpublished writings, with biographical narrative, illustrations, facsimiles, and appendixes.

1982a *Aspects of the Feminine.* (Princeton/Bollingen Paperback.) Princeton University Press. (Paperback.) London: Routledge & Kegan Paul. pp. 179. 1986: (Ark Paperback.) London: Routledge & Kegan Paul. Contents:
1. "The Worship of Woman and the Worship of the Soul." (5–23) CW 6, pars. 375–606 repub. [From sec. 4, "The Type Problem in Poetry."]
2. "The Love Problem of a Student." (25–40) CW 10,5.
3. "Marriage as a Psychological Relationship." (41–53) CW 17,8.
4. "Woman in Europe." (55–75) CW 10,6.

5. "Anima and Animus." (77–100) CW 7 (2d ed.), pars. 296–350.
6. "Psychological Aspects of the Mother Archetype." (101–40) CW 9i,4.
7. "The Psychological Aspects of the Kore." (143–64) CW 9i,7.
8. "The Shadow and the Syzygy." (165–79) CW 9ii, ch. II, III.

1983a *The Zofingia Lectures.* Supplementary vol. A to the CW. See Part II, following CW 20.

1983b *The Essential Jung.* Sel. and intro. by Anthony Storr. Princeton University Press (simult. cloth and paperback; not in B.S.); London: Fontana Paperbacks (Fontana Pocket Reader, entitled *Jung: Selected Writings*). pp. 447. Anthology of 44 brief extracts and 9 complete works, from CW, E. 1962a, E. 1973b, E. 1974b, and E. 1975b, interspersed with editorial commentary. The complete works are:
1. "Psychoanalysis and Neurosis." (46–54) CW 4,11.
2. "Introduction" to *Psychological Types.* (129–33) CW 6,2.
3. "Psychological Typology." (133–46) CW 6,8.
4. "The Practical Use of Dream-Analysis." (168–89) CW 16,12.
5. "The Development of Personality." (191–210) CW 17,7.
6. "Conscious, Unconscious, and Individuation." (212–26) CW 9i,10.
7. "Mandalas." (235–38) CW 9i,13.
8. "Introduction to the Religious and Psychological Problems of Alchemy." (253–86) CW 12,2,1.
9. "The Undiscovered Self." (349–403) CW 10,14.

1983c *Memories, Dreams, Reflections.* Recorded and ed. by Aniela Jaffé. Paperback edn. London: Flamingo. pp. 440. E. 1962a (London edn.) repub.

1984a *Selected Letters of C. G. Jung, 1909–1961.* Sel. and ed. [with a new pref.] by Gerhard Adler. (Princeton/Bollingen Paperback.) Princeton University Press. pp. 218. 150 letters from E. 1973b and E. 1975b.

1984b *Psychology and Western Religion.* (Princeton/Bollingen Paperback.) Princeton University Press. pp. 297. 1988: (Ark Paperback.) London: Routledge & Kegan Paul. Contents:

1. "A Psychological Approach to the Dogma of the Trinity." (3–96) CW 11,2.
2. "Transformation Symbolism in the Mass." (97–192) CW 11,3.
3. "Psychotherapists or the Clergy." (195–216) CW 11,7.
4. "Psychoanalysis and the Cure of Souls." (217–24) CW 11,8.
5. "Brother Klaus." (225–32) CW 11,6.
6. "Letter to Père Lachat." (233–46) CW 18,99.
7. "On Resurrection." (247–51) CW 18,100.
8. "Jung and Religious Belief." (253–97) CW 18,103.

1984c *Dream Analysis. Notes of the Seminar Given in 1928–1930.* (B.S. 99: [1].) See Part III, 1984 (p. 196).

1988a With Sigmund Freud: *The Freud/Jung Letters* . . . (Paperback.) Cambridge, Mass.: Harvard University Press. Reprint (reset) of E. 1974b, third printing (1979), with new preface by William McGuire, which cites a corr. in the trans.

1989a *Essays on Contemporary Events. The Psychology of Nazism.* With a fwd. by Andrew Samuels. Princeton University Press. (Ark Paperback.) London: Routledge.† pp. 93. E. 1947a, with new subtitle, repub. in the Hull trans. from CW 10 and CW 16.

† In 1989 the imprint Routledge & Kegan Paul changed to Routledge, a section of Routledge, Chapman and Hall, Inc., London.

1989b *Aspects of the Masculine.* With intro. by John Beebe. (Princeton/Bollingen Paperback.) Princeton University Press. (Ark Paperback.) London: Routledge. pp. 173. With editorial commentary, set in the same typeface as the texts from CW (sources omitted in this publication). Contents:
I. The Hero
   1. "The Origin of the Hero." (3–7) CW 5, pars. 251, 297–99.
   2. "The Battle for Deliverance from the Mother." (9–23) CW 5, pars. 441–60.
II. Initiation and the Development of Masculinity
   3. "The Stages of Life." (25–35) CW 8, pars. 759–90, 795.
   4. "On the Psychology of the Unconscious." (37–44) CW 7,1, pars. 167–83.
   5. "Lecture VIII, 13 March 1929." (45–50) *Dream Analysis* (Seminar, 1928–1930; see Part III), pp. 170–75.
   6. "The Love Problem of a Student." (51–59) CW 10,5, pars. 216–35.

III. The Father
    7. "The Significance of the Father in the Destiny of the Individual." (61–71) CW 4,14, pars. 707–44.
    8. "The Personal and the Collective Unconscious." (73–84) CW 7,2, ch. 1.
IV. Logos and Eros: Sol and Luna
    9. "The Personification of the Opposites." (85–108) CW 14, pars. 224–26, 104–33.
V. The Masculine in Women
    10. [Letter of 12 November 1957.] (109) E. 1975b, p. 402.
    11. "The Houston Films." (110) E. 1977b,4, p. 294.
    12. "From Esther Harding's Notebooks: 1922, 1925." (111–14) E. 1977b, pp. 25–30.
VI. The Anima
    13. "Concerning the Archetypes, with Special Reference to the Anima Concept." (115–22) CW 9i,3, pars. 134–47.
    14. "The Personification of the Opposites: Interpretation and Meaning of Salt." (123–25) CW 14, pars. 330–33.
    15. [Letter of 26 August 1943.] (126) E.1973b, pp. 334–35.
    16. "Lecture V, 19 February 1930." (127–39) *Dream Analysis* (Seminar, 1928–1930; see Part III), pp. 479–91.
VII. The Spirit
    17. "The Phenomenology of the Spirit in Fairy Tales." (141–48) CW 9i,8, pars. 401–9.
    18. "The Spirit Mercurius." (149–73) CW 13,4.

1990a *The Undiscovered Self* with *Symbols and the Interpretation of Dreams.* With new intro. by William McGuire. (Princeton/Bollingen Paperback.) Princeton University Press. pp. 144. Contents:
    1. "The Undiscovered Self (Present and Future)." (1–61) CW 10,14 repub.
    2. "Symbols and the Interpretation of Dreams." (63–144) CW 18,2 repub.

1991a With Sigmund Freud: *The Freud/Jung Letters.* . . . Abridged. (Paperback.) London: Penguin Books. Reprint of E. 1979a.

1991b *Psyche and Symbol: A Selection from the Writings of C. G. Jung.* Sel. and intro. by Violet S. de Laszlo. (Princeton/Bollingen Paperback.) Princeton University Press. pp. 144. E. 1958b repub. in the Hull trans. from CW.

1991c *The Basic Writings of C. G. Jung.* Selected and intro. by Violet S. de Laszlo. (Princeton/Bollingen Paperback.) pp. 561. E. 1959a repub. in the Hull trans. from CW. Selections from CW 6 have been expanded.

1992a *Psychology of the Unconscious. A Study of the Transformations and Symbolisms of the Libido.* Trans. by Beatrice M. Hinkle. Supplementary vol. B of the CW. E. 1916 repub. See Part II, following CW 20.

1992b *The Gnostic Jung.* Sel. and intro. by Robert A. Segal. Princeton University Press (simult. cloth and paperback; not in B.S.). pp. 284. Anthology of 22 brief extracts, 7 letters, and 6 complete works from CW, E. 1966a,19, and E. 1975b, interspersed with editorial commentary. The complete works are:
1. "Gnostic Symbols of the Self." (55–91) CW 9ii, ch. XIII.
2. "Foreword to Neumann: *Depth Psychology and a New Ethic.*" (91–92) CW 18,77.
3. "Address at the Presentation of the Jung Codex." (98–101) CW 18,135.
4. "Foreword to Quispel: *Tragic Christianity.*" (103–6) CW 18,91.
5. "Religion and Psychology: A Reply to Martin Buber." (155–63) CW 18,96.
6. "Seven Sermons to the Dead" ["Septem Sermones ad Mortuous"]. (181–93) E. 1966a,19.

FRENCH

1907a "Associations d'idées familiales." *Archs. psychol.*, VII:26 (Oct.), 160–68. The content of this paper considerably overlaps that of E. 1910a,2; in addition, "some material reused in ETH lectures, *Modern Psychology*, April 1934–July 1935."

1908a A summary of *Diagnostische Associationsstudien*, Vol. I. *Année psychologique*, XIV, 453–55. Summarized from G. 1906a. Each article summarized individually in 1 or 2 paragraphs.

1909a "L'Analyse des rêves." *Année psychologique*, XV, 160–67. TR.—English: CW 4,3.

1913a "Contribution à l'étude des types psychologiques." *Archs. psychol.*, XIII:52 (Dec.), 289–99. Lecture delivered to the Fourth Psychoanalytic Congress, Munich, 7–8 Sept. 1913, in German and then rev. into French by the author. Cf. GW 6,4 for the German version. TR.—English: 1916a,12.

1913b "La Psycho-analyse." *Encéphale*, VIII, 263–66. Summary of a report read in English to the 17th International Congress of Medicine, London, August 1913. Cf. E. 1916a,9.

1916a "La Structure de l'inconscient." *Archs. psychol.*, XVI:62 (Dec.), 152–79. Trans. by M. Marsen from a German ms. subsequently pub. as GW 7,4. Delivered in German as a lecture to the Zurich School of Analytical Psychology, 1916. TR.—English: CW 7,4 (1st edn.). Cf. GW 7,4.

1932b "La psychanalyse devant la poésie. Existe-t-il une poésie de signe 'freudien'?" *Journal des poètes*, III:5 (11 Dec.), 1. Written in German in reply to the question in the title and trans. by ?. Cf. CW 18,111 and GW 18,111.

1939a *Phénomènes occultes*. Paris: Montaigne (Aubier). pp. 122. Trans. by E. Godet and Yves Le Lay. Relevant contents:

1. Préface. (v–vii) Trans. from the German ms., written for this edn. Dated 1938. Cf. CW 18,5.

1943a *L'homme à la découverte de son âme. Structure et fonctionnement de l'inconscient.* (Action et Pensée, 10.) Geneva: Éditions du Mont-Blanc. pp. 403. 1946: 2d edn., rev. & corrected. pp. 354. Trans. by R. Cahen-Salabelle. Pub., rev. & exp., as Fr. 1962a. Relevant contents:

  9. "Epilogue." (401–03) Written for this edn. and dated Jan. 1944. Repub., trans. rev., as Fr. 1962a,9. TR.—English: CW 18,72/German: GW 18,72.

1948a *Aspects du drame contemporain.* Geneva: Georg. pp. 233. Trans. from the German by Roland Cahen-Salabelle. Relevant contents:

  1. "Avertissement de l'auteur." (69–74) Written for this edn. TR.—None recorded.

1954b "C. G. Jung et l'astrologie.' *Astrologie moderne.* Pub. here in the form of an "Interview du 26 Mai 1954 de André Barbault et Jean Carteret" but actually taken from a letter in French to André Barbault (26 May 1954), written in response to a questionnaire. Letter trans. as E. 1970d and in E. 1976a and G. 1972b.

1956b Letters to Père Bruno. Père Bruno de Jésus-Marie, with the collaboration of Ch. Baudouin, C. G. Jung, and R. Laforgue: "Puissance de l'archétype." pp. 13–18. *Élie le prophète.* Vol. II, pp. 11–33. Ed. by Père Bruno de Jésus-Marie. (Les Études Carmélitaines.) Paris: Desclée de Brouwer. Written in French to Père Bruno and dated 5 Nov. 1953 (pp. 13–17) and 22 Dec. 1953 (error for 1954) (pp. 17–18). TR.—English: CW 18,98/German: GW 18,98.

1958d "Hors des lieux communs." *Le Jura libre,* 8 Aug. 1 p. TR.—None recorded.

1959a "Préface." Georges Duplain: *Aux frontières de la connaissance. Entretien avec le professeur C.-G. Jung à propos d'une étude sur les "soucoupes volantes."* Lausanne: Gazette de Lausanne. 1 p. (t.p. verso) Reprint ("separatum") of interview by Duplain, pub. in the *Gazette,* Aug. 24, Sept. 1 and 8, 1959, with addition of Jung's "Préface," which appears only in this reprint, not in the original articles. TR.—English: 1977b.

1961d   "Réponse à la question du bilinguisme." *Flinker Almanac 1961*. pp. 21. Paris: Librairie Française et Etrangère. Letter to the editor, Martin Flinker, written in response to a question. TR.—English: CW 18,123/German: GW 18,123.

1962a   *L'homme à la découverte de son âme. Structure et fonctionnement de l'inconscient.* (Action et Pensée, 10.) 6th edn., rev. and exp. Geneva: Éditions du Mont-Blanc. pp. 354. 1963: Reset. (Petite Bibliothèque Payot, 53.) Paris: Payot. pp. 341. (Lacks index.) Trans. by Roland Cahen. Fr. 1943a, rev. and exp. Relevant contents (pagination of 1962 and 1963 edns. respectively):

      9. "Épilogue." (333–34) (339–40) Fr. 1943a,9 repub., trans. rev.

HEBREW

1950/51a "Alkhimiah we-psykhologiah." *Encyclopaedia Hebraica.* Vol. 3, pp. 606–08. Jerusalem: Encyclopedia Publishing Co. Written especially for this volume and trans. by a member of the editorial board from the English text pub., slightly rev., as CW 18,106. Cf. GW 18,106.

1958a *Psykhologiah analytit we-khinukh.* Tel Aviv: Dvir. pp. 143. Trans. from G. 1946b by Netta Blech. Contains a foreword dated 1955 especially written for this edition. TR.—English: (foreword only) CW 18,133. Cf. GW 18,133.

1974a "Ma-amar Jung le-ktav Mishmar be-shweits lifnei 29 shanim." *Al Hamishmar,* 15 Nov. [What did Jung say to *Mishmar's* correspondent in Switzerland 29 years ago?] Trans. by an unknown hand from a letter written in German to Eugen Kolb (14 Sept. 1945), Swiss correspondent for *Al Hamishmar,* in response to questions on Hitler. Cf. CW 18,74 / GW 18,74.

HUNGARIAN

1948a *Bevezetés a tudattalan pszichológiájába.* Budapest: Bibliotheca. pp. 177. Trans. from G. 1943a by Peter Nagy. Contains a foreword written especially for the Hungarian edn., dated Jan. 1944. Cf. CW 18,36 / GW 18,36.

ITALIAN

1908a "Le nuove vedute della psicologia criminale. Contributo al metodo della 'Diagnosi della conoscenza del fatto' (Tatbestandsdiagnose)." *Rivista di psicologia applicata*, IV: 4 (July–Aug.), 285–304. Trans. from a German ms. by L. Baroncini. Partially incorporated into E. 1910a,1. TR.—English: CW 2,16 // German: GW 2,16.

1959c *Il problema dell'inconscio nella psicologia moderna.* Turin: Einaudi. Italian 1942 tr. of G. 1931a, repub. with the addn. of a foreword to this Italian repr. dated March 1959. pp. 307. TR.—(Foreword only) English: CW 18,67. Cf. GW 18,67.

SPANISH

1934a *Tipos psicológicos.* (Col. Piragra, 23.) Buenos Aires: Sudamericana. pp. 566. Trans. from G. 1921a by Ramón Gómez de la Serna. In later edns., paging and format vary. 1945: pp. 552; 1960: pp. 483; 1964: pp. 659; 1965: 2 vols. Contains a foreword written for this edn. and dated October 1934. TR.—(Foreword only) English: CW 6,3.

1947a "Prefacio" and "Prólogo . . . a la edición española." Jolande Jacobi: *La psicología de C. G. Jung.* pp. 25–26 and p. 27. Madrid: Espasa-Calpe. Preface trans. from G. 1940c and the prologue (written especially for this edn.) from the German ms. by José M. Sacristán. TR.—English: (Prologue only) CW 18,41. Cf. GW 18,41.

II

THE COLLECTED WORKS OF C. G. JUNG

DIE GESAMMELTEN WERKE
VON C. G. JUNG

The contents of the two editions are coordinated on facing pages. Paragraph numbers (column at right) are given only for the *Collected Works*; they are the same for the *Gesammelte Werke* except for discrepancies in volumes 6, 8, 11, and 14, which are explained in each volume. Page numbers are given in ( ) following each title. The cross-references indicate, in general, the immediate derivation of each work, with further references as may be useful.

For the volumes of the *Gesammelte Werke*, the listings from GW 19 have been substituted (updated insofar as feasible), with the permission of Walter-Verlag, Olten, Switzerland. In references to the bibliographical entries, "D" (Deutsch) = "G" (German).

The Collected Works of C. G. Jung. Edited by †Herbert Read, Michael Fordham, and †Gerhard Adler; executive editor (from 1967), William McGuire. Translated by †R.F.C. Hull, except as otherwise noted. New York: Pantheon Books for Bollingen Foundation, 1953–1960; Bollingen Foundation (distributed by Pantheon Books, a Division of Random House), 1961–1967. Princeton, New Jersey: Princeton University Press, 1967– . (Bollingen Series XX.) London: Routledge & Kegan Paul, 1953– ; from 1989, Routledge. (The New York/Princeton and London edns. are identical except for title-pages and binding. Reprintings vary.)

CW 1 *Psychiatric Studies.* (Collected Works, 1.) 1957: 1st edn. 1970: 2d edn. 1983: Princeton/Bollingen Paperback.

1.	"On the Psychology and Pathology of So-Called Occult Phenomena." (3–88) Trans. from G. 1902a.	1–150
2.	"On Hysterical Misreading." (89–92) Trans. from G. 1904b.	151–65
3.	"Cryptomnesia." (95–106) Trans. from G. 1905a.	166–86
4.	"On Manic Mood Disorder." (109–34) Trans. from G. 1903a.	187–225
5.	"A Case of Hysterical Stupor in a Prisoner in Detention." (137–56) Trans. from G. 1902b.	226–300
6.	"On Simulated Insanity." (159–87) Trans. from G. 1903b.	301–55
7.	"A Medical Opinion on a Case of Simulated Insanity." (188–205) Trans. from G. 1904c.	356–429
8.	"A Third and Final Opinion on Two Contradictory Psychiatric Diagnoses." (209–18) Trans. from G. 1906d.	430–77
9.	"On the Psychological Diagnosis of Facts." (219–21) Trans. from G. 1905d.	478–84

CW 2 *Experimental Researches.* (Collected Works, 2.) 1973. Trans. by Leopold Stein in collaboration with Diana Riviere. 1981: Princeton/Bollingen Paperback.

1.	"The Association of Normal Subjects." (3–196) By C. G. Jung and Franz Riklin. Trans. from G. 1906a,1.	1–498

Die Gesammelten Werke von C. G. Jung. Herausgegeben von †Marianne Niehus-Jung, †Lena Hurwitz-Eisner, †Franz Riklin, †Lilly Jung-Merker, Elisabeth Rüf und Leonie Zander. Zürich: Rascher, 1958–1970. Olten: Walter, 1971– .

GW 1 *Psychiatrische Studien.* (Gesammelte Werke, 1.) 1966.

1. «Zur Psychologie und Pathologie sogenannter okkulter Phänomene.» (1–98) D. 1902a neuhg.
2. «Über hysterisches Verlesen.» (99–102) D. 1904b neuhg.
3. «Kryptomnesie.» (103–15) D. 1905a, leicht rev.
4. «Über manische Verstimmung.» (117–46) D. 1903a neuhg.
5. «Ein Fall von hysterischem Stupor bei einer Untersuchungsgefangenen.» (147–67) D. 1902b neuhg.
6. «Über Simulation von Geistesstörung.» (169–201) D. 1903b neuhg.
7. «Ärztliches Gutachten über einen Fall von Simultation geistiger Störung.» (203–21)(D. 1904c neuhg.
8. «Obergutachten über zwei widersprechende psychiatrische Gutachten.» (223–33) D. 1906d neuhg., mit leichter Titeländerung.
9. «Zur psychologischen Tatbestandsdiagnostik.» (235–37) D. 1905d neuhg.

GW 2 *Experimentelle Untersuchungen.* (Gesammelte Werke, 2.) 1979. Mit Übersetzungen aus dem Englischen von Sabine Lucas.

1. «Experimentelle Untersuchungen über Assoziationen Gesunder.» (13–213) Mit Franz Riklin. D. 1906a,1 neuhg.

Appendix:
15. «Statistisches von der Rekrutenaushebung.» (605–9) D. 1906c neuhg.
16. «Neue Aspekte der Kriminalpsychologie.» (610–20) Üb. von CW 2,16.
17. «Die an der Psychiatrischen Klinik in Zürich gebräuchlichen psychologischen Untersuchungsmethoden.» (621) D. 1910r neuhg.
18. «Ein kurzer Überblick über die Komplexlehre.» (622–28) Erstmals pub. aus Ms.
19. «Zur psychologischen Tatbestandsdiagnostik: Das Tatbestandsexperiment im Schwurgerichtsprozeß Näf.» (629–38) D. 1937b neuhg.

GW 3 *Psychogenese der Geisteskrankheiten.* (Gesammelte Werke, 3.) 1968.
1. «Über die Psychologie der Dementia praecox: Ein Versuch.» (1–170) D. 1907a neuhg.
2. «Der Inhalt der Psychose.» (171–215) D. 1914a neuhg. (Eingeschlossen Nachtrag: «Über das psychologische Verständnis pathologischer Vorgänge.»)
3. «Kritik über E. Bleuler: Zur Theorie des schizophrenen Negativismus.» (217–24) D. 1911c neuhg.
4. «Über die Bedeutung des Unbewußten in der Psychopathologie.» (225–34) Üb. aus. dem E. 1914b von Klaus Thiele-Dohrmann, und leicht rev.
5. «Über das Problem der Psychogenese bei Geisteskrankheiten.» (235-52) Üb. aus dem E. 1919a von Klaus Thiele-Dohrmann.
6. «Geisteskrankheit und Seele.» (253–59) D. 1928c neuhg. mit Originaltitel des Ms.
7. «Über die Psychogenese der Schizophrenie.» (261–81) Üb. aus dem E. 1939d von Klaus Thiele-Dohrmann.
8. «Neuere Betrachtungen zur Schizophrenie.» (283–91) D. 1959f neuhg.
9. «Die Schizophrenie.» (293–312) D. 1958i neuhg.

11. "Letter to the Second International Congress 553–584
of Psychiatry Symposium on Chemical Con-
cepts of Psychosis, 1957." (272) E. 1958d repub. Written to Max Rinkel (Apr. 1957). TR.—
German: 1973a.

CW 4 *Freud and Psychoanalysis.* (Collected Works, 4.) 1961. 1985: Prince-
ton/Bollingen Paperback.

1. "Freud's Theory of Hysteria: A Reply to 1–26
Aschaffenburg." (3–9) Trans. from G. 1906g.
2. "The Freudian Theory of Hysteria." (10–24) 27–63
Trans. from G. 1908m.
3. "The Analysis of Dreams." (25–34) Trans. 64–94
from Fr. 1909a by Philip Mairet and rev. by
R.F.C. Hull.
4. "A Contribution to the Psychology of Ru- 95–128
mour." (35–47) Trans. from G. 1910q.
5. "On the Significance of Number Dreams." 129–53
(48–55) Trans. from G. 1911e.
6. "Morton Prince, *The Mechanism and Interpreta-* 154–93
tion of Dreams: A Critical Review." (56–73)
Trans. from G. 1911b.
7. "On the Criticism of Psychoanalysis." (74–77) 194–96
Trans. from G. 1910o.
8. "Concerning Psychoanalysis." (78–81) Trans. 197–202
from G. 1912g.
9. "The Theory of Psychoanalysis." (83–226) 203–522
Trans. from G. 1955b.
10. "General Aspects of Psychoanalysis." (229–42) 523–56
Trans. from the German ms., a version of
which was subsequently pub. as GW 4,10.
11. "Psychoanalysis and Neurosis." (243–51) E. 557–75
1916a,9, trans. slightly rev., with title change.
12. "Some Crucial Points in Psychoanalysis: A 576–669
Correspondence between Dr. Jung and Dr.
Loÿ." (252–89 Trans. from G. 1914b.
13, a and b. "Prefaces to *Collected Papers on Analyti-* 670–92
cal Psychology." (290–97) E. 1916a,1 and E.
1917a,1, trans. slightly rev.
14. "The Significance of the Father in the Destiny 693–744
of the Individual." (301–23) Trans. from G.

GW 4 *Freud und die Psychoanalyse.* (Gesammelte Werke, 4.) 1969.

1. «Die Hysterielehre Freuds. Eine Erwiderung auf die Aschaffenburgsche Kritik.» (1–10) D. 1906g neuhg.
2. «Die Freudsche Hysterietheorie.» (11–28) D. 1908m neuhg.
3. «Die Traumanalyse.» (29–40) Üb. aus dem Fr. 1909a von Klaus Thiele-Dohrmann.
4. «Ein Beitrag zur Psychologie des Gerüchtes.» (41–57) D. 1910q neuhg.
5. «Ein Beitrag zur Kenntnis des Zahlentraumes.» (59–69) D. 1911e neuhg.
6. «Morton Prince, M.D.: *The Mechanism and Interpretation of Dreams.* Eine kritische Besprechung.» (71–93) D. 1911b neuhg.
7. «Zur Kritik über Psychoanalyse.» (95–100) D. 1910o neuhg.
8. «Zur Psychoanalyse.» (101–6) D. 1912g neuhg.
9. «Versuch einer Darstellung der psychoanalytischen Theorie.» (107–255) D. 1955b neuhg.
10. «Allgemeine Aspekte der Psychoanalyse.» (257–73) Nach unpub. deutschem Ms. Vgl. E. 1913d.
11. «Über Psychoanalyse.» (275–86) Üb. aus dem E. 1916a,8 von Klaus Thiele-Dohrmann.
12. «Psychotherapeutische Zeitfragen. Ein Briefwechsel zwischen C. G. Jung und R. Loÿ.» (287–331) D. 1914b neuhg.
13. «Vorreden zu den *Collected Papers on Analytical Psychology.*» (333–44) (Text der 2. Vorrede nach deutschem Ms.) Üb. aus dem E. 1916a,1 und E. 1917a,1 von Klaus Thiele-Dohrmann.
14. «Die Bedeutung des Vaters für das Schicksal des Einzelnen.» (345–70) D. 1949a neuhg.

CW 6 *Psychological Types.* (Collected Works, 6.) 1971. [No. 4:] A revision by R.F.C. Hull of the trans. by H. G. Baynes (cf. E. 1923a). Trans. from G. 1921a. 1976: Princeton/Bollingen Paperback.

1. Foreword to the First Swiss Edition. (xi–xii)
2. Foreword to the Seventh and Eighth Swiss Editions. (xii–xiii)
3. Foreword to the Argentine Edition. (xiv–xv) Trans. from Sp. 1934a.
4. Psychological Types.

Introduction. (3–7)	1–7
I. The Problem of Types in the History of Classical and Medieval Thought. (8–66)	8–100
II. Schiller's Ideas on the Type Problem. (67–135)	101–222
III. The Apollonian and the Dionysian. (136–46)	223–42
IV. The Type Problem in Human Character. (147–65)	243–74
V. The Type Problem in Poetry. (166–372)	275–460
VI. The Type Problem in Psychopathology. (273–88)	461–83
VII. The Type Problem in Aesthetics. (289–99)	484–504
VIII. The Type Problem in Modern Philosophy. (300–21)	505–41
IX. The Type Problem in Biography. (322–29)	542–55
X. General Description of the Types. (330–407) Repub. as E. 1917a,8.	556–671
XI. Definitions. (408–86)	672–844
Epilogue. (487–95)	845–57

Appendix: Four Papers on Psychological Typology.

5. "A Contribution to the Study of Psychological Types (1913)." (499–509) Trans. from the German ms. Cf. GW 6,4. and Fr. 1913a.	858–82
6. "Psychological Types (1923)." (510–23) Trans. from GW 6,5 (2d edn.).	883–914
7. "A Psychological Theory of Types (1931)." (524–41) E. 1933a,4, repub. trans. slightly rev.	915–59

8. "Psychological Typology (1936)." (542–55)   960–87
Trans. from GW 6,7 (2d edn.)

CW 7 *Two Essays on Analytical Psychology.* (Collected Works, 7.) 1953: 1st edn. 1956: Paperback 1st edn. New York: Noonday (Meridian). 1966: 2d edn. (fully reset). 1972: (2d edn.) Princeton/Bollingen Paperback. First Edition:

1. "The Psychology of the Unconscious." (3–117)   1–201
Trans. from G. 1943a, with omission of some prefatory matter.
   a) "Preface to the First Edition." (3–4) Dated Dec. 1916.
   b) "Preface to the Second Edition." (4–5) Dated Oct. 1918.
   c) "from Preface to the Third Edition." (5–6) Dated 1925.
   e) "Preface to the Fifth Edition." (6–7) Dated Apr. 1942.
2. "The Relations between the Ego and the Un-   202–406
conscious." (121–239) Trans. from G. 1935a.
   a) "Preface to the Second Edition." (121–32) Dated Oct. 1934.

Appendixes:
3. "New Paths in Psychology." (243–62) A trans.   407–36
of an incomplete version of G. 1912d. For trans. of complete version, see CW 7,3, 2d edn.
4. "The Structure of the Unconscious." (263–92)   437–507
Trans. from Fr. 1916a by Philip Mairet. For a trans. of the orig. German ms., see CW 7,4, 2d edn.

Second Edition:
1. "On the Psychology of the Unconscious." (1–   1–201
119) Contains the same prefaces as CW 7, 1st edn., although paging differs, with the following addition:
   d) "Preface to the Fourth Edition (1936)." (7) Trans. from G. 1943a.

146

GW 7 *Zwei Schriften über Analytische Psychologie.* (Gesammelte Werke, 7.) 1964. 4., vollständig revidierte Auflage 1989.

1. «Über die Psychologie des Unbewußten.» (1–130) D. 1943a neuhg. Vorworte zur ersten bis fünften Auflage.
2. «Die Beziehungen zwischen dem Ich und dem Unbewußten.» (131–264) D. 1935 a neuhg.

Vorrede zur 2. Auflage.

Anhang:

3. «Neue Bahnen der Psychologie.» (267–91) D. 1912d neuhg.
4. «Die Struktur des Unbewußten.» (292–337) Gehalten als Vortrag an der Zürcher Schule für Analytische Psychologie, 1916. Originalms. betitelt: «Über das Unbewußte und seine Inhalte.» Vgl. CW 7,4. Zuerst pub. in französischer Üb. Pub., rev. und erw., in D. 1928a.

Cf. CW 7,3, below.

GW 8 *Die Dynamik des Unbewußten.* (Gesammelte Werke, 8.) 1967. Vollst. rev. 1976 mit veränd. Paginierung.

1. «Über die Energetik der Seele.» (11–78) D. 1948b,2 neuhg.
2. «Die transzendente Funktion.» (78–108) D. 1958b neuhg.
3. «Allgemeines zur Komplextheorie.» (109–23) D. 1948b,3 neuhg.
4. «Die Bedeutung von Konstitution und Vererbung für die Psychologie.» (125–33) D. 1929i neuhg.
5. «Psychologische Determinanten des menschlichen Verhaltens.» (135–48) Ursprüngl. Vortrag auf englisch (vgl. E. 1937a) nach unpub. deutschem Ms.
6. «Instinkt und Unbewußtes.» (149–60) D. 1948b,6 neuhg.
7. «Die Struktur der Seele.» (161–82) D. 1931a,7 neuhg.
8. «Theoretische Überlegungen zum Wesen des Psychischen.» (183–261) D. 1954b,8 neuhg.
9. «Allgemeine Gesichtspunkte zur Psychologie des Traumes.» (263–308) D. 1948b, 4 neuhg.
10. «Vom Wesen der Träume.» (309–27) D. 1948b,5 1983a neuhg.

7. «Zum psychologischen Aspekt der Korefigur.» (197–220) D. 1951b,2 neuhg.
8. «Zur Phänomenologie des Geistes im Märchen.» (221–69) D. 1948a,2 neuhg.
9. «Zur Psychologie der Tricksterfigur.» (271–90) D. 1954a neuhg.
10. «Bewußtsein, Unbewußtes und Individuation.» (291–307) D. 1950a,4 neuhg.
11. «Zur Empirie des Individuationsprozesses.» (309–72) D. 1950a,4 neuhg.
12. «Über Mandalasymbolik.» (373–407) D. 1950a,5 neuhg.
13. «Mandalas [Appendix].» (409–14) D. 1955e neuhg.

GW 9,ii *Aion; Beiträge zur Symbolik des Selbst.* (Gesammelte Werke, 9,ii.) 1976. Jungs Beitrag zu D. 1951a neuhg.: Titel und Untertitel anders angeordnet.

    Vorrede. (9–11) Dat. Mai 1950.
    I. Das Ich. (12–16)
    II. Der Schatten. (17–19)
    III. Die Syzygie: Anima und Animus. (20–31)
    IV. Das Selbst. (32–45)
    V. Christus, ein Symbol des Selbst. (46–80)
    VI. Das Zeichen der Fische. (81–103)
    VII. Die Prophezeiung des Nostradamus. (104–11)
    VIII. Über die geschichtliche Bedeutung des Fisches. (112–26)
    IX. Die Ambivalenz des Fischsymbols. (127–35)
    X. Der Fisch in der Alchemie. (136–65)
    XI. Die alchemistische Deutung des Fisches. (166–85)

GW 10 *Zivilisation im Übergang.* (Gesammelte Werke, 10.) 1974.

16. «Das Gewissen in psychologischer Sicht.» (475–95) D. 1958c Neuausg.
17. «Gut und Böse in der analytischen Psychologie.» (497–510) GW 11,19 Neuausg.
18. «Vorrede zu: Toni Wolff, *Studien zu C. G. Jungs Psychologie.*» (511–18) D. 1959e Neuausg.
19. «Die Bedeutung der schweizerischen Linie im Spektrum Europas.» (519–30) D. 1928e Neuausg.
20. «Der Aufgang einer neuen Welt.» Eine Besprechung von: H. Keyserling, *Amerika. Der Aufgang einer neuen Welt.* (531–37) D. 1930e Neuausg.
21. «Ein neues Buch von Keyserling, *La Révolution mondiale et la responsibilité de l'esprit.*» (539–45) D. 1934i Neuausg.
22. «Komplikationen der amerikanischen Psychologie.» (547–61) Üb. aus CW 10,22 von Elisabeth Rüf.
23. «Die träumende Welt Indiens.» (563–74) Üb. aus E. 1939b von Elisabeth Rüf.
24. «Was Indien uns lehren kann.» (575–80) Üb. aus E. 1939c von Elisabeth Rüf. «Verschiedenes.»
25. «Geleitwort.» (*Zentralblatt* VI, 1933) (581–82) D. 1933e Neuausg.
26. «Zeitgenössisches.» (*Neue Zürcher Zeitung* CLV, 1934) (583–93) D. 1934f und D. 1934g Neuausg.
27. «Rundschreiben.» (*Zentralblatt* VII, 1934) (595–96) D. 1934j Neuausg.
28. «Geleitwort.» (*Zentralblatt* VIII, 1935) (597–602) D. 1935j Neuausg.
29. «Vorbemerkung des Herausgebers.» (*Zentralblatt* VIII, 1935j) (603–4) D. 1935k Neuausg.
30. «Begrußungsansprache [des Präsidenten] zum Achten Allgemeinen Ärztlichen Kongreß in Bad Nauheim (1935).» (605–7) 27.–30. März 1935.
31. «Votum.» (*Schweizerische Ärztezeitung* XVI, 1935) (609–12) D. 1935h Neuausg. mit leichter Titelabweichg.
32. «Begrüßungsansprache [des Präsidenten] zum Neunten Internationalen Ärztlichen Kongreß für Psychotherapie in Kopenhagen (1937).» (613–15) 2.–4. Okt. 1937.

ms. pub. as GW 10,32. Congress held 2–4 Oct. 1937.

33. "Presidential Address to the 10th Interna-   1069–73
tional Medical Congress for Psychotherapy,
Oxford, 1938." (564–67) Given in English.
Summary pub. as E. 1938b.

CW 11 *Psychology and Religion: West and East.* (Collected Works, 11.) 1958:
1st edn. 1969: 2d edn. With 1 plate (frontisp.).

1. "Psychology and Religion." (3–105) E. 1938a,   1–168
combined with a trans. of G. 1940a. Repub. as
E. 1959a,11.
2. "A Psychological Approach to the Dogma of   169–295
the Trinity." (107–200) Trans. from G.
1948a,4.
3. "Transformation Symbolism in the Mass."   296–448
(201–96) Trans. from G. 1954b,6. Cf. E.
1955b.
4. "Foreword to White's *God and the Unconscious*."   449–67
(299–310) E. 1952c, trans. slightly rev.
5. "Foreword to Werblowsky's *Lucifer and Prome-*   468–73
theus." (311–15) E. 1952b, trans. slightly rev.
6. "Brother Klaus." (316–23) Trans. from G.   479–87
1933c.
7. "Psychotherapists or the Clergy." (327–47)   488–538
Trans. from G. 1932a.
8. "Psychoanalysis and the Cure of Souls." (348–   539–52
54) Trans. from G. 1928g.
9. "Answer to Job." (355–470) E. 1954a repub.   553–758
with the addn. of E. 1956c as "Prefatory
Note," both sl. rev. Repub. as E. 1971a,15.
Pub. without "Prefatory Note" as E. 1960a and
E. 1965aa. "Important phrase" restored to
"Prefatory Note" (2d sentence, 4th par.) in the
2d ptg. of the 2d edn. of this vol. (1973) and
repub. in this form as E. 1973a. Cf. E. 1975b,
letter to S. Doniger (Nov. 1955), for orig. version of "Prefatory Note."
10. "Psychological Commentary on *The Tibetan*   759–830
Book of the Great Liberation." (475–508) E.
1954e repub. Pt. 1 (par. 759–87).

33. «Begrüßungsansprache [des Präsidenten] zum Zehnten Internationalen Ärztlichen Kongreß für Psychotherapie in Oxford (1938).» (617–20) 29. Juli–2. Aug. Üb. aus CW 10,33 von Elisabeth Rüf.

GW 11 *Zur Psychologie westlicher und östlicher Religion.* (Gesammelte Werke, 11.) 1963. 5., vollständig revidierte Auflage 1988, ohne Anhang und mit neuer Paginierung.

1. «Psychologie und Religion.» (xvii–117) D. 1940a Neuausg. (17–125)

2. «Versuch einer psychologischen Deutung des Trinitätsdogmas.» (119–218) D. 1948a,4. Neuausg. mit leichter Titelabweichg. (127–215)

3. «Das Wandlungssymbol in der Messe.» (219–323) D. 1954b,6 Neuausg. (217–310)

4. «Geleitwort zu V. White: *Gott und das Unbewußte.*» (325–39) D. 1957h Neuausg. (313–23)

5. «Vorrede zu Z. Werblowsky: *Lucifer and Prometheus.*» (340–44) Originaltext aus deutschem Ms. zuerst in englischer Üb. pub. (324–27)

6. «Bruder Klaus.» (345–52) D. 1933c Neuausg. (328–34)

7. «Über die Beziehung der Psychotherapie zur Seelsorge.» (355–76) D. 1932a Neuausg. mit leichter Titelabweichg. (337–55)

8. «Psychoanalyse und Seelsorge.» (377–83) D. 1928g Neuausg. (356–62)

9. «Antwort auf Hiob.» (385–506) D. 1961a Neuausg. «Nachwort» (pp. 505–6) ohne Paragraphierung, einem Brief an Simon Doniger (Nov. 1955) entnommen. (263–474)

10. «Psychologischer Kommentar zu: *Das tibetische Buch der großen Befreiung.*» (511–49) D. 1955d Neuausg. (477–511)

CW 12 *Psychology and Alchemy.* (Collected Works, 12.) 1953: 1st edn. 1968: 2d edn. (fully reset). With 270 text illus. Trans. from G. 1952d, except no. 1 in 2d edn. 1980: Princeton/Bollingen Paperback; Routledge & Kegan Paul, Paperback.

11. «Psychologischer Kommentar zum Bardo Thödol (Das tibetanische Totenbuch.)» (550–67) D. 1935f Neuausg. (512–27)
12. «Yoga und der Westen.» (571–80) Originaltext aus deutschem Ms. zuerst in engl. Üb. (531–29)
13. «Vorwort zu D. T. Suzuki: *Die große Befreiung.*» (581–602) D. 1939c Neuausg. (540–59)
14. «Zur Psychologie östlicher Meditation.» (603–21) D. 1948a,5 Neuausg. (560–76)
15. «Über den indischen Heiligen. Einführung zu H. Zimmer: *Der Weg zum Selbst.*» (622–32) D. 1944b Neuausg. (578–86)
16. «Vorwort zum *I Ging.*» (633–54) Text des deutschen Originalms. Engl. Fassung in E. 1950d weicht davon ab. (587–606)
Anhang (nicht in CW 11, auch nicht in 1988 Auflage):
17. «Antwort an Martin Buber.» (657–65) D. 1952j Neuausg. mit Titelabweichg. GW 18,96.
18. «Zu *Psychologie und Religion.*» (665–67) Aus einem Brief an einen protestantischen Theologen, geschrieben 1940.
19. «Gut und Böse in der analytischen Psychologie.» (667–81) D. 1959b Neuausg. Neu hg. aus GW 10,17.
20. «Zum Problem des Christussymbols.» (681–85) Üb. von Aniela Jaffé aus englisch geschriebenem Brief an Victor White (24. Nov. 1953). Text des Originalbriefes ersch. in E. 1975b.
21. «Zu *Antwort auf Hiob.*» (685–86) Aus einem Brief an Hans Schär (16. Nov. 1951). Ganzer Text des Briefes ersch. in D. 1972b.
22. «Zu *Antwort auf Hiob.*» (687) Aus einem Brief an Dorothée Hoch (28. Mai 1952). Ganzer Text des Briefes ersch. in D. 1972b.
23. «Klappentext zur ersten Auflage von *Antwort auf Hiob.*» (687) April 1952 GW 18,95.
24. «Aus einem Brief an einen protestantischen Theologen.» (688) Aus einem Brief an Hans Wegmann (19. Dez. 1943). Ganzer Text ersch. in D. 1972a.
25. «Brief an *The Listener.* Januar 1960.» (689–90) Üb. aus E. 1960c von Marianne Niehus-Jung. Neuausg. in D. 1973a.
26. «Zu *Die Reden Gotamo Buddhos.*» (690–93) D. 1956c Neuausg. mit Titelabweichg. GW 18,101.

GW 12 *Psychologie und Alchemie.* (Gesammelte Werke, 12.) 1972. Mit 271 Textillus. D. 1952d Neuausg.

First Edition:
1. Foreword to the Swiss Edition. (vii)
2. Psychology and Alchemy.
    I. Introduction to the Religious and Psycho-   1–43
    logical Problems of Alchemy. (1–37)
    II. Individual Dream Symbolism in Relation   44–331
    to Alchemy. (39–213).
    III. Religious Ideas in Alchemy. (215–451)   332–554
    Epilogue. (453–63)   555–65

Second Edition:
1. "Prefatory Note to the English Edition." (v)
    Trans. from the unpublished ms.
2. "Foreword to the Swiss Edition." (x)
3. "Psychology and Alchemy.
    I. Introduction to the Religious and Psycho-   1–43
    logical problems of Alchemy. (1–37)
    II. Individual Dream Symbolism in Relation   44–331
    to Alchemy. (39–223) Repub. as
    E. 1971a,11 and E. 1974a,6.
    III. Religious Ideas in Alchemy. (225–471)   332–554
    Epilogue. (473–83)   555–65

CW 13 *Alchemical Studies.* (Collected Works, 13.) 1967. With 50 plates (1 col.) and 4 text illus. 1983: Princeton/Bollingen Paperback; Routledge & Kegan Paul, Paperback.

1. "Commentary on *The Secret of the Golden*   1–84
    Flower." (1–56) Trans. from G. 1957b,1 and 3.
2. "The Vision of Zosimos." (57–108) Trans.   85–144
    from G. 1954b,5.
3. "Paracelsus as a Spiritual Phenomenon." (109–   145–238
    89) Trans. from G. 1942a,2, with the addition
    of 2 footnotes derived from posthumous pa-
    pers.
4. "The Spirit Mercurius." (191–200) Trans.   239–303
    from G. 1948a,3.
5. "The Philosophical Tree." (251–349) Trans.   304–482
    from G. 1954b,7.

CW 14 *Mysterium Coniunctionis. An Inquiry into the Separation and Synthesis of Psychic Opposites in Alchemy.* (Collected Works, 14.) 1963: 1st edn.

1970: 2d edn. (par. 518a added). With 10 plates. Trans. from G. 1955a and 1956a. 1977: Princeton/Bollingen Paperback.

NOTE: M.-L. von Franz, *Aurora Consurgens: A Document Attributed to Thomas Aquinas on the Problem of Opposites in Alchemy*, published as vol. III ("supplementary vol.") in the original Swiss edition of *Mysterium Coniunctionis*, was published separately in English, translated by R.F.C. Hull and A.S.B. Glover (B.S. 77, 1966). 1966: Routledge & Kegan Paul.

CW 15 *The Spirit in Man, Art, and Literature.* (Collected Works, 15.) 1966. 1971: Princeton/Bollingen Paperback. 1984: Ark Paperback, Routledge & Kegan Paul.

beit von Marie-Louise von Franz. (Gesammelte Werke, 14.) In zwei Bänden. 1968. 4., vollständig revidierte Auflage 1984. Bd. 2 enthält 7 Tafeln und 3 Textillustr. D. 1955a und 1956a Nachdr., mit neugestalteter Titelseite und zusätzlich mit Üb. griechischer und lateinischer Textstellen, Bibliographie und einem Vorwort der Herausgeber. Inhalt siehe D. 1955a und D. 1956a. Paragraphennummern stimmen mit D. 1955a und D. 1956a überein, weichen aber von CW 14 ab. Vollständig rev. Neuausgabe erscheint 1984.

/I   Vorwort
    I. Die Komponenten der Coniunctio
    II. Die Paradoxa
    III. Die Personifikationen der Gegensätze

/II   IV. Rex und Regina
    V. Adam und Eva
    VI. Die Konjunktion
    Nachwort

/III   «*Aurora Consurgens.*» *Ein dem Thomas von Aquin zugeschriebenes Dokument der alchemistischen Gegensatzproblematik,* von Dr. M.-L. von Franz. (Gesammelte Werke, 14, Ergänzungsband.) Olten: Walter. 1973.

GW 15   *Über das Phänomen des Geistes in Kunst und Wissenschaft.* (Gesammelte Werke, 15.) 1971.

1. «Paracelsus.» (11–20) D. 1934b,5 Neuausg. vgl. D. 1952c.
2. «Paracelsus als Arzt.» (21–41) D. 1942a,1 Neuausg.
3. «Sigmund Freud als kulturhistorische Erscheinung.» (43–51) D. 1934b,6 Neuausg.
4. «Sigmund Freud.» (53–62) D. 1939d Neuausg.
5. «Zum Gedächtnis Richard Wilhelms.» (63–73) D. 1957b,2 Neuausg.
6. Über die Beziehungen der analytischen Psychologie zum dichterischen Kunstwerk.» (75–96) D. 1931a,3 Neuausg.
7. «Psychologie und Dichtung.» (97–120) D. 1950a,2 mit zusätzlicher «Vorrede» hier erstmals nach Ms. in der ursprünglichen deutschen Fassg., die postum gefunden wurde.

troduction trans. from a ms. found posthumously and pub. as the "Vorrede" to GW 15,7.

8. " 'Ulysses': A Monologue." (109–34) Trans.   163–203
from G. 1934b,7. Letter to James Joyce (27
Sept. 1932), included in the Appendix, pp.
133–34, is E. 1966d repub.

9. "Picasso." (135–41) Trans. from G. 1932g.   204–14

CW 16 *The Practice of Psychotherapy. Essays on the Psychology of the Transfer-*
ence and Other Subjects. (Collected Works, 16.) 1954: 1st edn. 1966:
2d edn. (no. 13 fully reset). With 3 plates and 10 text illus. 1985:
Princeton/Bollingen Paperback.

1. "Foreword to the Swiss Edition (1958)." Trans.
from GW 16,1. (2d edn. only.)

Part One.   1–27
2. "Principles of Practical Psychotherapy." (3–20)
Trans. from G. 1935k.

3. "What is Psychotherapy?" (21–28) Trans. from   28–45
G. 1935g.

4. "Some Aspects of Modern Psychotherapy."   46–65
(29–35) E. 1930b repub.

5. "The Aims of Psychotherapy." (36–52) Trans.   66–113
from G. 1931a,5.

6. "Problems of Modern Psychotherapy." (53–75)   114–74
Trans. from G. 1931a,2.

7. "Psychotherapy and a Philosophy of Life."   175–91
(76–83) Trans. from G. 1943e.

8. "Medicine and Psychotherapy." (84–93) Trans.   192–211
from G. 1945e.

9. "Psychotherapy Today." (94–110) Trans. from   212–29
G. 1945f.

10. "Fundamental Questions of Psychotherapy."   230–54
(111–25) Trans. from G. 1951d.

Part Two.   255–93
11. "The Therapeutic Value of Abreaction." (129–
38) E. 1928a,11, trans. slightly rev. and with title change.

12. "The Practical Use of Dream-Analysis." (139–   294–352
61) Trans. from G. 1934b,4.

8. « ‹Ulysses› Ein Monolog.» (121–49) D. 1934b,7 Neuausg.
«Anhang» (pp. 146–49) einschließlich einer Üb. von Elisabeth
Rüf eines Briefes an James Joyce auf englisch. (27. Sept.
1932). Originalbrief in CW 15,8 und E. 1973b.
9. «Picasso». (151–57) D. 1934b,8 Neuausg.

GW 16 *Praxis der Psychotherapie. Beiträge zum Problem der Psychotherapie und
zur Psychologie der Übertragung.* (Gesammelte Werke, 16.) 1958. 5.,
vollständig revidierte Auflage 1991, mit neuer Paginierung. Mit 3
Tafeln und 11 Textillustr.

1. «Geleitwort des Autors.» (ix–x) Dat. Aug. 1957. Erster Teil:
Allgemeine Probleme der Psychotherapie. (11–12)
2. «Grundsätzliches zur praktischen Psychotherapie.» (1–20) D.
1935l Neuausg. (15–32)
3. «Was ist Psychotherapie?» (21–29) D. 1935g Neuausg. (33–40)
4. «Einige Aspekte der modernen Psychotherapie.» (30–37) Üb.
aus CW 16,4 von den Hg. (41–47)
5. «Ziele der Psychotherapie.» (38–55) D. 1931a,5; 1983a
Neuausg. (48–63)
6. «Die Probleme der modernen Psychotherapie.» (57–81) D.
1931a,2 Neuausg. (64–85)
7. «Psychotherapie und Weltanschauung.» (82–89) D. 1946a,4
Neuausg. (86–93)
8. «Medizin und Psychotherapie.» (90–99) D. 1945e Neuausg.
(94–102)
9. «Die Psychotherapie in der Gegenwart.» (100–117) D.
1946a,3 Neuausg. (103–18)
10. «Grundfragen der Psychotherapie.» (118–33) D. 1951d
Neuausg. (119–32)

Zweiter Teil: Spezielle Probleme der Psychotherapie.
11. «Der therapeutische Wert des Abreagierens.» (137–47) Üb.
aus E. 1921a von den Hg. (135–44)
12. «Die praktische Verwendbarkeit der Traumanalyse.» (148–
71) D. 1934b,4, 1983a Neuausg. (145–65)

13. «Die Psychologie der Übertragung.» (173–345) D. 1946c
Neuausg. (167–319)

GW 17 *Über die Entwicklung der Persönlichkeit.* (Gesammelte Werke, 17.)
1972.
1. «Über Konflikte der kindlichen Seele.» (11–47) D. 1946b,2
Neuausg.
2. «Einführung zu Frances G. Wickes *Analyse der Kindeseele.*»
(49–58) D. 1931e Neuausg. mit Titelabweichg.
3. «Die Bedeutung der Analytischen Psychologie für die Erziehung.» (59–76) D. 1971a,4, 1983a Neuausg.
4. «Analytische Psychologie und Erziehung.» (77–153) D.
1946b,1 Neuausg.
5. «Der Begabte.» (155–68) D. 1946b,3 Neuausg.
6. «Die Bedeutung des Unbewußten für die individuelle Erziehung.» (169–87) D. 1971a,5 Neuausg.
7. «Vom Werden der Persönlichkeit.» (189–211) D. 1934b,9,
1983a Neuausg.
8. «Die Ehe als psychologische Beziehung.» (213–27) D.
1931a,11.

GW 18 *Das symbolische Leben. Verschiedene Schriften.* (Gesammelte Werke,
18.) 1981. In zwei Bänden. Wo nicht anders vermerkt, Übersetzungen aus dem Englischen von Sabine Lucas, aus dem Französ-
ischen und Italienischen von Elisabeth Rüf.

/I
1. «Über Grundlagen der Analytischen Psychologie. Die Tavistock Lectures.» (13–198) Stark rev. Neuausg. von D. 1969a.
2. «Symbole und Traumdeutung.» (199–285) Jungs Beitrag
aus D. 1968a, mit ursprünglichem Titel, weitgehend nach
dem Original rev.

3. «Das symbolische Leben.» (287–314) Üb. aus E. 1954c.
4. «Über spiritistische Erscheinungen.» (317–33) Neuausg. von D. 1905e.
5. «Vorrede zu Jung: *Phénomènes occultes.*» (335–37) Geschrieben für Fr. 1939a,1; hier erstmals deutsch, nach Ms.
6. «Psychologie und Spiritismus.» (338–43) Neuausg. von D. 1948e.
7. «Vorrede und Beitrag zu Moser: *Spuk: Irrglaube oder Wahrglaube?*» (344–55) Neuausg. von D. 1950e.
8. «Vorwort zu Jaffé: *Geistererscheinungen und Vorzeichen. Eine psychologische Deutung.*» (356–58) Neuausg. von D. 1958e.
9. «Der gegenwärtige Stand der angewandten Psychologie in den einzelnen Kulturländern.» (361–62) Neuausg. von D. 1908o.
10. «Über Dementia praecox.» (363) Neuausg. von D. 1910s.
11. «Besprechung von Sadger: *Konrad Ferdinand Meyer.*» (364–66) Neuausg. von D. 1909h.
12. «Besprechung von Waldstein: *Das unbewußte Ich und sein Verhältnis zur Gesundheit und Erziehung.*» (367–70) Neuausg. von D. 1909i.
13. «Blick in die Verbrecherseele.» (371–74) Nachdruck von D. 1933a.
14. «Zur Frage der ärztlichen Intervention.» (375–76) Nachdruck von D. 1950g.
15. «Vorrede zu Custance: *Wisdom, Madness and Folly.*» (377–80) Deutsch geschrieben für E. 1952a.
16. «Vorwort zu Perry: *The Self in Psychotic Process.*» (381–84) Üb. aus E. 1953e.
17. «Geleitwort zu Schmaltz: *Komplexe Psychologie und körperliches Symptom.*» (385–86) Nachdruck von G. 1955c.
18. «Sigmund Freud: Über den Traum.» (389–97) Nach deutschem Vortragsms. von 1901.

19. «Besprechung von Hellpach: *Grundlinien einer Psychologie der Hysterie.*» (398–402) Nachdruck von D. 1905b.

20. «Besprechungen von psychiatrischer Literatur.» (403–17) Nachdruck von D. 1906e, f und h; 1907b, c und d; 1908e, f, g, h und k; 1909d–g; 1910a–j.

21. «Über die Bedeutung der Lehre Freuds für Neurologie und Psychiatrie.» (418–19) Nachdruck von D. 1908d.

22. «Wilhelm Stekel: *Nervöse Angstzustände und ihre Behandlung.*» (420–21) Nachdruck von D. 1908j.

23. «Vorbemerkung der Redaktion» zum *Jahrbuch.* (422) Nachdruck von D. 1909b.

24. «Randbemerkungen zu Wittels: *Die sexuelle Not.*» (423–26) Nachdruck von D. 1910 l.

25. «Besprechung von Wulffen: *Der Sexualverbrecher.*» (427) Nachdruck von D. 1910p.

26. «Referate über psychologische Arbeiten schweizerischer Autoren (bis Ende 1909).» (428–51) Nachdruck von D. 1910m.

27. «Besprechung von Hitschmann: *Freuds Neurosenlehre.*» (452) Nachdruck von D. 1911d.

28. «Jahresbericht des Präsidenten der Internationalen Psychoanalytischen Vereinigung über das Vereinsjahr 1910/11.» (453–56) Nachdruck von D. 1911g.

29. «Zwei Briefe zur Psychoanalyse.» (457–60) Nachdruck von D. 1912e und f.

30. «Über die psychoanalytische Behandlung nervöser Leiden.» (461–63) Nachdruck von D. 1912h.

31. «Eine Bemerkung zur Tauskschen Kritik der Nelkenschen Arbeit.» (464–68) Nachdruck von d. 1913d.

32. «Antworten auf Fragen über Freud.» (469–71) Üb. aus E. 1968f (dat. 7. Aug. 1953).

/II
33. «Uber Ambivalenz.» (475–77) Nachdruck von D. 1911h.
34. «Beiträge zur Symbolik.» (478) Nachdruck von D. 1911f.
35. «Anpassung, Individuation und Kollektivität.» (481–86) Zwei Typoskripte, dat. Okt. 1916, gefunden im Psychologischen Club Zürich.
36. «Vorwort zur ungarischen Ausgabe [Jung] *Über die Psychologie des Unbewußten.*» (487–88) Dat. Jan. 1944. Vgl. Ung. 1948a.
37. «*Vorworte zu [Jung] Über psychische Energetik und das Wesen der Träume.*» (491–92). Nachdruck von D. 1948b,1.
38. «Über Halluzination.» (493) Nachdruck von D. 1933f.
39. «Geleitwort zu Schleich: *Die Wunder der Seele.*» (494–99) Nachdruck von D. 1934e.
40. «Geleitwort zu Jacobi: *Die Psychologie von C. G. Jung.*» (500–501) Dat. Aug. 1939. Nachdruck von D. 1940c.
41. «Vorwort zur spanischen Ausgabe» von 40. (501). Nach deutschem Typoskript. Vgl. Span. 1947a.
42. «Vorwort zu Harding: *Psychic Energy.*» (502–3) Nach deutschem Ms., dat. Juli 1947. Vgl. E. 1947e.
43. «Rede anläßlich der Gründungssitzung des C. G. Jung-Institutes Zürich, am 24. April 1948.» (504–9) Deutsches Typoskript.
44. «Lexikonartikel ‹Tiefenpsychologie›.» (510–20) Nachdruck von D. 1951c.
45. «Geleitwort zu den ‹Studien aus dem C. G. Jung-Institut Zürich›.» (521–22) Nachdruck von D. 1949e.
46. «Vorwort zu Frieda Fordham: *Introduction to Jung's Psychology.*» (523–24) Üb. von Johanna Meier-Fritzsche aus E. 1953d.
47. «Vorwort zu Michael Fordham: *New Developments in Analytical Psychology.*» (525–28) Nach deutschem Ms.; vgl. E. 1957g.

48. «Ein astrologisches Experiment.» (529–36) Nachdruck von D. 1958f.
49. «Briefe über Synchronizität.» (537–44) (An Markus Fierz: 21. Feb. 1950, 2. März 1950, 20. Okt. 1954, 28. Oktober 1954; an Michael Fordham, englisch geschrieben: 1. Juli 1955.)
50. «Die Zukunft der Parapsychologie.» (545–46) Üb. aus E. 1963e.
51. «Die Hypothese des kollektiven Unbewußten.» (549–50) Nachdruck von D. 1932i.
52. «Geleitwort zu Adler: *Entdeckung der Seele.*» (551) Nachdruck von D. 1934d.
53. «Geleitwort zu Harding: *Frauen-Mysterien.*» (552–55) Nach deutschem Typoskript, dat. Aug. 1948. Vgl. D. 1949d.
54. «Vorwort zu Neumann: *Ursprungsgeschichte des Bewußtseins.*» (556–57) Nachdruck von D. 1949f.
55. «Vorwort zu Adler: *Zur analytischen Psychologie.*» (558–60) Dat. Mai 1949. Nachdruck von D. 1952g.
56. «Vorwort zu Jung: *Gestaltungen des Unbewußten.*» (561–62) Nachdruck von G. 1950a,1.
57. «Vorwort zu Wickes: *Von der inneren Welt des Menschen.*» (563–64) Nachdruck von D. 1953b.
58. «Vorrede zu Jung: *Von den Wurzeln des Bewußtseins.*» (565–66) Nachdruck von D. 1954b,1.
59. «Vorwort zu van Helsdingen: *Beelden uit het onbewuste.*» (567–68) Nachdruck von D. 1957f.
60. «Vorwort zu Jacobi: *Komplex, Archetypus, Symbol in der Psychologie C. G. Jungs.*» (569–70) Nachdruck von D. 1957g.
61. «Vorwort zu Bertine: *Menschliche Beziehungen.*» (571–73) Nachdruck von D. 1957d.
62. «Vorwort zu de Laszlo: *Psyche and Symbol.*» (574–79) Nachdruck von Üb. aus E. 1958a,1.
63. «Vorwort zu Brunner: *Die Anima als Schicksalsproblem des Mannes.*» (580–85) Nachdruck von D. 1963a.
64. «Bericht über Amerika.» (589) Nachdruck von D. 1910n.

65. «Zur Psychologie des Negers.» (590) Nachdruck von D. 1913c.
66. «Radiogespräch München.» (591–95) Nach unpub. Ms., dat. 19. Jan. 1930.
67. «Vorworte zu Jung: *Seelenprobleme der Gegenwart.*» (596–98) Nachdruck von D. 1931a,1 [und Neuaufl., dat. Dez. 1930 und Juli 1932]; nach deutschen Typoskript: It. 1959c [dat. März 1959].
68. «Vorwort zu Aldrich: *The Primitive Mind and Modern Civilization.*» (599–601) Üb. aus E. 1931b.
69. «Pressemitteilung beim Besuch der Vereinigten Staaten.» (602–3) Üb. aus unpub. Ms., dat. Sept. 1936.
70. «Psychologie und nationale Probleme.» (604–21) Üb. aus unpub. Vortragsms., dat. 14. Okt. 1936.
71. «Rückkehr zum einfachen Leben.» (621–29) Nachdruck aus D. 1941e.
72. «Epilog zu Jung: *L'Homme à la découverte de son âme.*» (630–31) Deutsches Ms. Vgl. Fr. 1944a.
73. «Randglossen zur Zeitgeschichte.» (632–45) Nach unpub. Typoskript, dat. 1945. Die letzten 9 Paragr. desselben pub. als D. 1946g.
74. «Antworten an *Mishmar* über Adolf Hitler.» (646–47) Brief an Eugen Kolb, dat. 14. Sept. 1945. Vgl. Hebr. 1974a.
75. «Techniken für einen dem Weltfrieden dienlichen Einstellungswandel. (Memorandum für die UNESCO).» (648–56) Üb. aus unpub. Typoskript, englisch geschrieben auf Anfrage der UNESCO.

76. «Die Wirkung der Technik auf das seelisch-geistige Leben.» (657–58) Nachdruck von D. 1949g.
77. «Geleitwort zu Neumann: *Depth Psychology and a New Ethic.*» (659–66) Nach deutschem Typoskript, dat. März 1949. Vgl. E. 1969e.
78. «Vorwort zu Baynes: *Analytical Psychology and the English Mind.*» (667–68) Nach deutschem Typoskript; vgl. E. 1950b.
79. «Lebensregeln.» (669–70) Nachdruck von D. 1954f.
80. «Über ‹Flying Saucers›.» (671–76) Nachdruck von D. 1954e.
81. «An die United Press International.» (676–77) Nachdruck von D. 1958h.
82. «Brief an Keyhoe.» (677–79) Üb. aus E. 1959g.
83. «Die menschliche Natur ist idealistischen Ratschlägen nicht leicht zugänglich.» (680–81) Üb. aus E. 1955h.
84. «Das geistige Europa und die ungarische Revolution.» (682) Nachruck von D. 1956f und 1957c; hier zusammen.
85. «Über Psychodiagnose.» (683–84) Nachdruck von D. 1958g.
86. «Wenn Christus heute auf Erden wandelte.» (685) Üb. aus E. 1958i.
87. «Vorwort zu *Hugh Crichton-Miller 1877–1959.*» (686–88) Üb. aus E. 1961b.
88. «Warum adoptiere ich nicht die ‹katholische Wahrheit›?» (691–93) Aus einem Brief (Typoskript) vom 22. Sept. 1944 an H. Irminger, der nie abgesandt wurde. Vgl. dazu D. 1972a.
89. «Lexikonartikel ‹Dämonie›.» (694) Nachdruck von D. 1949h
90. «Vorwort zu Jung: *Symbolik des Geistes.*» (695–96) Dat. Juni 1947. Nachdruck von D. 1948a,1.
91. «Vorwort zu Quispel: *Tragic Christianity.*» (697–99) Deutsch geschrieben, dat. Mai 1949. Das Buch ist nie erschienen.
92. «Geleitwort zu Abegg: *Ostasien denkt anders.*» (700–701) Nachdruck von D. 1950d.
93. «Vorrede zu Allenby: *A Psychological Study of the Origins of Monotheism.*» (702–6) Deutsch geschrieben, dat. Mai 1950. Das Buch ist nie erschienen.

94. "The Miraculous Fast of Brother Klaus." 1497–98
(660–61) Trans. from G. 1951e. Rev. from a
letter to Fritz Blanke (10 Nov. 1948). Cf. E.
1973b for a trans. of entire orig. letter.

95. "Concerning 'Answer to Job'." (662) Trans. 1498a
from GW 11,23 by Ruth Horine. Jung's description, printed on the dust jacket of the
orig. edn., ca. 1 April 1952. Cf. G. 1952a.

96. "Religion and Psychology: A Reply to Martin 1499–1513
Buber." (663–70) E. 1973e repub. (German
text pub. in GW 11.)

97. "Address at the Presentation of the Jung Co- 1514–17
dex." (671–72) Given in Zurich, 15 Nov.
1953. Trans. from a German ms. pub. as G.
1975a,4. (Cf. no. 135, below.)

98. "Letter to Père Bruno." (673–78) Trans. from 1518–31
Fr. 1956b by A.S.B. Glover and Jane A. Pratt.
Dated 5 Nov. 1953. Cf. letters to Bruno (22
Dec. 1954; 20 Nov. 1956) in E. 1975b.

99. "Letter to Père Lachat." (679–91) Trans. from 1532–57
the French by A.S.B. Glover. Dated 27 March
1954. Cf. Letters to Lachat (18 Jan. and 29
June 1955) in E. 1975b.

100. "On Resurrection." (692–96) Written in En- 1558–74
glish in reply to an inquiry and dated 19 Feb.
1954.

101. "On the Discourses of the Buddha." (697–99) 1575–80
Trans. from G. 1956c. (German text pub. as
GW 11,26.)

102. "Foreword to Froboese-Thiele: *Träume—eine* 1581–83
Quelle religiöser Erfahrung?" (700–01) Trans.
from G. 1957e.

103. "Jung and Religious Belief." (702–44) E. 1584–1690
1958c repub., with minor stylistic rev., addl.
footnotes, and addn. of title. Cf. letter to
H. L. Philp (11 June 1957) in E. 1975b.

104. "Foreword to a Catalogue on Alchemy." (747) 1691
E. 1968d repub., sl. rev. and with the addn.
of a title.

105. "Faust and Alchemy." (748–50) Trans. from 1692–99
G. 1950b by Hildegard Nagel.

94. «Das Fastenwunder des Bruder Klaus.» (707–8) Nachdruck von D. 1951e.
95. «Zu Jung: *Antwort auf Hiob.*» (709) Klappentext auf dem Buchumschlag der Originalausgabe. Vgl. D. 1952a.
96. «Religion und Psychologie. Eine Antwort auf Martin Buber.» (710–17) Nachdruck von D. 1952j.
97. «Ansprache bei der Überreichung des ‹Jung Codex›.» (718–20) 15. Nov. 1953. Vgl. unten, 135.
98. «Brief an Père Bruno O.C.D.» (721–27) Üb. aus dem Original (5. Nov. 1953). Vgl. Fr. 1956b.
99. «Brief an Pasteur Lachat.» (728–41) Üb. aus dem Original (27. März 1954). Vgl. D. 1972b.
100. «Über die Auferstehung.» (742–47) Dat. 19. Febr. 1954; geschrieben als Antwort auf Fragen. Üb. aus dem Englischen.
101. «Zu K. E. Neumann: *Die Reden Gotamo Buddhos.*» (748–51) Nachdruck von D. 1956c.
102. «Vorrede zu Froboese-Thiele: *Träume—eine Quelle religiöser Erfahrung?*» (752–53) Nachdruck von D. 1957e.
103. «Jung und der religiöse Glaube.» (754–801) Üb. von E. 1958c. Vgl. D. 1973a, Brief vom 11. Juni 1957 an H. L. Philp.
104. «Vorwort zu einem Buchkatalog über Alchemie.» (805–6) Dat. Mai 1946. Vgl. E. 1968d.
105. «Faust und die Alchemie.» (807–9) Nachdruck von 1950b.

106. "Alchemy and Psychology." (751–53) Written in English for the *Encyclopedia Hebraica*, and pub. here with minor stylistic rev. TR.—Hebrew: 1950/51a.   1700–04

107. "Memorial to J. S." (757–58) E. 1955c repub. Spoken in English in memory of Jerome Schloss, 1927.   1705–10

108. "Foreword to Schmid-Guisan: *Tag und Nacht*." (759–60) Trans. from G. 1931d.   1711–12

109. "Hans Schmid-Guisan: In Memoriam." (760–61) Trans. from G. 1932d.   1713–15

110. "On the Tale of the Otter." (762–64) Trans. from G. 1932b.   1716–22

111. "Is There a Freudian Type of Poetry?" (765–66) Trans. from the unpub. German ms. Cf. Fr. 1932b.   1723–24

112. "Foreword to Gilbert: *The Curse of the Intellect*." (767) Written in English for the book, which was never pub., and dated Jan. 1934.   1725–26

113. "Foreword to Jung: *Wirklichkeit der Seele*." (768–69) Trans. from G. 1934b,1.   1727–29

114. "Foreword to Mehlich: *J. H. Fichtes Seelenlehre und ihre Beziehung zur Gegenwart*." (770–72) Trans. from G. 1935e.   1730–36

115. "Foreword to von Koenig-Fachsenfeld: *Wandlungen des Traumproblems von der Romantik bis zur Gegenwart*." (773–75) Trans. from G. 1935d.   1737–41

116. "Foreword to Gilli: *Der dunkle Bruder*." (776–78) Trans. from G. 1938d.   1742–47

117. "Gérard de Nerval." (779) Trans. from G. 1946d.   1748

118. "Foreword to Fierz-David: *Dream of Poliphilo*." (780–81) E. 1950c repub., trans. rev.   1749–52

119. "Foreword to Crottet: *Mondwald*." (782–83) Trans. from G. 1949c.   1753–54

120. "Foreword to Jacobi: *Paracelsus: Selected Writings*." (784–85) E. 1951b repub., sl. rev.   1755–59

121. "Foreword to Kankeleit: *Das Unbewusste als Keimstätte des Schöpferischen*." (786) "Jung's Contribution." (786–87) Trans. from G. 1959d.   1760–68

106. «Alchemie und Psychologie.» Lexikonartikel für die *Encyclopaedia Hebraica*, 1948 deutsch geschrieben. Vgl. Hebr. 1950/51a.

107. «Jerome Schloss zum Gedächtnis.» (815–16) Englisch gesprochen in memoriam J. S., 1927.

108. «Vorwort zu Schmid-Guisan: *Tag und Nacht*.» (817–19) Nachdruck von D. 1931d.

109. «Dr. Hans Schmid-Guisan: In memoriam.» (819–20) Nachdruck von D. 1932d.

110. «Vorwort zu Schmitz' ‹Märchen vom Fischotter›.» (821–23) Nachdruck von D. 1932b.

111. «Existe-t-il une poésie de signe Freudien?» (824–25) Deutsch geschrieben, französisch pub. Vgl. Fr. 1932b.

112. «Vorwort zu Gilbert: *The Curse of Intellect*.» Üb. aus engl. Ms., dat. Jan. 1934. Das Buch ist nie erschienen.

113. «Vorwort zu Jung: *Wirklichkeit der Seele*.» (827–28) Nachdruck von D. 1934b,1.

114. «Vorwort zu Mehlich: *J. H. Fichtes Seelenlehre und ihre Beziehung zur Gegenwart*.» (829–31) Nachdruck von D. 1935e.

115. «Geleitwort zu von Koenig-Fachsenfeld: *Wandlungen des Traumproblems von der Romantik bis zur Gegenwart*.» (831–35) Nachdruck D. 1935d.

116. «Begleitwort zu Gilli: *Der dunkle Bruder*.» (836–38) Nachdruck von D. 1938d.

117. «Gérard de Nerval.» (839) Nachdruck von D. 1946d.

118. «Vorwort zu Fierz-David: *Der Liebestraum des Poliphilo*.» (840–42) Nachdruck von D. 1947b.

119. «Vorwort zu Crottet: *Mondwald*.» (843–44) Nachdruck von D. 1949c.

120. «Vorwort zu Jacobi: *Paracelsus: Selected Writings*.» (845–46) Deutsch geschrieben für E. 1951b.

121. «Geleitwort zu Kankeleit: *Das Unbewußte als Keimstätte des Schöpferischen*.» (847–48) «Jungs Beitrag» (848–49) Nachdruck von D. 1959d.

122. «Vorwort zu Serrano: *The Visits of the Queen of Sheba.*» (850) Üb. aus Typoskript. Vgl. E. 1960b und 1966c,1.
123. «Y a-t-il un vrai bilinguisme?» (851) Üb. aus Fr. 1961d.
124. «Besprechung von Heyer: *Der Organismus der Seele.*» (855–56) Nachdruck von D. 1933d.
125. «Besprechung von Heyer: *Praktische Seelenheilkunde.*» (856–58) Nachdruck von D. 1936d.
126. «Über das ‹*Rosarium philosophorum*›.» (859–62) Nachdruck aus D. 1938b.
127. «Vorwort zu einer indischen Zeitschrift für Psychotherapie [*Psychotherapy*, I/1].» (863) Üb. aus E. 1956e.
128. «Über Bilder in der psychiatrischen Diagnostik.» (864) Nachdruck von D. 1959h.
129. «Vorwort zu Evans: *The Problem of the Nervous Child.*» (867–68) Üb. aus engl. Ms., dat. Okt. 1919. Vgl. E. 1920a.
130. «Einleitung zu Harding: *The Way of All Women.*» (869–72) Deutsch geschrieben, dat. Feb. 1932. Vgl. E. 1933b.
131. «Ein Gespräch mit C. G. Jung über Tiefenpsychologie und Selbsterkenntnis.» (873–82) Nachdruck von D. 1943f.
132. «Geleitwort zu Spier: *The Hands of Children.*» (883–84) Deutsch geschrieben, dat. 1944. Vgl. E. 1944b.
133. «Vorrede zur hebräischen Ausgabe von [Jung]: *Psychologie und Erziehung.*» (885) Deutsch geschrieben, dat. Juni 1955. Vgl. Hebr. 1958a.

Addenda.

134. «Vorwort zu *Psychologische Abhandlungen*, Bd.I.» (889) Nachdruck von D. 1914c.
135. «Ansprache bei der Überreichung des Jung Codex [längere Fassung].» Vgl. 97, oben.

GW 19 *Bibliographie.* Ed. by Lilly Jung-Merker and Elizabeth Rüf. 1983. pp. 286.

GW 20 Index volume in preparation.

CW A *The Zofingia Lectures.* Trans. by Jan Van Heurck [from typescript prepared by the Jung family from the manuscript], with intro. by Marie-Louise von Franz. (Collected Works, Supplementary Vol. A, edited by William McGuire.) 1983. pp. 118. With 3 illustrs. and 2 facsimiles.

CW B *Psychology of the Unconscious. A Study of the Transformations and Symbolism of the Libido. A Contribution to the History of the Evolution of Thought.* Trans. by Beatrice M. Hinkle. (Collected Works, Supplementary Vol. B.) E. 1916b repub. in the format and typography of the CW, with intro. by William McGuire. 1992. pp. 447. With 6 plates. [Orig. intro. by Hinkle omitted.]

Author's Note (xxvii)

III

SEMINAR NOTES

SEMINAR NOTES

References are added, in square brackets, to the copies in the Kristine Mann Library, Analytical Psychology Club of New York. * = not examined.

1923 [*Human Relationships in Relation to the Process of Individuation.*] Unpub. typescript. 27 + 11 pp. Given at Polzeath, Cornwall, England, July 1923. Unauthorized longhand notes taken for their own use by M. Esther Harding and Kristine Mann. Also known as the "Cornwall Seminar." [KML 1]

1925a [*Analytical Psychology.*] *Notes on the Seminar in Analytical Psychology* ... [Comp. by Cary F. de Angulo and rev. by C. G. Jung.] Arranged by members of the class. Zurich: multigraphed typescript. pp. 227. Figs. [1925: 1st edn.] Given in Zurich, 23 Mar.–6 July 1925. Indexed. Cf. Sem. 1939 index. Spine title: *Analytical Psychology.* [KML 2]

Same. [n.d.: 2nd edn.] Retyped, typographical errors corrected, diagrams redrawn, otherwise seemingly unchanged. [Copy in V. A. Detloff Library, C. G. Jung Inst., San Francisco.]

[1989] Same. *Analytical Psychology.* Notes of the Seminar Given in 1925 by C. G. Jung. Ed., with intro., by William McGuire. With addenda. pp. 160, 1989. Princeton University Press (B.S. 99 [3]). London: Routledge.

1925b [*Dreams and Symbolism.*] Lectures at Swanage. Photocopied typescript. pp. 101. Given at Swanage, England, July–Aug. 1925. From unauthorized longhand notes taken by M. Esther Harding. Also known as "Swanage Seminar." [KML 3]

1928–30 *Dream Analysis.* Notes of the Seminars in Analytical Psychology ... [1930: 1st edn.] Zurich: multigraphed typescript. 6 pts. in 5 vols. 1938: New [2d, rev.] edn. 1958: 3d [unalt.] edn. Zurich: typewriter comp., offset. 2 vols. 1972: 4th [unalt.] edn. Given in Zurich, 7 Nov. 1928–25 June 1930.

Contents of 1st edn./2d edn. (by vols.):

1: 7 Nov.–12 Dec. 1928. Arranged by Anne Chapin. pp. 68. / Comp. and ed. by Mary Foote from notes of Anne Chapin and Ethel Taylor. pp. 67.

2: 23 Jan.–26 June 1929. Comp. and ed. by Charlotte H. Deady. pp. 285. / Same, ed. by Carol Baumann, with Jung's corrs. pp. 176.

3: 9 Oct.–11 Dec. 1929. Comp. and ed. by Mary Foote. pp. 212. / pp. 118.

4: 22 Jan.–26 Mar. 1930. Comp. and ed. by Mary Foote. pp. 190. / pp. 106.

5: 7 May–25 June 1930. Comp. and ed. by Mary Foote. Includes index of dreams in all vols. pp. 219. / Excludes index of dreams. pp. 120.

Contents of 3d edn. (by vols.):

1: 7 Nov. 1928–26 June 1929. As vols. 1–2 of 2d edn. pp. 215.

2: 9 Oct. 1929–25 June 1930. As vols. 3–5 of 2d edn. pp. 298.

4th edn. is identical with 3d.

[1984] Same. *Dream Analysis*. Notes of the Seminar Given in 1928–1930 by C. G. Jung. Ed., with intro., by William McGuire. 1984. Princeton University Press (B.S. 99: [1]); London: Routledge & Kegan Paul. pp. 767. "The text . . . is that of the 2nd edition, 1938 . . . ; the same text, unaltered, was privately issued in printed form, 1958 and 1972."

[1991] Same. *Traumanalyse*. Nach Aufzeichnungen des Seminars 1928–1930. [Supplementary vol. to the Gesammelte Werke.] Edited by William McGuire. Tr. from the foregoing [1984] by Brigitte Stein. Olten: Walter. p. 811.

1930–31 *Bericht über das deutsche Seminar* . . . Comp. and ed. by Olga von Koenig-Fachsenfeld. 1931–32, 2d ptg. Stuttgart: Privately printed. 2 vols. Given in Küsnacht/Zurich, 6 Oct. 1930–10 Oct. 1931. Contents (vols.):

1: 6–11 Oct. 1930. 113 pp. Figs. + 21 plates. Also contains R. Heyer: "Bericht über C. G. Jungs analytisches Seminar." *Zentralblatt für Psychotherapie* . . . , 4:1, 104–10.

2: 5–10 Oct. 1931. 153 pp. Figs. + 16 plates.

Spine title: *Deutsches Seminar*. ?Also known as *Zur Psychologie der Individuation*. [KML 8,9]

1930–34 [*Interpretation of Visions*.] Notes of the Seminars in Analytical Psychology. Ed. by Mary Foote. Autumn 1930–Winter 1934. Zurich: multigraphed typescript. 11 vols. + 1 of 29 plates. *1939–41: New edn. Given in Zurich, 15 Oct. 1930–21 Mar. 1934. Indexed in Sem. 1932b index and Sem. 1939 index. Spine title: *Visions*. [KML ?]

Excerpts pub. in 10 installments, each titled "The Interpretation of Visions. Excerpts from the Notes of Mary Foote." Selected and ed. by Jane A. Pratt. *Spring 1960–69*. New York: Analytical Psychology Club. Installments:

1. 30 Oct.–5 Nov. 1930. *Spring 1960*. pp. 107–48.
2. 12 Nov.–9 Dec. 1930. *Spring 1961*. pp. 109–51.
3. 13 Jan.–25 Mar. 1931. *Spring 1962*. pp. 107–57.
4. 6 May–24 June 1931. *Spring 1963*. pp. 102–47.
5. 11 Nov.–16 Dec. 1931. *Spring 1964*. pp. 97–138.
6. 16 Dec.–10 Feb. 1932. *Spring 1965*. pp. 100–41.
7. 17 Feb.–9 Mar. 1932. *Spring 1966*. pp. 121–53.
8. 9 Mar.–22 June 1932. *Spring 1967*. pp. 86–147.
9. 1 June 1932–18 Jan. 1933. *Spring 1968*. pp. 53–132.
10. 25 Jan.–21 June 1933. *Spring 1969*. pp. 7–72.

Republ. as *The Visions Seminars*. With parts 11–13 ed. by Patricia Berry. Zurich: Spring Publs., 1976. 2 vols. pp. 534, 28 pls.

1932a With J. W. Hauer: *The Kundalini Yoga*. Notes on the seminar given by J. W. Hauer with Psychological Commentary by C. G. Jung. Comp. by Mary Foote. Autumn 1932. [1st edn.] Zurich: multigraphed typescript. pp. 216. illus. 1940: New [2d] edn. Given at the Psychologischer Club Zurich, by Hauer 3–8 Oct. and by Jung 12, 19, and 26 Oct. and 2 Nov. 1932. 1st edn. contains the following material of Jung's:

1. "Psychological Commentary." Lectures I–IV. (131–216) Lectures I–III given in English. Lecture IV given in German, "arranged by [Toni] Wolff for the report of the German seminar, with additional material from Dr. Jung," and trans. by Cary F. Baynes.

Also known as the "Tantra Yoga Seminars." [KML 10]

Lectures I–IV repub., sl. rev., as "Psychological Commentary on Kundalini Yoga," *Spring 1975*, 1–32 and *1976*, 1–31. Zurich: Analytical Psychology Club of New York.

Also issued in a German version: *Bericht über das Seminar von Prof. Dr. J. W. Hauer.* 3–8 Oktober 1932 im Psychologischer Club Zurich. 1933: Zurich: multigraphed typescript. Contains the following Jung material:

1. "Erstes-Viertes englische(s) Seminar(e)." (105–48) [?Trans. and] ed. by Linda Fierz and Toni Wolff from the notes of the English seminars, with the exception of the fourth seminar, as noted above under the English version.

2. "Westliche Parallelen zu den tantrischen Symbolen." (153–58) Condensed version of seminar given during the same period as those above.

1932b [*Index to Dream Analysis and Interpretation of Visions; Notes of the English Seminars,*] Autumn 1928–Spring 1932. Comp. by Carol Sawyer [Baumann]. 1932: Zurich: multigraphed typescript. 36 pp. Includes chronological list of dreams and visions, and list of reference books mentioned. Incorporated in Sem. 1939, index. Paging corresponds to that of the first edns. Spine title: *Index to Dreams and Visions, 1928–32.*

1933 *Bericht über das Berliner Seminar* . . . 1933. [1st edn.]. Berlin: multigraphed typescript. 199 pp. 1950's, 2d ptg. Zurich. 165 pp. Given in Berlin, 26 June–1 July 1933. Contains the following Jung material:

1. "Stenogramm des Seminars . . ." (1–165) Shorthand notes of the seminars.

2. "Stenogramm des Zwiegesprächs von . . . Jung und A. Weizsäcker in der Funkstunde Berlin," 26 June 1933. (166–73) Interview broadcast over Berlin radio. TR.: English: 1977b,1.

Also known as the "Berliner Seminare" and possibly as "Über Träume." A 2d vol. of seminars given in Berlin in 1934 is said to exist.

1933–41 *Modern Psychology.* Notes on lectures . . . [1934?–42, 1st edn.] Zurich: multigraphed typescript. 6 vols. 1959–60: 2d edn. Zurich: Private printed [typewriter comp., offset]. 6 vols. in 3. Given at the Eidgenössische Technische Hochschule, Zurich, 20 Oct. 1933–11 July 1941.

Arrangement of contents in the 1st edn. (vols.):

1: *Modern Psychology.* 20 Oct. 1933–23 Feb. 1934. 77 pp.

2: *Modern Psychology.* 20 Apr. 1934–12 July 1935. 163 pp. Both these vols. comp. and trans., from shorthand notes, by Elizabeth Welsh and Barbara Hannah.

3: *Process of Individuation: [Eastern Texts].* 28 Oct. 1938–23 June 1939. 166 pp. Comp. and trans. by Barbara Hannah.

4: *Process of Individuation: Exercitia Spiritualia of St. Ignatius of Loyola.* 16 June 1939–8 Mar. 1940. pp. 142. Comp. and trans. from the shorthand notes of Riwkah Schärf by Barbara Hannah. 1977/1978: Excerpts (16 June–7 July 1939) in *Spring 1977* (Zurich: Analytical Psychology Club of New York), pp. 183–200, and *1978* (Irving, Texas: Spring Publications), pp. 28–36.

5: *Process of Individuation: Alchemy I.* 8 Nov. 1940–28 Feb. 1941. pp. 157. Comp. and trans. from the shorthand notes of Riwkah Schärf by Barbara Hannah.

6: *Process of Individuation: Alchemy II.* 2 May–11 July 1941. pp. 129 plus index, 130–52. Comp. and trans. from the shorthand notes of Riwkah Schärf by Barbara Hannah.

Arrangement of contents in the 2d edn. (vols.):

1/2: *Modern Psychology.*

3/4: *The Process of Individuation: [Eastern Texts].* (11–101) *The Process of Individuation: Exercitia Spiritualia of St. Ignatius of Loyola.* (102–264)

5/6: *The Process of Individuation: Alchemy I.* (11–130) *The Process of Individuation: Alchemy II.* (135–231). Index (235–53). [KML 15, 16]

1934–39 *Psychological Analysis of Nietzsche's Zarathustra.* Notes on Seminars . . . Ed. by Mary Foote. Spring 1934–Winter 1939. 1st edn. Zurich: multigraphed typescript. 10 vols. + index vol. *[n.d.: 2d edn.] Given in Zurich. Vol. 1–3 typed double-spaced; 4–10 single-spaced.* In the 2d edn., spacing is the same in all vols. [KML 17, 18]

Extracts of vol. 7 pub. as follows: [1] "Answer by Dr. Jung to a Question Concerning the Archaic Elements in the Self. Zurich Seminar June 3, 1936." *Bull. APC*, 30:5 (May), 14–19. A version, taken from some student's notes, of Jung's spoken reply given in the course of his seminar, Zurich, 3 June 1936. (The seminar notes above contain a dif. version, Pt. 7, pp. 80–85.) [2] "Comments on a Passage from Nietzsche's Zarathustra (1936)." *Spring 1972*. pp. 149–61. Zurich: Analytical Psychology Club of New York. Excerpted from the seminar notes, Pt. 7, Lecture 2 (13 May 1936), pp. 18–29, and slightly re-edited.

Index vol.: *Index of the Notes on Psychological Analysis of Nietzsche's Zarathustra* . . . Vols. 1–10, 1934–1939 [1st edn.]. Comp. by Mary Briner. 1942, Zurich: multigraphed typescript. 58 pp. [KML 19]

[1988] Same. *Nietzsche's "Zarathustra."* Notes of the Seminar Given in 1934–1939 by C. G. Jung. Ed., with intro., by James L. Jarrett. 1988. Princeton University Press (B.S. 99: [2]); London: Routledge & Kegan Paul. Vol. I, pp. 1–764; Vol. II, pp. 767–1546. "The text . . . is that of the multigraphed version which Mary Foote . . . issued privately in ten volumes from approximately 1934 to 1940."

1934 *[Bericht über das Basler Seminar.]* 1–6 October 1934. No editor named. Basel, 1935: multigraphed typescript, untitled. pp. 89.

1935 *Fundamental Psychological Conceptions. A Report of Five Lectures* . . . Ed. by Mary Barker and Margaret Game for the Analytical Psychology Club, London, 1936. London: multigraphed typescript. 235 pp. Given under the auspices of the Institute of Medical Psychology, London, 30 Sept.–4 Oct. 1935. Pub., sl. rev., with title change, as E. 1968a and CW 18,1. Also known as the "London Lectures" and as the "Tavistock Lectures." [KML 20] TR.: GW 18,1.

1935–36 *Lectures at the ETH, Zurich, Oct. 1935–July 1936. Comp. by Barbara Hannah, Una Gauntlett Thomas, and Elizabeth Baumann.

1936–37a *Dream Symbols of the Individuation Process.* Ed. from members' notes by Kristine Mann, M. Esther Harding, and Eleanor Bertine, with the help of Sallie Pinckney. New York: multigraphed typescript. 1937–38. 2 vols. Based on shorthand transcripts "as near verbatim as possible." Contents (vols.):
    1. Seminar at Bailey Island, Maine. 20–25 Sept. 1936. Also known as the "Bailey Island Seminar."
    2. Seminar in New York City, 16–18, 25–26 Oct. 1937. Also known as the "New York Seminar." [KML 22]

1936–37b *Seminar über Kinderträume und ältere Literatur über Traum-Interpretation.* Ed. by Hans H. Baumann. [?1937] Zurich: multigraphed typescript. 115 pp. Given at the Eidgenössische Technische Hochschule, Zurich, Winter Semester 1936–37. Spine title: *Kinderträume. W.S. 1936–37.* [KML 21] Cf. below, [1987], II and VI.

Excerpt trans. and pub. as follows: "A Seminar with C. G. Jung: Comments on A Child's Dream (1936–37)." *Spring 1974.* pp. 200–23. Zurich: Analytical Psychology Club of New York. Trans. by Eugene H. Henley from the seminar above.

1937 * *Bericht über die Berliner Vorträge.* 28–29 September 1937. Ed. by Marianne Stark. Berlin, 1937: multigraphed typescript. pp. 55, with 52 photographs.

1938–39 *Psychologische Interpretation von Kinderträumen und ältere Literatur über Träume.* Ed. by Liliane Frey and Riwkah Schärf from stenographic transcripts. [n.d. 1st edn.] [1950's] 2d edn. Zurich: [Privately printed for the C. G. Jung-Institut] Eidgenössische Technische Hochschule. 217 pp. Given at the ETH, Zurich, 25 Oct. 1938–7 Mar. 1939. Spine title: *Kinderträume, W.S. 1938/39.* A supplementary vol. of students' papers, made up for the 1st edn., has been added to the 2d edn. as an "Anhang." [KML 24, 25] Trans. as follows: *Psychological Interpretation of Children's Dreams.* Notes on Lectures ... 1938–39. Zurich: multigraphed typescript. 143 pp. Trans. from the German above by Mary Foote, with the help of Cornelia Brunner. Spine title: *Children's Dreams.* [KML 23] Cf. below, [1987], I and III.

1939 [*Index to Analytical Psychology, Dream Analysis, and Interpretation of Visions*; Notes of the English Seminars, 1925–Winter 1934.] Comp. by Mary Briner. 1939. Zurich: multigraphed typescript. 59 pp. Incorporates Sem. 1932b index. Includes list of dreams and visions, list of reference books mentioned, and word index. Paging corresponds to that of the 1st edns. Spine title: *Index 1925–1934.* [KML 4]

1939–40 *Psychologische Interpretation von Kinderträumen.* Ed. by Liliane Frey and Aniela Jaffé from the stenographic transcripts of Riwkah Schärf. Date of 1st edn. not known. 1950's: 2d edn. Zurich: [Privately printed for the C. G. Jung-Institut] Eidgenössische Technische Hochschule. 195 pp. Given at the Hochschule, Zurich, Winter Semester 1939–40. Spine title: *Kinderträume. W.S. 1939/40.* A supplementary vol. of students' papers, made up for the 1st edn., has been added to the 2d edn. as an "Anhang." [KML 26, 27] Cf. below, [1987], IV.

1940–41 *Kindertraumseminar.* Winter 1940–41. Ed. by Rivkah Kluger-Schärf and M.-L. von Franz, from the notes of Ignaz Reichstein, Walter Huber, K. W. Bash, Margrit Ostrowski-Sachs, E. Levy, M.-L. von Franz, and Carol Baumann. Privately printed. 1976. pp. 173. Given at the Eidgenossische Technische Hochschule, Zurich. Cf. below, [1987], V.

[1987] *Kinderträume.* Seminare. [Supplementary vol. to the Gesammelte Werke.] Ed. by Lorenz Jung and Maria Meyer-Grass. Olten: Walter. pp. 678. Contents:

    I. Zur Methodik der Trauminterpretation.† (15–41)
    II. Seminar über Kinderträume (WS 1936/37). (42–107)
    III. Psychologische Interpretation von Kinderträumen und ältere Literatur über Träume (WS 1938/39). (108–249)
    IV. Psychologische Interpretation von Kinderträumen (WS 1939/40). (250–391)
    V. Kindertraumseminar (WS 1940/41). (392–588)
    VI. Anhang: Ältere Literatur über Traum-Interpretation (WS 1936–37). (589–643)

† Transcript of the seminar meetings of 25 Oct. and 8 Nov. 1938.

INDEX 1: TITLES

The contents of composite volumes (anthologies, paperback extracts, etc.) published after 1975 are not indexed. Names of authors for whose books Jung wrote a foreword, *Vorwort*, preface, etc., are included in Index 2. Abbreviations: Fr. = French, He. = Hebrew, Hu. = Hungarian, It. = Italian, Sp. = Spanish.

A

Abstracts, *Folia neuro-biologica*: Jung, Métral, Lombard, Claparède, Flournoy, Leroy, Lemaître, G. 1908c; Piéron, Revault d'Allones, Hartenberg, Dumas, Dromard, Marie, Janet, Pascal, Vigouroux et Juquelier, G. 1908i; Varendonck, Claparède, Katzaroff, Maeder, Rouma, G. 1908l

"Abstracts of the Psychological Works of Swiss Authors (1910)": CW 18,26

"Adaptation": E. 1970c,1, CW 18,35

"Adaptation, Individuation, Collectivity (1916)": CW 18,35

"Address at the Presentation of the Jung Codex": G. 1975a,4, CW 18,97

"Address Given at the Opening Meeting of the C. G. Jung Institute of Zurich, 24 April 1948": E. 1948b, CW 18,43

"Ärztliches Gutachten über einen Fall von Simulation geistiger Störung": G. 1904c, GW 1,7

"After the Catastrophe": E. 1946a,

1947a,6, CW 10,11

"Aims of Psychotherapy, The": E. 1933a,3, CW 16,5

Aion: G. 1951a, 1976b, E. 1959n, 1968j, GW 9,ii; CW 9,ii; Excerpts: E. 1950a, 1958a,2, 1971a,6

Alchemical Studies: E. 1967g, CW 13

"Alchemie und Psychologie": GW 18,106

"Alchemistic Text Interpreted As If It Were a Dream, An": E. 1947c

"Alchemy and Psychology": CW 18,106

Alchemy and the Occult. A Catalogue ..., Prefatory Note: E. 1968d, CW 18,104

"Alkhimiah we-psykhologiah": He. 1950/51a

"Allgemeine Aspekte der Psychoanalyse": G. 1972e,9, GW 4,10

"Allgemeine Beschreibung der Typen": G. 1972d,2, GW 6,3,10

"Allgemeine Gesichtspunkte zur Psychologie des Traumes": G. 1928b,3, 1948b,4, GW 8,9

Allgemeines zur Komplextheorie: G. 1934a, 1948b,3, GW 8,3

conscious," E. 1939a,3, 1959a,5,
CW 9,i,1
Aspects du drame contemporain: Fr.
1948a
Aspects of the Feminine: E. 1982a
Aspects of the Masculine: E. 1989b
"Association, Dream, and Hysteri-
cal Symptom": CW 2,7
"Association, Dream, and Hysteri-
cal Symptoms": E. 1918a,5
"Association Method, The": E.
1910a, 1916a,3, 1917a,3, CW
2,10
"Associations d'idées familiales":
Fr. 1907a
"Associations of Normal Subjects,
The": E. 1918a,1, CW 2,1
"Assoziation, Traum und hyste-
risches Symptom": G. 1906j,
1909a,1, GW 2,7
"Assoziationsmethode, Die": GW
2,10
"Astrological Experiment, An
(1958)": CW 18,48
"Astrologisches Experiment, Ein":
G. 1958f, GW 18,48
"Aufgang einer neuen Welt, Der":
G. 1930e, GW 10,20
Aufsätze zur Zeitgeschichte: G. 1946a;
Vorwort zu: GW 10,9; Nachwort
zu: GW 10,13
"Aus einem Brief an einen prote-
stantischen Theologen": GW
11,24
Aux frontières de la connaissance ...,
"Préface": Fr. 1959a

B

"Bailey Island Seminar": Seminar
Notes, 1936–37a
"Banalized beyond Endurance": E.
1958i
"Basic Postulates of Analytic Psy-

chology, The": E. 1933a,9, CW
8,13
Basic Writings of C. G. Jung: E.
1959a, 1991c
"Bedeutung der Analytischen Psy-
chologie für die Erziehung,
Die": G. 1971a,4, GW 17,3
"Bedeutung der Psychologie für
die Gegenwart, Die": G.
1934b,3, GW 10,7
"Bedeutung der schweizerischen
Linie im Spektrum Europas,
Die": G. 1928e, GW 10,19
"Bedeutung des Unbewussten für
die individuelle Erziehung, Die":
G. 1971a,5, GW 17,6
*Bedeutung des Vaters für das Schicksal
des Einzelnen, Die*: G. 1909c,
1949a, 1971a,1, GW 4,14
"Bedeutung von Konstitution und
Vererbung für die Psychologie,
Die": G. 1929i, 1973c,2, GW 8,4
"Begabte, Der": 1946b,3, GW 17,5
"Begriff des kollektiven Unbewus-
sten, Der": GW 9,i,2
"Begrüssungsansprache zum Ach-
ten Internationalen Ärtzlichen
Kongress für Psychotherapie,
Bad Nauheim (1935)": GW
10,30
"Begrüssungsansprache zum
Neunten Internationalen Ärzt-
lichen Kongress für Psychother-
apie, Kopenhagen (1937)": GW
10,32
"Begrüssungsansprache zum
Zehnten Internationalen Ärtz-
lichen Kongress für Psycho-
therapie, Oxford (1938)": GW
10,33
"Beispiele europäischer Mandalas": G. 1929b,I,7, 1938a,4
"Beitrag zur Kenntnis des Zahlentraumes, Ein": G. 1911e,

"Beitrag" (*cont.*)
  1972e,5, GW 4,5
"Beitrag zur Psychologie des Ge-
  rüchtes, Ein": G. 1910q,
  1972e,4, GW 4,4
"Beiträge zur Symbolik": G. 1911f,
  GW 18,34
"Beiträge zur Symbolik des
  Selbst": G. 1951a, 1954c,4, GW
  9,ii
"Bemerkung zur Tauskschen Kri-
  tik der Nelkenschen Arbeit,
  Eine": G. 1913d, GW 18,31
"Bericht über Amerika": G. 1910n,
  GW 18,64
Bericht über das Basler Seminar:
  Seminar Notes, 1934
Bericht über das Berliner Seminar
  . . . : Seminar Notes, 1933
Bericht über das deutsche Seminar
  . . . : Seminar Notes, 1930–31
"Bericht über das Vereinsjahr
  1910–11": G. 1911g
Bericht über die Berliner Vorträge:
  Seminar Notes, 1937
"Berliner Seminare": Seminar
  Notes, 1933
"Besprechungen von psychia-
  trischer Literatur": GW 18,20
*Bevezetés a tudattalan pszichológiá-
  jába*: Hu. 1948a
Bewusstes und Unbewusstes: G. 1957a
"Bewusstsein, Unbewusstes und
  Individuation": G. 1939e, GW
  9,i,10
*Bezeihung der Psychotherapie zur Seel-
  sorge, Die*: G. 1932a
*Beziehungen zwischen dem Ich und
  dem Unbewussten, Die*: G. 1928a,
  1935a, 1990c, GW 7,2
"Blick in die Verbrecherseele. Das
  Doppelleben des Kriminellen
  . . .": G. 1933a, GW 18,13
"Bologna Enigma, The": E. 1946f

"Brief an Keyhoe": GW 18,82
"Brief an Pasteur Lachat": GW
  18,99
"Brief an Père Bruno O.C.D.":
  GW 18,98
"Brief an *The Listener*. Januar
  1960": GW 11,25
"Brief von Prof. C. G. Jung an den
  Verfasser": G. 1964a
"Brief zur Frage der Synchronizi-
  tät, Ein": G. 1961c
Briefe: I, 1906–45: G. 1972a; II,
  1946–55: G. 1972b; III, 1956–
  61: G. 1973a
"Briefe über Synchronizität": GW
  18,49
"Briefe von Carl Gustav Jung an
  Sabina Spielrein (1908–1919)":
  G. 1986d
Briefwechsel (with Freud): G. 1974a,
  1984g
"Brother Klaus": E. 1946c, CW
  11,6
"Bruder Klaus": G. 1933c, GW
  11,6

C

C. G. Jung: Bild und Wort: G. 1977a
C. G. Jung: Word and Image: E.
  1979b
"C. G. Jung et l'astrologie": Fr.
  1954b
*C. G. Jung im Gespräch. Interviews,
  Reden, Begegnungen*: G. 1986c
C. G. Jung Lesebuch, Das: G. 1983a
"C. G. Jung on Flying Saucers": E.
  1954h
"C. G. Jung on the Question of
  Flying Saucers": E. 1955i,
  1959i,3
*C. G. Jung Speaking: Interviews and
  Encounters*: E. 1977b
"Case of Hysterical Stupor in a

10,28; VIII (1935), CW 10,29
Editorial note to the series *Psycho-logische Abhandlungen*: G. 1914c
"Editorial Preface to the *Jahrbuch*":
CW 18,23
"Effect of Technology on the Human Psyche, The": CW 18,76
"Ehe als psychologische Beziehung, Die": G. 1925b, 1931a,11,
GW 17,8
Eidgenössische Technische Hochschule Lectures. *See* ETH Lectures
100 Briefe. Eine Auswahl: G. 1975b
Einführung in das Wesen der Mythologie: G. 1941c, 1951b
"Einige Aspekte der modernen Psychotherapie": G. 1972c,4,
GW 16,4
"Einige Bemerkungen zu den Visionen des Zosimos": G. 1938c
"Einleitung in die religionspsychologische Problematik der Alchemie": G. 1944a,2, 1957a,2,
GW 12,3,I
Einzelne in der Gesellschaft, Der: G. 1971a
"Entlarvung der viktorianischen Epoche. Freud kulturhistorisch gesehen": G. 1932f
"Entschleierung der Seele, Die":
G. 1931g
"Epilog zu Jung: *L'Homme à la découverte de son âme*": GW 18,72
"Epilogue to 'Essays on Contemporary Events' ": E. 1947a,7, CW 10,13
"Epilogue to Jung: *L'Homme à la découverte de son âme*": CW 18,72;
Fr. 1944a,9, 1962a,9
"Erdbedingtheit der Psyche, Die":
G. 1927a
Erinnerungen, Träume, Gedanken: G. 1962a

"Erklärung der Redaktion": G. 1913b
"Erlösungsvorstellungen in der Alchemie, Die": G. 1937a, 1944a,4,
GW 12,3,III
Erlösungsvorstellungen in der Alchemie. (Psychologie und Alchemie 2.): G. 1984f
Essays on a Science of Mythology ... :
E. 1949a, 1963a, 1969a
Essays on Contemporary Events: E.
1947a, 1989a; "Preface": E.
1947a,1, CW 10,9
Essential Jung, The: E. 1983b
ETH Lectures: Seminar Notes,
1933–41, 1935–36
"Europäischer Kommentar." *Das Geheimnis der goldenen Blüte*: G.
1938a,3, 1957b,3
"Examples of European Mandalas": E. 1931a,2, CW 13,1, pp. 56ff.
"Excerpts from Selected Letters":
E. 1971b
Excerpts of letters to Illing (26 Jan. & 10 Feb. 1955): G. 1956d
"Existe-t-il une poésie de signe Freudien?": GW 18,111
"Experiences Concerning the Psychic Life of the Child": E. 1910a,3
"Experimental Observations on the Faculty of Memory": CW 2,4
Experimental Researches: E. 1973f,
CW 2
"Experimentelle Beobachtungen über das Erinnerungsvermögen": G. 1905c, GW 2,4
Experimentelle Untersuchungen: G. 1979a, GW 2
"Experimentelle Untersuchungen über Assoziationen Gesunder":
G. 1904a, 1906a,1, GW 2,1

F

Psychological Problems of Al-
chemy": E. 1959a,10, CW 12,2,I
(1st edn.), 3,I (2nd edn.)
"Introduction to Toni Wolff's
Studies in Jungian Psychology":
CW 10,18
"Introductions by C. G. Jung": E.
1950e
"Is There a Freudian Type of Po-
etry?": CW 18,111
"Is There a True Bilingualism?":
CW 18,123

J

"Jahresbericht des Präsidenten der
Internationalen Psychoanaly-
tischen Vereinigung über das
Vereinsjahr 1910/11": GW 18,28
"Jerome Schloss zum Gedächtnis":
GW 18,107
"Jung and Religious Belief": CW
18,103
"Jung on Freud": E. 1962a, 1&6
"Jung on Life after Death": E.
1962a,12
"Jung on the UFO . . .": E. 1959i
"Jung und der religiöse Glaube":
GW 18,103
"Jungian Method of Dream Analy-
sis": E. 1947d
"Jung's Commentary to Brother
Klaus": E. 1946c
"Jung's View of Christianity": E.
1962a,13

K

"Kampf mit dem Schatten, Der":
GW 10,12
Kinderträume. Seminare: G. 1987b;
Seminar Notes, 1936–37b,

1938–39, 1939–40, 1940–41,
[1987]
"Klappentext zur ersten Auflage
von Antwort auf Hiob": GW 11,23
"Kommentar zu Das Geheimnis der
Goldenen Blüte": GW 13,1
"Komplexe und Krankheitsur-
sachen bei Dementia praecox":
G. 1908b
"Kritik über E. Bleuler: 'Zur Theo-
rie des schizophrenen Negativis-
mus' ": G. 1911c, GW 3,3
"Kryptomnesie": G. 1905a,
1971c,3, GW 1,3
Kundalini Yoga, The: Seminar
Notes, 1932a
"Kurzer Überblick über die Kom-
plexlehre, Ein": GW 2,18

L

"Leben die Bücher noch?": G.
1952h
"Lebensregeln": GW 18,79
"Lebenswende, Die": G. 1931a,10,
GW 8,16
Lectures at the ETH: Seminar
Notes, 1933–41, 1935–36
"Letter from Dr. Jung": E. 1913c
"Letter on Parapsychology and
Synchronicity, A . . .": E. 1961a
"Letter to Keyhoe": CW 18,82
"Letter to Miss Pinckney": E.
1948c
"Letter to Père Lachat": CW 18,99
Letter to the editor [of the Lis-
tener]: E. 1960c
Letter to the editors [of Zürcher
Student] on the effect of technol-
ogy on the psyche: G. 1949g
"Letter to the Second Interna-
tional Congress for Psychiatry
. . . 1957": CW 3,11

word to the English Edition": E.
1951b; Foreword to: CW 18,120
"Paracelsus als Arzt": G. 1941f,
1942a,1, GW 15,2
"Paracelsus als geistige Erscheinung": G. 1942a,2, GW 13,3
"Paracelsus as a Spiritual Phenomenon": CW 13,3
"Paracelsus the Physician": CW
15,2
"Parapsychologie hat uns mit
unerhörten Möglichkeiten be-
kanntgemacht, Die": G. 1956b
Persönlichkeit und Übertragung: G.
1984c
Phénomènes occultes: Fr. 1939a;
Foreword to: CW 18,5; Vorrede
zu, GW 18,5
"Phenomenology of the Spirit in
Fairy Tales, The": E. 1954b,1,
1958a,3, 1970a,3, CW 9,i,8
"Philosophical Tree, The": CW
13,5
"Philosophische Baum, Der": G.
1945g, 1954b,7, GW 13,5
"Picasso": G. 1932g, 1934b,8, GW
15,9; E. 1940a, 1953i, CW 15,9
"Plight of Woman in Europe,
The": E. 1930d
Portable Jung, The: E. 1971a
"Practical Use of Dream-Analysis,
The": E. 1974a,5, CW 16,12
Practice of Psychotherapy, The . . . : E.
1954i, 1966g, CW 16
"Praktische Verwendbarkeit der
Traumanalyse, Die": G. 1931c,
1934b,4, GW 16,12
Praxis der Psychotherapie: G. 1958d,
GW 16
"Préface." Georges Duplain: *Aux
frontières de la connaissance*: Fr.
1959a
"Preface," *Psychotherapy* (Calcutta):
E. 1956e, CW 18,127

"Preface by C. G. Jung": E. 1954g
"Preface by C. G. Jung: *Ostasien
Denkt Anders* . . .": E. 1953f
"Preface by Dr. Jung": E. 1960d
"Preface to an Indian Journal of
Psychotherapy": CW 18,127
"Preface to de Laszlo: *Psyche and
Symbol*": CW 18,62
"Preface to 'Essays on Contempo-
rary Events' ": CW 10,9
"Prefaces to *Collected Papers on An-
alytical Psychology*": CW 4,13
"Prefacio" and "Prólogo . . . a la
edición española" to Jacobi: *La
psicologia de C. G. Jung*: Sp.
1947a
"Present State of Applied Psychol-
ogy, The": CW 18,9
"Presidential Address . . . 1935":
CW 10,30
"Presidential Address . . . 1937":
CW 10,32
"Presidential Address . . . 1938":
E. 1938b, CW 10,33
"Press Communiqué on Visiting
the United States": CW 18,69
"Pressemitteilung beim Besuch der
Vereinigten Staaten": GW 18,69
"Principles of Practical Psychother-
apy": CW 16,2
*Problema dell'inconscio nella psicologia
moderna, Il*: It. 1959c
"Probleme der modernen Psy-
chotherapie, Die": G. 1929d,
1931a,2, GW 16,6
Probleme der Psychotherapie: G.
1972c
"Problems of Modern Psychother-
apy": E. 1931d, 1933a,2, CW
16,6
Process of Individuation: Alchemy I:
Seminar Notes, 1933–41
Process of Individuation: Alchemy II:
Seminar Notes, 1933–41

Process of Individuation: [Eastern
Texts]: Seminar Notes, 1933–41
Process of Individuation: Exercitia
Spiritualia . . . : Seminar Notes,
1933–41
"Psychanalyse devant la poésie, La.
Existe-t-il une poésie de signe
'freudien'?": Fr. 1932b
Psyche and Symbol. A Selection from
the Writings of C. G. Jung: E.
1958a, 1991b; "Preface": E.
1958a,1, CW 18,62
Psychiatric Studies: E. 1957k, 1970e,
CW 1
Psychiatrie und Okkultismus: G.
1971c
Psychiatrische Studien: G. 1966a,
GW 1
"Psychic Conflicts in a Child": E.
1969c,1, CW 17,1
"Psychoanalyse": G. 1912e
"Psycho-analyse, La": Fr. 1913b
"Psychoanalyse und Assoziations-
experiment": G. 1906a,4, 1906i,
GW 2,5
"Psychoanalyse und Seelsorge": G.
1928g, 1971d,3, GW 11,8
"Psycho-analysis": E. 1913d, 1915d
"Psychoanalysis": E. 1915d,
1916a,8, 1917a,8
"Psycho-Analysis and Association
Experiments": E. 1918a,4
"Psychoanalysis and Association
Experiments": CW 2,5
"Psychoanalysis and Neurosis":
CW 4,11
"Psychoanalysis and the Cure of
Souls": CW 11,8
Psychoanalytic Years, The: E. 1974f
Psychogenese der Geisteskrankheiten:
G. 1968c, GW 3
Psychogenesis of Mental Disease, The:
E. 1960f, CW 3
Psychological Analysis of Nietzsche's

Zarathustra. Notes on the Seminar:
Seminar Notes, 1934–39
"Psychological Approach to the
Dogma of the Trinity, A": CW
11,2
"Psychological Aspects of the
Kore, The": E. 1949a,2,
1963a,2, 1969a, CW 9,i,7
"Psychological Aspects of the
Mother Archetype, The": E.
1943a, 1959a,6, 1970a,1, CW
9,i,4
"Psychological Commentary." The
Kundalini Yoga: Seminar Notes,
1932a
"Psychological Commentary." The
Tibetan Book of the Great Libera-
tion: E. 1954e, CW 11,10
"Psychological Commentary on
'The Tibetan Book of the
Dead,' ": E. 1957f, 1958a,8, CW
11,11
"Psychological Diagnosis of Evi-
dence, The": CW 2,6
"Psychological Factors Determin-
ing Human Behavior": E. 1937a,
CW 8,5
"Psychological Foundations of Be-
lief in Spirits, The": E. 1920b,
1928a,9, CW 8,11
Psychological Interpretation of Chil-
dren's Dreams . . . : Seminar
Notes, 1938–39
"Psychological Methods of Investi-
gation . . . , The": CW 2,17
Psychological Reflections . . . : E.
1953a, 1970b
" 'Psychological Reflections' on
Youth and Age": E. 1972e
"Psychological Theory of Types,
A": E. 1933a,4, CW 6,7
"Psychological Types": E. 1925b,
1928a,12, 1971c, CW 6,6
Psychological Types, or, The Psychol-

ogy of Individuation: E. 1923a,
CW 6; Excerpts: E. 1959a,4,
1971a,8
"Psychological View of Conscience,
A": CW 10,16
Psychologie der Übertragung, Die: G.
1946c, 1991b, GW 16,13
*Psychologie der unbewussten Prozesse,
Die. Ein Überblick . . .* : G. 1917a,
1918a
Psychologie und Alchemie: G. 1944a,
1952d, 1972f, 1984,e,f, GW 12
"Psychologie und Dichtung": G.
1930a, 1950a,2, 1954c,2, GW
15,7
Psychologie und Erziehung: G.
1946b; Foreword to the Hebrew
edn. of: He. 1958a; CW 18,133
"Psychologie und nationale Probleme": GW 18,70
"Psychologie und Religion": G.
1971d,1, GW 11,1
Psychologie und Religion . . . : G.
1940a, 1971d, 1991c
"Psychologie und Spiritismus": G.
1948e, GW 18,6
Psychologische Abhandlungen: 1: G.
1914c; 3: 1931a; 4: G. 1934b; 5:
G. 1944a; 6: G. 1948a; 7: G.
1950a; 8: G. 1951a; 9: G. 1954b;
10: G. 1955a; 11: G. 1956a
Psychologische Abhandlungen. Editorial note to the series: G. 1914c
Psychologische Betrachtungen: G.
1945a
"Psychologische Determinanten
des menschlichen Verhaltens":
G. 1973c,3, GW 8,5
"Psychologische Diagnose des
Tatbestandes, Die": G. 1905f,
1906k, GW 2,6
*Psychologische Diagnose des Tatbe-
standes, Die*: G. 1941d
*Psychologische Interpretation von Kin-

derträumen . . .* : Seminar Notes,
1938–39
"Psychologische Typen": G. 1925c,
1972d,4, GW 6,5
Psychologische Typen: G. 1921a,
1960a, 1967d, GW 6
"Psychologische Typologie"
(1931): G. 1931a,6, GW 6,6
"Psychologische Typologie"
(1936): G. 1936b, GW 6,7
"Psychologischen Aspekte des
Mutterarchetypus, Die": G.
1939b, 1954b,4, GW 9,i,4
"Psychologischen Grundlagen des
Geisterglaubens, Die": G.
1928b,5, 1948b,7, GW 8,11
"Psychologischer Kommentar." *Das
tibetische Buch der grossen Be-
freiung*: G. 1955d
"Psychologischer Kommentar zu:
*Das tibetische Buch der grossen Be-
freiung*": GW 11,10
"Psychologischer Kommentar zum
Bardo Thödol": G. 1935f,2, GW
11,11
Psychology and Alchemy: E. 1953j,
1968h, CW 12
Psychology and Education: E. 1969c
"Psychology and Literature": E.
1933a,8, CW 15,7
"Psychology and National Prob-
lems": CW 18,70
"Psychology and Poetry": E. 1930c
"Psychology and Religion": E.
1959a,11, CW 11,1
Psychology and Religion: E. 1938a
*Psychology and Religion: West and
East*: E. 1958k, 1968k, CW 11
"Psychology and Spiritualism": CW
18,6
Psychology and the East: E. 1978b
Psychology and the Occult: E. 1977a
Psychology and Western Religion: E.
1984b

"Recent Thoughts on Schizophrenia": CW 3,9

"Recollections of . . . the U. S.": E. 1971b,4

"Rede anlässlich der Gründungssitzung des C. G. Jung-Institutes Zürich, am 24. April 1948": GW 18,43

Reden Gotamo Buddhos, Die: Statement in publisher's brochure (on): G. 1956c, GW 11,26

"Referate über psychologische Arbeiten schweizerischer Autoren (bis Ende 1909)": G. 1910m, GW 18,26

"Rejoinder to Dr. Bally": G. 1934f; CW 10,26

"Relation of the Ego to the Unconscious, The": E. 1928b,2

"Relations between the Ego and the Unconscious, The": E. 1971a,5, CW 7,2; Excerpts: E. 1959a,3

"Released to United Press from Dr. Jung": E. 1958h

"Religion and Psychology: A Reply to Martin Buber": E. 1973e, CW 18,96

"Religion und Psychologie. Eine Antwort auf Martin Buber": G. 1952j, GW 18,96

"Réponse à la question du bilinguisme": Fr. 1961d

"Report on America (1910)": CW 18,64

"Return to the Simple Life": E. 1945b, CW 18,71

"Review of the Complex Theory, A": CW 8,3

"Reviews of Psychiatric Literature (1906–10)": CW 18,20

"Révolution Mondiale, La": CW 10,21

"Richard Wilhelm": G. 1930c,

1931b, 1962a,15,vii

"Richard Wilhelm: In Memoriam": CW 15,5

"Rise of a New World, The": CW 10,20

"Role of the Unconscious, The": CW 10,1

"Rückkehr zum einfachen Leben": G. 1941e, GW 18,71

"Rules of Life": CW 18,79

"Rundschreiben" (*Zentralblatt* VII, 1934): GW 10,27

S

"Schatten, Animus und Anima": G. 1948f

"Schizophrenia": CW 3,10

"Schizophrenie, Die": G. 1958i, 1973d,5, GW 3,9

Schweizer Lexikon: G. 1949h

Secret of the Golden Flower, The: E. 1931a, 1962b

"Seele und Erde": G. 1931a,8, GW 10,2

"Seele und Tod": G. 1934b,10&h, GW 8,17

"Seelenproblem des modernen Menschen, Das": G. 1928f, 1929e, 1931a,14, GW 10,4

Seelenprobleme der Gegenwart: G. 1931a, 1991f; Forewords to: CW 18,67

"Seelischen Probleme der menschlichen Altersstufen, Die": G. 1930d

Selected Letters of C. G. Jung, 1909–1961: E. 1984a

Seminar über Kinderträume . . . : Seminar Notes, 1936–41

"Seminar with C. G. Jung, A . . .": Seminar Notes, 1936–37b

VII Sermones ad Mortuos . . . : G. 1916a; E. 1925a, 1967b

T

U

"Über die psychoanalytische Behandlung nervöser Leiden": G. 1912h, GW 18,30
"Über die Psychogenese der Schizophrenie": GW 3,7
Über die Psychologie der Dementia praecox: Ein Versuch: G. 1907a, GW 3,1
Über die Psychologie des Unbewussten: G. 1943a, GW 7,1; Foreword to the Hungarian Edn. of: CW 18,36
"Über die psychophysischen Begleiterscheinungen im Assoziationsexperiment": GW 2,12
"Über die Reproduktionsstörungen beim Assoziationsexperiment": G. 1907e, 1909a,2, GW 2,9
"Über 'Flying Saucers' ": GW 18,80
Über Grundlagen der Analytischen Psychologie: G. 1969a
"Über Grundlagen der Analytischen Psychologie. Die Tavistock Lectures": GW 18,1
"Über Halluzination": GW 18,38
"Über hysterisches Verlesen . . .": G. 1904b, 1971c,2, GW 1,2
"Über Komplextheorie": G. 1934a
Über Konflikte der kindlichen Seele: G. 1910k, 1916b, 1939a, 1946b,2, GW 17,1
"Über Mandalasymbolik": G. 1950a,5, GW 9,i,12
"'Über manische Verstimmung'": G. 1903a, 1971c,4, GW 1,4
Über psychische Energetik und das Wesen der Träume: G. 1948b
"Über Psychoanalyse": G. 1972e,10, GW 4,11
"Über Psychoanalyse beim Kinde": G. 1912b
"Über Psychodiagnose": GW 18,85
"Über Psychologie": G. 1933b

"Über Psychotherapie und Wunderheilungen": G. 1959a
"Über Simulation von Geistesstörung": G. 1903b, GW 1,6
"Über spiritistische Erscheinungen": G. 1905e, GW 18,4
"Über Synchronizität": G. 1952f, GW 8,19
". . . Über Tiefenpsychologie und Selbsterkenntnis": G. 1943f, 1947c
"Über Träume": Seminar Notes, 1933
"Über Wiedergeburt": G. 1950a,3, GW 9,i,5
"UFO," E. 1959g
"Ulysses: A Monologue": E. 1953h, CW 15,8
"Ulysses, A Monologue": E. 1949c
"Ulysses . . .": G. 1932e, 1934b,7, GW 15,8
Unbewusste im normalen und kranken Seelenleben, Das . . . Ein Überblick . . . : G. 1926a
"Unconscious in the Normal and Pathological Mind, The": E. 1928b,1
Undiscovered Self, The: E. 1958b, 1990a
"Undiscovered Self (Present and Future), The": CW 10,14

V

"Verschiedenen Aspekte der Wiedergeburt, Die": G. 1940b
Versuch einer Darstellung der psychoanalytischen Theorie. Neun Vorlesungen . . . : G. 1913a, 1955b, 1973b, 1973b,1, GW 4,9
"Versuch einer psychologischen Deutung des Trinitätsdogmas": GW 11,2

1925a, 1938b, 1991g
"Wandlungssymbol in der Messe,
Das": G. 1942c, 1954b,6,
1971d,4, GW 11,3
"Warum adoptiere ich nicht die
'katholische Wahrheit'?": GW
18,88
"Was Indien uns lehren kann":
GW 10,24
"Was ist Psychotherapie?": G.
1935g, 1972c,3, GW 16,3
"Weitere Untersuchungen über
das galvanische Phänomen und
die Respiration bei Normalen
und Geisteskranken": GW 2,14
Welt der Psyche: G. 1954c
"Wenn Christus heute auf Erden
wandelte": GW 18,86
"Westliche Parallelen zu den tan-
trischen Symbolen": Seminar
Notes, 1932a
"What India Can Teach Us": E.
1939c, CW 10,24
"What Is Psychotherapy?": CW 16,3
"Why and How I Wrote My *Answer
to Job*": E. 1956c
"Why I Am Not a Catholic": CW
18,88
Wirklichkeit der Seele: G. 1934b,
1990i; Foreword to: CW 18,113
"Wirklichkeit und Überwirklich-
keit": G. 1932h, GW 8,15
"Wirkung der Technik auf das
seelisch-geistige Leben, Die":
GW 18,76
"Wo leben die Teufel? . . .": G
1950f
"Woman in Europe": E. 1928a,5,
1928c, CW 10,6
"Wotan": G. 1936c, 1946a,2, GW
10,10; E. 1937c, 1947a,3, CW
10,10
"Wotan und der Rattenfänger
. . .": G. 1956e

Y

"Y a-t-il un vrai bilinguisme?": GW
18,123
"Yoga and the West": E. 1936c,
CW 11,12
"Yoga und der Westen": GW 11,12
"Yoga, Zen, and Koestler": E.
1961c
"Your Negroid and Indian Behav-
ior": E. 1930a

Z

"Zeichen am Himmel . . .": G.
1958h
"Zeitgenössisches. (*Neue Zürcher
Zeitung*, CLV, 1934)": G. 1934f;
CW 10,26
"Ziele der Psychotherapie": G.
1929c, 1931a,5, GW 16,5
Zivilisation im Übergang: G. 1974b,
GW 10
Zofingia Lectures, The: E. 1983a,
CW A
"Zu *Antwort auf Hiob*" (1951), GW,
11,21; (1952), GW 11,22
"Zu *Die Reden Gotamo Buddhos*":
GW 11,26
"Zu Jung: *Antwort auf Hiob*": GW
18,95
"Zu *Psychologie und Religion*": GW
11,18
"Zu unserer Umfrage 'Leben die
Bücher noch?' ": G. 1952h
"Zugang zum Unbewussten": G.
1968a
"Zukunft der Parapsychologie,
Die": GW 18,50
"Zum Gedächtnis Richard Wil-
helms": G. 1938a,2, 1957b,2,
GW 15,5
"Zum Problem des Christussym-
bols": GW 11,20

INDEX 2: PERSONAL NAMES

Names of editors, compilers, co-authors, authors for whose books Jung wrote reviews or forewords, persons eulogized, translators, and recipients of letters published elsewhere than in the *Letters* or *Briefe* (which are separate from the CW)—in the German and English entries.

A

Abegg, Lily: G. 1950d; E. 1953f;
  CW/GW 18,92
Adler, Alfred: G. 1934d
Adler, Gerhard: G. 1934d, 1952g;
  E. 1966e, 1973b, 1975b, 1984a,
  CW/GW 18,52, CW/GW 18,55;
  Fr. 1957a; CW ed.
Aldrich, Charles Robert: E.
  1928a,13, 1931b, CW/GW 18,68
Allenby, Amy I.: CW/GW 18,93
Alt, Franz: G. 1983a, 1986a, 1989b
Anshen, Ruth Nanda: E. 1942a
Aschaffenburg, Gustav: G. 1906g,
  GW 4,1; CW 4,1

B

Bach, Georg R.: G. 1956d
Bailey, Paul C.: E. 1968c
Bally, Gustav: G. 1934f; CW 10,26
Barbault, André: G. 1972b; E.
  1970d, 1975b; Fr. 1954b
Barker, Mary: E. 1968a; Seminar
  Notes, 1935
Baroncini, L.: It. 1908a
Barz, Helmut: G. 1984a
Bash, K. W.: E. 1942c; Seminar
  Notes, 1940–41
Baumann, Carol: E. 1947b, 1947c;
  Seminar Notes, 1928–30,2,

1932b, 1940–41
Baumann, Elizabeth: Seminar
  Notes, 1935–36
Baumann, Hans H.: Seminar
  Notes, 1936–37b
Baumgardt, Ursula: G. 1984a
Baynes, Cary F.: E. 1928a&b,
  1931a&d, 1932b, 1933a&b,
  1936c, 1943a, 1950d, 1953a,
  1962b; Seminar Notes, 1932a
Baynes, H. G.: E. 1920b, 1923a,
  1923b, 1924a&b, 1928a&b,
  1950b, 1953a, CW 6, CW/GW
  18,78
Bechterew, W. von: G. 1910d; CW/
  GW 18,20
Becker, Th.: G. 1910h; CW/GW
  18,20
Beebe, John: E. 1989b
Bender, Hans: G. 1958f, 1961c,
  1973a; E. 1975b
Bertine, Eleanor: G. 1957d,
  1972b; E. 1958e, 1971b,8,
  1973b; It. 1961a; CW/GW
  18,61; Seminar Notes, 1936–37a
Betschart, Ildefons: G. 1963b
Bezzola, Dumeng: G. 1907f
Binswanger, Hilde: G. 1969a
Bitter, Wilhelm: G. 1959a&b,
  1973a; E. 1975b
Blanke, Fritz: G. 1951e, 1972b; E.
  1973b, CW/GW 18,94

E

Eaton, Ralph M.: E. 1932a
Ebon, Martin: E. 1963e
Eder, Edith: E. 1913b, 1914a, 1915b, 1916a
Eder, M. D.: E. 1913b, 1914a, 1915b, 1916a, 1918a
Ehrenfels, Christian von: G. 1909g, 1910a; CW/GW 18,20
Einstein, Albert: E. 1971b,5
Eissler, Kurt R.: G. 1973a, 1974a; E. 1974b, 1975b
Ellmann, Richard: E. 1959l
Ermatinger, Emil: G. 1930a
Eschle, Franz: G. 1908e; CW/GW 18,20
Evans, Elida: E. 1920a, CW/GW 18,129
Evans, Richard I.: G. 1967c, 1986c; E. 1964b, 1977b,4
Evans-Wentz, W. Y.: G. 1935f, 1955d; E. 1954e, 1957f

F

Feifel, Herman: E. 1959c
Fichte, J. H.: G. 1935e
Fierz, Markus: CW/GW 18,49,i
Fierz-David, Linda: G. 1947b; E. 1950c, CW/GW 18,118; Seminar Notes, 1932a
Flesch-Brunningen, Hans: G. 1961b
Flinker, Martin: G. 1957j; Fr. 1961d
Flournoy, Théodore: G. 1908c,5, 1962a,15,vi
Foote, Mary: E. 1974e, 1975b; Seminar Notes, 1928–30,1,3,4,5, 1930–34, 1932a, 1934–39, 1938–39, [1988]
Fordham, Frieda: G. 1959c; E. 1953d, CW/GW 18,46; CW ed.

Fordham, Michael: E. 1957g, CW/GW 18,47&49,ii
Forel, August: G. 1910j, 1968b, 1972a; E. 1973b, CW/GW 18,20
Forryan, Barbara: CW 20
Frank, Ludwig: G. 1907f
Franz, Marie-Louise von: G. 1951a, 1955a, 1968a; E. 1964a; GW 14; CW A; Seminar Notes, 1940–41
Freeman, John: G. 1968a, 1986c,4; E. 1964a, 1964c, 1977b,6
Frei, Gebhard: G. 1957h, 1972b, 1991e,10; E. 1952c, 1973b; Sp. 1955b
Freud, Sigmund: G. 1906g, 1908d,k&m, 1932f, 1934d, 1939d, 1962a,15,ii, 1969b, 1972a, 1972e,2, 1974a, 1984g; E. 1932b, 1933a,6, 1961e, 1962a,15, 1968f, 1971b,3, 1973b&d,1, 1974b&d, 1979a, 1988a, 1991a; GW 4; CW 4, CW/GW 18,18,21,32; It. 1974a
Frey, Liliane: Seminar Notes, 1938–39, 1939–40
Frey-Wehrlin, C. T.: E. 1965a
Froboese-Thiele, Felicia: G. 1940a, 1957e, CW/GW 18,102

G

Galliker, A.: G. 1952h, 1972b; E. 1975b; Seminar Notes, 1935
Game, Margaret: E. 1968a
Gerster, Georg: G. 1953a, 1954e, 1986c,5; E. 1977b,7
Gilbert, J. Allen: CW/GW 18,112
Gilli, Gertrud: G. 1938d; CW/GW 18,116
Glover, A.S.B.: CW/GW 18,72,98,&99
Glover, Janet M.: CW 20
Godet, E.: Fr. 1939a

1979b, 1983c; GW 11,20; CW/
GW 18,8; Seminar Notes, 1939–
40
Janet, Pierre: G. 1908i,7
Jarosy, Ivo: E. 1953i
Jarrett, James L.: Seminar Notes,
[1988]
Jolas, Eugene: E. 1930c
Jones, Ernest: G. 1972b, 1974a; E.
1914b, 1974b, 1975b
Joyce, James: G. 1972a, GW 15,8;
E. 1959l, 1966d, 1973b, CW
15,8
Jung, Emma: G. 1934b,
1962a,15,i&iii; E. 1962a,16&17,
1975a
Jung, Lorenz: G. 1990c; Seminar
Notes, [1987]
Jung, Marianne, see Niehus-Jung,
Marianne
Jung-Merker, Lilly: GW 19, GW
ed.
Juquelier, P.: G. 1908i,9

K

Kankeleit, Otto: G. 1959d; CW/
GW 18,121
Katzaroff, Dimitre: G. 1908l,3
Kennedy, William H.: E. 1950a
Kerényi, Karl: G. 1941a,b,&c,
1951b, 1954a; E. 1949a, 1956a,
1963a, 1969a; Fr. 1953b, 1958a;
It. 1948b, 1965a, 1972a
Keyhoe, Donald: E. 1958g,
1959i,2, CW/GW 18,82
Keyserling, Hermann, Graf: G.
1925b, 1927a, 1928e, 1930e,
1934i, 1991e,7; E. 1926a, 1959k,
1975a
Kirkham, Ethel D.: E. 1948a,
1954g
Kirsch, Hildegard: E. 1972d
Kirsch, James: G. 1946h, 1972a&b,
1973a; E. 1946d,2, 1972c&d,

1973b, 1975a, 1975b
Kitchin, Derek: E. 1954c
Klaus, Bruder, see Niklaus von der
Flüe
Kleist, Karl: G. 1909d; CW/GW
18,20
Kluger-Schärf, Rivkah: Seminar
Notes, 1940–41
Knapp, Albert: G. 1907c; CW/GW
18,20
Koenig-Fachsenfeld, Olga von: G.
1935d; CW/GW 18,115; Seminar
Notes, 1930–31
Koestler, Arthur: G. 1961b, 1973a;
E. 1961c
Kolb, Eugen: CW/GW 18,74; He.
1974a
Kranefeldt, W. M.: G. 1930b,
1934b, GW 4,15; E. 1932a, CW
4,15
Krich, A. M.: E. 1928a, 14

L

Lachat, Père William: G. 1972b; E.
1975b, 1984b, CW/GW 18,99
Lasky, Melvin J.: G. 1956e, 1961b,
1973a, 1991e,10; E. 1961c,
1963f, 1975b
Le Lay, Yves: Fr. 1939a
Lemaître, Aug.: G. 1908c,7
Leonard, M.: G. 1973a; E. 1960c,
1975b
Leroy, E.-Bernard: G. 1908c,6
Levy, E.: Seminar Notes, 1940–41
Loewenfeld, L.: G. 1909e; CW/GW
18,20
Lombard, Emile: G. 1908c,3
Lomer, Georg: G. 1908g; CW/GW
18,20
London, Louis S.: G. 1972a; E.
1937aa, 1973b
Long, Constance E.: E. 1916a,
1917a
Lorenz, Theodor: E. 1944a

1955a; Sp. 1961a

Payne, Virginia: G. 1972b; E. 1971b,4, 1973b

Perry, John Weir: E. 1953e, CW/GW 18,16

Peterson, Frederick: E. 1970b, CW 2,13

Phelan, Gladys: E. 1953b

Philp, Howard L.: G. 1973a; E. 1958c, 1975b, CW/GW 18,103

Picasso, Pablo: G. 1932g, 1934b,8; E. 1940a, 1953i; GW 15,9; CW 15,9

Piéron, H.: G. 1908i,1

Pilcz, Alexander: G. 1910b; CW/GW 18,20

Pinckney, Sallie M.: G. 1972b; E. 1948c, 1973b; Seminar Notes, 1936–37a

Pöldinger, Walter: G. 1959h, CW/GW 18,128

Pope, A. R.: E. 1957a

Pratt, Jane A.: E. 1973b, 1975b, CW/GW 18,98; Seminar Notes, 1930–34

Prince, Morton: G. 1911b, GW 4,6; E. 1925b, CW 4,6

Q

Quispel, Gilles: G. 1975a; CW/GW 18,91

R

Radin, Paul: G. 1954a; E. 1956a; Fr. 1958a; It. 1965a

Ramakrishna, Sri: E. 1936c

Rank, Otto: G. 1910n, 1911f

Reibmayer, Albert: G. 1910f; CW/GW 18,20

Reichardt, M.: G. 1907d; CW/GW 18,20

Reichstein, Ignaz: Seminar Notes, 1940–41

Reinecke, Elisabeth: E. 1968c

Remmler, Helmut: G. 1984a

Ress, Lisa: CW/GW 18,134&135, 19

Revault d'Allones, G.: G. 1908i,2

Rhees, Jean: CW 2,10&11

Ricksher, Charles: E. 1908a, CW 2,14

Riklin, Franz: G. 1904a, 1906a,1, 1911h; E. 1918a,1; GW ed.

Rinkel, Max: G. 1973a; E. 1958d, CW 3,11

Riviere, Diana: CW 2

Rolfe, Constance: G. 1989c,2, 1991e,6,8; E. 1949d

Rosenthal, Hugo: G. 1934b

Rouma, Georges: G. 1908l,5

Rudin, Joseph: G. 1964a; E. 1968c

Rüf, Elisabeth: GW 10,12,15,22,&33, GW 15,8, GW 19; GW ed.

Rychlak, Joseph F.: G. 1972a; E. 1968b, 1975b

Rychner, Max: G. 1932c, 1972a; E. 1973b

S

Sacristán, José M.: Sp. 1947a

Sadger, Isidor: G. 1909h; CW/GW 18,11

Samuels, Andrew: E. 1989a

Sandwich, Earl of: G. 1973a; E. 1971b,10, 1975b

Sauerlander, Wolfgang: G. 1974a, 1984g; CW/GW 18,9,21,22,28,33&34

Schär, Hans: G. 1972b, GW 11,21; E. 1975b

Schärf, Riwkah: G. 1948a; Seminar Notes, 1933–41, 1938–39, 1939–40

Schleich, Carl Ludwig: G. 1934e; CW/GW 18,39

White, Victor: G. 1957h, 1972b; E.
1952c, 1975b; GW 11,4&20; CW
11,4; Sp. 1955b
Whitmont, Edward: E. 1955e
Wickes, Frances G.: G. 1931e,
1953b, 1972a; E. 1927a, 1966c,
1971b,2, 1973b; GW 17,2; CW
17,2, CW/GW 18,57
Wilhelm, Richard: G. 1929b&h,
1930c, 1931b, 1938a, 1957b,
1962a,15,vii; E. 1931a, 1950d,
1962a,18, 1962b; It. 1936a
Wilhelm, Salome: E. 1962b
Wilson, William G.: G. 1973a; E.
1963d, 1968e, 1975b
Winston, Clara: E. 1962a
Winston, Richard: E. 1962a
Wittels, Fritz: G. 1910l; E.

1973d,2; CW/GW 18,24
Wolff, Toni: G. 1940a, 1959e; E.
1938a; GW 10,18, CW 10,18;
Seminar Notes, 1932a
Woods, Ralph L.: E. 1947d
Wulffen, Erich: G. 1910p; CW/GW
18,25

Z

Zacharias, Gerhard P.: G. 1954c
Ziegler, K. A.: G. 1946f; E. 1946b;
CW/GW 18,104
Zimmer, Heinrich: G. 1944b,
1962a,15,viii, GW 11,15
Zosimos: G. 1938c, 1954b,5; CW
13,2

THE COLLECTED WORKS OF

C. G. JUNG

EDITORS: SIR HERBERT READ, MICHAEL FORDHAM, AND GER-
HARD ADLER; *EXECUTIVE EDITOR*, WILLIAM McGUIRE. *TRANS-
LATED BY* R.F.C. HULL, EXCEPT WHERE NOTED.

In the following list, dates of original publication are given in pa-
rentheses (of original composition, in brackets). Multiple dates indicate
revisions.

(continued)

The Theory of Psychoanalysis (1913)
General Aspects of Psychoanalysis (1913)
Psychoanalysis and Neurosis (1916)
Some Crucial Points in Psychoanalysis: A Correspondence between Dr. Jung and Dr. Loÿ (1914)
Prefaces to "Collected Papers on Analytical Psychology" (1916, 1917)
The Significance of the Father in the Destiny of the Individual (1909/1949)
Introduction to Kranefeldt's "Secret Ways of the Mind" (1930)
Freud and Jung: Contrasts (1929)

5. SYMBOLS OF TRANSFORMATION ([1911–12/1952] 1956; 2nd edn., 1967)

PART I
Introduction
Two Kinds of Thinking
The Miller Fantasies: Anamnesis
The Hymn of Creation
The Song of the Moth

PART II
Introduction
The Concept of Libido
The Transformation of Libido
The Origin of the Hero
Symbols of the Mother and of Rebirth
The Battle for Deliverance from the Mother
The Dual Mother
The Sacrifice
Epilogue
Appendix: The Miller Fantasies

6. PSYCHOLOGICAL TYPES ([1921] 1971)

A revision by R.F.C. Hull of the translation by H. G. Baynes

Introduction
The Problem of Types in the History of Classical and Medieval Thought
Schiller's Ideas on the Type Problem
The Apollinian and the Dionysian
The Type Problem in Human Character
The Type Problem in Poetry
The Type Problem in Psychopathology

(continued)

6. (*continued*)

Psychological Aspects of the Mother Archetype (1938/1954)
Concerning Rebirth (1940/1950)
The Psychology of the Child Archetype (1940)
The Psychological Aspects of the Kore (1941)
The Phenomenology of the Spirit in Fairytales (1945/1948)
On the Psychology of the Trickster-Figure (1954)
Conscious, Unconscious, and Individuation (1939)
A Study in the Process of Individuation (1934/1950)
Concerning Mandala Symbolism (1950)
Appendix: Mandalas (1955)

9. PART II. AION ([1951] 1959; 2nd ed., 1968)
   RESEARCHES INTO THE PHENOMENOLOGY OF THE SELF
   The Ego
   The Shadow
   The Syzygy: Anima and Animus
   The Self
   Christ, a Symbol of the Self
   The Sign of the Fishes
   The Prophecies of Nostradamus
   The Historical Significance of the Fish
   The Ambivalence of the Fish Symbol
   The Fish in Alchemy
   The Alchemical Interpretation of the Fish
   Background to the Psychology of Christian Alchemical Symbolism
   Gnostic Symbols of the Self
   The Structure and Dynamics of the Self
   Conclusion

10. CIVILIZATION IN TRANSITION (1964; 2nd edn., 1970)
    The Role of the Unconscious (1918)
    Mind and Earth (1927/1931)
    Archaic Man (1931)
    The Spiritual Problem of Modern Man (1928/1931)
    The Love Problem of a Student (1928)
    Woman in Europe (1927)
    The Meaning of Psychology for Modern Man (1933/1934)
    The State of Psychotherapy Today (1934)
    Preface and Epilogue to "Essays on Contemporary Events" (1946)
    Wotan (1936)
    After the Catastrophe (1945)
    The Fight with the Shadow (1946)

(continued)

16. (*continued*)

The Psychology of the Transference (1946)
Appendix: The Realities of Practical Psychotherapy ([1937] added 1966)

17. THE DEVELOPMENT OF PERSONALITY (1954)
Psychic Conflicts in a Child (1910/1946)
Introduction to Wickes's "Analyses der Kinderseele" (1927/1931)
Child Development and Education (1928)
Analytical Psychology and Education: Three Lectures (1926/1946)
The Gifted Child (1943)
The Significance of the Unconscious in Individual Education (1928)
The Development of Personality (1934)
Marriage as a Psychological Relationship (1925)

18. THE SYMBOLIC LIFE (1954)
Translated by R.F.C. Hull and others
Miscellaneous writings

19. COMPLETE BIBLIOGRAPHY OF C. G. JUNG'S WRITINGS (1976; 2nd edn., 1992)

20. GENERAL INDEX TO THE COLLECTED WORKS (1979)

THE ZOFINGIA LECTURES (1983)
Supplementary Volume A to The Collected Works. Edited by William McGuire, translated by Jan van Heurck, introduction by Marie-Louise von Franz

PSYCHOLOGY OF THE UNCONSCIOUS ([1912] 1992)
A STUDY OF THE TRANSFORMATIONS AND SYMBOLISMS OF THE LIBIDO.
A CONTRIBUTION TO THE HISTORY OF THE EVOLUTION OF THOUGHT
Supplementary Volume B to the Collected Works. Translated by Beatrice M. Hinkle, introduction by William McGuire

Related publications:

THE BASIC WRITINGS OF C. G. JUNG
Selected and introduced by Violet S. de Laszlo

C. G. JUNG: LETTERS
Selected and edited by Gerhard Adler, in collaboration with Aniela Jaffé.
Translations from the German by R.F.C. Hull.
VOL. 1: 1906–1950
VOL. 2: 1951–1961

C. G. JUNG SPEAKING: Interviews and Encounters
Edited by William McGuire and R.F.C. Hull

C. G. JUNG: Word and Image
Edited by Aniela Jaffé

THE ESSENTIAL JUNG
Selected and introduced by Anthony Storr

THE GNOSTIC JUNG
Selected and introduced by Robert A. Segal

PSYCHE AND SYMBOL
Selected and introduced by Violet S. de Laszlo

Notes of C. G. Jung's Seminars:

DREAM ANALYSIS ([1928–30] 1984)
Edited by William McGuire

NIETZSCHE'S *ZARATHUSTRA* ([1934–39] 1988)
Edited by James L. Jarrett (2 vols.)

ANALYTICAL PSYCHOLOGY ([1925] 1989)
Edited by William McGuire

Printed in the USA
CPSIA information can be obtained
at www.ICGtesting.com
JSHW081930040224
56474JS00004B/5

9 780691 259437